The Tozer Topical Reader
Volume One

The TOZER Topical Reader

Volume One

COMPILED BY
RON EGGERT

Christian Publications
CAMP HILL, PENNSYLVANIA

Christian Publications
3825 Hartzdale Drive, Camp Hill, PA 10711
www.cpi-horizon.com

Faithful, biblical publishing since 1883

The Tozer Topical Reader
In Two Volumes

ISBN: 0-87509-838-X
Copyright 1998, by Ron Eggert
All rights reserved
Printed in the United States of America

99 00 01 02 03   5 4 3 2 1

Selected quotations as submitted from
*The Knowledge of the Holy, The Attributes of God:
Their Meaning in the Christian* by A.W. Tozer
Copyright © 1961 by Alden Wilson Tozer.
Copyright Renewed.
Reprinted by permission of
HarperCollins Publishers, Inc.

Selected quotations are taken from
Keys to the Deeper Life by A.W. Tozer.
Copyright © 1987 by
Zondervan Publishing House.
Used by permission of Zondervan Publishing House.

Scripture taken from the Holy Bible:
King James Version.

Scripture also taken from the HOLY BIBLE:
NEW INTERNATIONAL VERSION ®.
© 1973, 1978, 1984 by the
International Bible Society.
Used by permission of
Zondervan Bible Publishers.

To Denny and Barb Butcher;
Buzz and Diana Fisher

Better friends could never be found
this side of heaven

To Dianna

My patient and loving wife of over thirty years
The one exception to the above statement

Foreword

"How many a man has dated a new era in his life from the reading of a book!"

So wrote Henry David Thoreau in chapter 3 of *Walden* nearly a century and a half ago, and many of us agree with him. I recall what happened to me when as a young minister I first read A.W. Tozer's *The Pursuit of God*. It was like the dawning of a new day as the blinders were removed from the eyes of my heart. Since then, I have steadily added Dr. Tozer's books to my library, read them and re-read them, quoted from them in my sermons and books, and given thanks to God for this unique man whose prophetic ministry is still needed by the church today.

And now we have *The Tozer Topical Reader* which assembles and indexes treasures from Dr. Tozer's books and makes them readily accessible to all of us. Thank you, Ron Eggert, for giving us this valuable guide to the spiritual wealth Dr. Tozer bequeathed so generously to God's people.

Dr. Tozer repeatedly warned us that the best books aren't the ones that do our thinking for us, but the ones that make us stop and think and then look deeper into the Scriptures. Reading a single sentence in a Tozer book has more than once led me into the green pastures of the Word to find there the encouragement and nourishment I've needed for my own life and ministry.

To the glory of God, may that be our experience as we use this book, trusting the Spirit to teach us the truth as it is in Jesus.

Warren W. Wiersbe

Introduction

I finally had to quit quoting Tozer in my preaching. It got to the point where as soon as I mentioned his name people began to chuckle, as in "Here he goes again." And I could just hear Larry Colclasure, grinning on the right front pew, thinking, "Does Eggert ever read anybody else?"

The fact is, over the years I have collected, read and quoted from everything published by A.W. Tozer (42 different books, I think). No matter what I was preaching I found he contributed an incredibly insightful, up-to-date, poignant thought. Though he died in 1963 his prophetic pronouncements touched me right where my current concerns were.

I'm probably out of step with the current thrust of the church, with its constant emphasis on success, growth and numbers. Tozer's message may not be what we want to hear. But when I read what he says about worship, what he writes about the current condition of the church, where his heart pants for the knowledge of the holy, I cry out that we today might recapture some of his spirit.

In *The Tozer Topical Reader* I have sought to capture the essence of A.W. Tozer. These are eminently quotable excerpts, but beyond that I trust they are passages that will give the reader a sense of the passion that consumed Tozer throughout his ministry. My prayer is that these volumes will serve not only as a rich source of quotable material for pastors and teachers, but also, more than that, my strong desire is that people across the church spectrum will find here a rich source of devotional encouragement and spiritual stimulation. If Tozer was right as he lamented the weak condition of the evangelical church (And what would he think of the church today?), we desperately need to hear his challenge. We desperately need to get back to a pursuit of God, a knowledge of the holy. We desperately need to retrieve our harp for its intended purpose. (See entry 1361.)

Ron Eggert
November, 1998

A

1. Absolutes

I have been around long enough and preached often enough to have been called some interesting names. For instance, I have been called an absolutist.

My response? Of course I am an absolutist, and so is every other believer if he or she is worth anything to God and to His testimony. None of us should be scared or offended if we are called absolutists. We must never let words bother us.

Of course we believe in something absolute. Of course we believe in something permanent. We believe in God, the fixed Absolute, to whom we pray, "Our Father, who art in heaven."

Matthew 6:9; John 17:15-18; 2 Corinthians 6:17,18; 3 John 4
Men Who Met God, 94.

2. Accountability; America: greatness

I find myself indignant concerning much preaching and teaching which portrays the Christ as a soft and pliant friend of everybody, a painted, plastic figure without any spine and involved in no way with justice. . . .

Every one of us is going to be finally accountable to the One who gave us being. We are accountable to the One from whose heart we came and who laid His laws upon us. We are accountable to God! . . .

It was the belief in the accountability of man to his maker that made America a great nation. Among those earlier leaders was Daniel Webster whose blazing eyes and fiery oratory often held the Senate spellbound. In those days the Congress was composed of strong, noble statesmen who carried the weight of the nation in their hearts and minds.

Someone asked: "Mr. Webster, what do you consider the most serious thought that has ever entered your mind?"

"The most solemn thought that has ever entered my mind is my accountability to my Maker," he replied.

John 5:24-27; Acts 10:42-43; Acts 17:30-31; Romans 2:16; 2 Corinthians 5:10
Echoes from Eden, 124,129,130.

3. Activity: moratorium on; Busyness; Church: activities

I think we are the busiest bunch of eager beavers ever seen in the religious world. The idea seems to be that if we are not running in a circle, breathing down the back of our own neck, we are not pleasing God! . . .

I heard a Christian leader warn recently that we are suffering from a rash of amateurism in Christian circles. Christianity has leveled down and down and down. We are as light as butterflies—though we flit, flit, flit around in the sunshine and imagine that we are eagles flapping our broad wings.

Sometimes I think the Church would be better off if we would call a moratorium on activity for about six weeks and just wait on God to see what He is waiting to do for us. That's what they did before Pentecost.

Psalm 46:10; Habakkuk 2:20; Mark 16:15; Luke 24:49; Acts 1:12-14;1 Peter 1:3-5
The Counselor, 95.

4. Activity: moratorium on; Church: spiritual condition

I suppose my suggestion will not receive much serious attention, but I should like to suggest that we Bible-believing Christians announce a moratorium on religious activity and set our house in order preparatory to the coming of an afflatus from above. So carnal is the body of Christians which composes the conservative wing of the Church, so shockingly irreverent are our public services in some quarters, so degraded are our religious tastes in still others, that the need for power could scarcely have been greater at any time in history. I believe we should profit immensely were we to declare a period of silence and self-examination during which each one of us searched his own heart and sought to meet every condition for a real baptism of power from on high.

Psalm 4:4; Psalm 139:23,24; 1 Corinthians 3:1-3
The Pursuit of Man, 94.

5. Activity: religious; Busyness

Today the Christian emphasis falls heavily on the "active" life. People are more concerned with earth than with heaven; they would rather "do something" than to commune with God. The average Christian feels a lot nearer to this world than to the world above. The current vogue favors "Christian action." The favorite brand of Christianity is that sparked by the man in a hurry, hard hitting, aggressive and ready with the neat quip. We are neglecting the top side of our souls. The light in the tower burns dimly while we hurry about the grounds below, making a great racket and giving the impression of wonderful devotion to our task.

Isaiah 55:1,2; Luke 10:38-42; John 6:27
The Price of Neglect, 46, 47.

6. Activity: religious; Busyness

Many of our Christians are activists—they are good at footwork and they are engaged in many religious journeys, but they do not seem to move up any closer to Jesus in heart and in spirit. This modern religious emphasis on activity reminds me of the Japanese mice that I have seen in the windows of the pet store. Don't stop and look at them if you are the nervous type. I do not know why they call them dancing mice because they don't waltz—they just run continually. I think they must be fundamentalists, brethren—they are on the go all the time! Some Christians seem to feel that it is a mark of spirituality to attend banquets and seminars and workshops and conferences and courses, night after night, week after week. . . .

It is not enough just to be rushing somewhere to another meeting, another discussion, another dialogue. Jesus commended Mary for knowing the value of the one thing that is necessary—that God should be loved and praised above all other business which may occupy us bodily or spiritually. Mary was fervently occupied in spirit about the love of His Godhead. I like that—although I know it sounds strange and almost heretical to our modern activists.

Psalm 4:4; Psalm 27:4; Luke 10:38-42; 2 Timothy 3:1-7
I Talk Back to the Devil, 137,138,139.

7. Activity: religious; Busyness; Worship: meaningless

There is all around us, however, a very evident and continuing substitute for worship. I speak of the compelling temptation among Christian believers to be constantly engaged, during every waking hour, in religious activity.

We cannot deny that it is definitely a churchly idea of service. Many of our sermons and much of our contemporary ecclesiastical teaching lean toward the idea that it is surely God's plan for us to be busy, busy, busy—because it is the best cause in the world in which we are involved.

But if there is any honesty left in us, it persuades us in our quieter moments that true spiritual worship is at a discouragingly low ebb among professing Christians.

Do we dare ask how we have reached this state? . . .

How can our approach to worship be any more vital than it is when so many who lead us, both in the pulpit and in the pew, give little indication that the fellowship of God is delightful beyond telling?

Psalm 42:1-2; Psalm 63:1-2; Isaiah 1:11-20; Isaiah 55:1,2
Whatever Happened to Worship?, 26, 27.

8. Activity: religious; Externalism; Current conditions: shallowness

"The accent in the Church today," says Leonard Ravenhill, the English evangelist, "is not on devotion, but on commotion." Religious extroversion has been carried to such an extreme in evangelical circles that hardly anyone has the desire, to say nothing of the courage, to question the soundness of it. Externalism has taken over. God now speaks by the wind and the earthquake only; the still small voice can be heard no more. The whole religious machine has become a noisemaker. The adolescent taste which loves the loud horn and the thundering exhaust has gotten into the activities of modern Christians. The old question, "What is the chief end of man?" is now answered, "To dash about the world and add to the din thereof.". . .

We must begin the needed reform by challenging the spiritual validity of externalism. What a man is must be shown to be more important than what he does. While the moral quality of any act is imparted by the condition of the heart, there may be a world of religious activity which arises not from within but from without and which would seem to have little or no moral content. Such religious conduct is imitative or reflex. It stems from the current cult of commotion and possesses no sound inner life.

1 Kings 19:12; Matthew 12:34-37
The Root of the Righteous, 75.

9. Activity: religious; Sermon on the Mount

It is more than probable that in the whole history of the United States there was never at any one time so much religious activity as there is today. And it is also very likely that there was never less true spirituality.

For some reason, religious activity and godliness do not always go together. To discover this, it is only necessary to observe the current religious scene. . . .

If this should strike you as being uncharitable, make this little test: kneel down and read reverently the Sermon on the Mount. Let it get hold of your heart. Catch the spiritual "feeling" of it. Try to conceive what kind of person he or she would be who would embody its teachings. Then compare your conception with the product of the modern religious mill. You will find a wide world of difference both in conduct and in spirit.

Matthew 5-7; Romans 10:1-3
We Travel an Appointed Way, 49.

10. Activity: religious; Service: motives for

Much religious work is being done these days that is not owned by our Lord and will not be accepted or rewarded in that great day. Superior human gifts are being mistaken for the gifts of the Holy Spirit, and neither they who exercise these gifts nor the Christian public before whom they are exercised are aware of the deception. Never has there been more activity in religious circles and, I confidently believe, never has there been so little of God and so much of the flesh. Such work is a snare because it keeps us busy and at the same time prevents us from discovering that it is our work and not God's.

1 Corinthians 3:12-14; 1 Corinthians 4:3-5; 1 Corinthians 15:9-10; Philippians 2:12-13; Colossians 1:28-29; 1 Timothy 4:7,8
The Size of the Soul, 53.

11. Activity: religious; Spiritual goals

It is possible to have motion without progress, and this describes much of the activity among Christians today. It is simply lost motion.

In God there is motion, but never wasted motion; He always works toward a predetermined end. Being made in His image, we are by nature constituted so that we are justifying our existence only when we are working with a purpose in mind. Aimless activity is beneath the worth and dignity of a human being. Activity that does not result in progress toward a goal is wasted; yet most Christians have no clear end toward which they are striving. On the endless religious merry-go-round they continue to waste time and energy, of which, God knows, they never had much and have less each hour.

Genesis 1:26-27; 1 Corinthians 9:22,23; Philippians 3:13,14; Hebrews 12:1,2
Born After Midnight, 101.

12. Activity: test of Godliness; Busyness

Working for Christ has today been accepted as the ultimate test of godliness among all but a few evangelical Christians. Christ has become a project to be promoted or a cause to be served instead of a

Lord to be obeyed. Thousands of mistaken persons seek to do for Christ whatever their fancy suggests should be done, and in whatever way they think best. The *what* and the *how* of Christian service can only originate in the sovereign will of our Lord, but the busy beavers among us ignore this fact and think up their own schemes. The result is an army of men who run without being sent and speak without being commanded.

Jeremiah 1:5; Acts 9:6; Acts 26:13-19
The Set of the Sail, 140.

13. Adoration; Worship: adoration

The admonition to "love the Lord thy God with all thy heart, . . . and with all thy mind" (Matthew 22:37) can mean only one thing. It means to adore Him.

I use the word "adore" sparingly, for it is a precious word. I love babies and I love people, but I cannot say I adore them. Adoration I keep for the only One who deserves it. In no other presence and before no other being can I kneel in reverent fear and wonder and yearning and feel the sense of possessiveness that cries "Mine, mine!". . .

Consecration is not difficult for the person who has met God. Where there is genuine adoration and fascination, God's child wants nothing more than the opportunity to pour out his or her love at the Savior's feet.

Psalm 63:1-2; Matthew 22:37-39
Whatever Happened to Worship?, 88, 89.

14. Affections; Satisfaction

The human heart lives by its sympathies and affections. In the day that will try every man's works how much we know will not come in for much consideration. What and whom we have loved will be about all that matters then. For this reason we can never give too great care to the condition of our inner lives. . . .

The human heart with its divine capacity for holy pleasure must no longer be allowed to remain the victim of fear and bad teaching. Christ died for our hearts and the Holy Spirit wants to come and satisfy them.

Let us emulate Isaac and open again the wells our fathers digged and which have been stopped up by the enemy. The waters are there, cool, sweet and satisfying. They will spring up again at the touch of the honest spade. Who will start digging?

Genesis 26:15-25; John 4:13-14;
2 Timothy 1:6-7
The Root of the Righteous, 67, 69.

15. America: liberty; Current issues: loss of freedom

Plato has somewhere said that in a democratic society the price wise men pay for neglecting politics is to be ruled by unwise men. . . .

In America, for instance, there are millions of plain men and women, decent, honest and peace loving, who take their blessings for granted and make no effort to assure the continuance of our free society. These persons are without doubt far in the majority. They constitute the main body of our population, but for all their numbers they are not going to determine the direction our country will go in the next few years. Their weakness lies in their passivity. They sit back and allow radicals and those in the minority but who shout the loudest to set the course for the future. If this continues much longer we have no assurance that we can retain that liberty which was once purchased for us at such appalling cost.

The Price of Neglect, 5.

16. America: problems; Modern day; Progress

I challenge the idea that we are advanced. I know the majority of modern educators, newspaper writers, TV personalities, radio reporters, politicians and all the rest do not agree with me. Nevertheless, I challenge the idea that we are any further advanced than they were in the days of Jesus.

If we are so advanced, then I want to ask some questions. Why do we kill thousands of human beings each year with automobiles? Because we ride automobiles instead of donkeys, we are advanced? If we are so advanced in our day, why are the penitentiaries packed full and the mental hospitals crowded? If we are so advanced, why is the whole world a powder keg? If we are so advanced, how is it that we have weapons that can annihilate the world? If we are so advanced, why is it that people cannot walk alone in the parks anymore? Why is it that workers who get out at midnight never walk home alone anymore? Why is it in this advanced age that drugs, violence, abortion and divorce are soaring?

There is a mind-set that thinks every motion is progress. Every time you move you are progressing. Then there is the mind-set that thinks whenever you move in a straight line you are going forward, forgetting that you can move in a straight line and be going backward.

Ecclesiastes 1:4-10; Romans 3:10-18;
2 Timothy 3:1-7
Rut, Rot or Revival: The Condition of the Church, 101, 102.

17. America: sinfulness

I am among those who believe that our Western civilization is on its way to perishing. It has many commendable qualities, most of which it has borrowed from the Christian ethic, but it lacks the element of moral wisdom that would give it permanence. Future historians will record that we of the twentieth century had intelligence enough to create a great civilization but not the moral wisdom to preserve it.

Deuteronomy 32:28; Isaiah 5:8-23; Romans 1:24-25
Man: The Dwelling Place of God, 49.

18. Angels: denial of

Anyone who wants to can put a film of unbelief over his or her eyes and thus deny the existence and activity of angels. But in doing so, he or she is denying clear biblical teaching.

Some protest the discussion of angels, saying, "Let's be practical!" By which they mean, "Let's limit our considerations to three-dimensional, sense-perceived objects." There is a day coming when the answers to our questions will be plain. On that day we will discover that the ministries of the angelic beings are indeed practical and very real. . . .

We are living in a world full of God's created beings—many of them not seen by us or those around us. We ought to thank God for the angels and for God's providential circumstances every day. As one of the old saints long ago remarked, "If you will thank God for your providences, you will never lack a providence to thank God for!"

Job 38:7; Psalm 34:6-7; Psalm 91:11-12;
Luke 2:13; Hebrews 1:13-14; Hebrews 12:22-24
Jesus, Our Man in Glory, 52, 53, 57.

19. Angels: ignorance about

Our Protestant churches have never been very enthusiastic about the Bible references to the many kinds of angels and angelic beings which make up the Lord's heavenly host. Because we do not see them, we generally do not discuss them. There seem to be many Christians who are not sure what they should believe about God's heavenly messengers.

In short, where the matter of Bible teaching about angels is concerned, we have come into a sad state of neglect and ignorance.

Personally, I despise the cynical references to angels and the comic jokes about them. The preacher who reported his guardian angel had had a hard time keeping up with him as he sped over the highway spoke in bad taste and probably in ignorance. If that is the best a preacher can say about the guardian angels or God's angelic host, he needs to go back to his Bible.

Genesis 32:1-2; Isaiah 6:1-2; Matthew 18:10; Hebrews 1:6-8; Hebrews 13:1-3
Jesus, Our Man in Glory, 47.

20. Anger; Temper: loss of credibility

Some people have a temper. We blame it on our Irish grandfather or on something else; but it's a plague spot. I remember a man who had a very high spiritual testimony and became a leading pastor in his denomination. One night at a board meeting, he lost his temper like a mule driver and after that, nobody believed in him.

One time, a man I thought was a fine Christian had a new car and somebody came along and dented his fender. He blew like a little bomb. I never believed in him again. Whenever I see a man blow his top, I never believe in that man unless I know he has gone to the Fountain that cleanses and gotten delivered. No man has any more right to go around with an uncleaned temper than he has to hold a rattlesnake in his jacket pocket. He has no more right to do that than he has to leave untreated a cancer on his tongue, because it will destroy his ministry. He can pray and testify, give and labor, but if one day he blows up, nobody will believe in him after that.

Proverbs 12:16; Proverbs 25:28; Proverbs 29:11; James 3:5-6
Success and the Christian, 60.

21. Anthropology; History: future more important

It is ironic that men will spend vast amounts both of time and of money in an effort to uncover the secrets of their past when their own future is all that should really matter to them.

No man is responsible for his ancestors; and the only past he must account for is the relatively short one he himself has lived here on earth. To learn how I can escape the guilt of sins committed in my brief yesterdays, how I can live free from sin today and enter at last into the blessed presence of God in a happy tomorrow—that is more important to me than anything that can be discovered by the anthropologist. It appears to me to be a strange perversion of interest to gaze backward at the dust when we are equipped to look upward at the glory.

Psalm 39:4-6; Luke 12:18-26; Romans 8:18-19; James 4:13-14
That Incredible Christian, 81, 82.

22. Antinomianism

Fundamental Christianity in our times is deeply influenced by that ancient enemy of righteousness, antinomianism. The creed of the antinomian is easily stated: We are saved by faith alone; works have no place in salvation; conduct is works, and is therefore of no importance. What we do cannot matter as long as we believe rightly. The divorce between creed and conduct is absolute and final. The question of sin is settled by the Cross; conduct is outside the circle of faith and cannot come between the believer and God. Such, in brief, is the teaching of the antinomian. And so fully has it permeated the Fundamental element in modern Christianity that it is accepted by the religious masses as the very truth of God.

Antinomianism is the doctrine of grace carried by uncorrected logic to the point of absurdity. It takes the teaching of justification by faith and twists it into deformity.

Romans 6:1; Galatians 5:13; James 2:17; James 2:26
Paths to Power, 40.

23. Apathy; Change

People who are in the rut, the circular grave, find that it is getting harder for them to change. They used to have spells when they were emotionally moved. Their wills got over on the side of God, and they really meant to make themselves into good Christians by the grace of God. But those times are getting fewer. They cannot afford to wait and say, "Oh, well, I will do it next Thanksgiving. I'll do it when I come home from vacation." No, they will either do it now or they will not do it at all. . . .

A beautiful sugar maple stands in front of our house up on Old Orchard Grove. It is one of the greenest trees I have ever seen. It hangs on to its leaves a long time, and then sometime in October I notice some leaves are missing and say to myself, "Oh well, there is still a mass of leaves. I do not need to worry." The next day I notice there are not as many leaves, and then I begin to notice some branches beginning to show. Before the snow flies there is not a leaf left. People in the rut never know when the last leaves are falling for them.

Deuteronomy 1:6-8; 1 Corinthians 1:10-12; 2 Corinthians 6:1-2
Rut, Rot or Revival: The Condition of the Church, 37, 38.

24. Apathy; Current conditions: apathy

The compelling message of John 3:17 is more than a statement of God's intention towards the human race, for in actuality it constitutes a "proclamation extraordinary!"...

Why is there a blank kind of indifference and why is there an incredible apathy to such an extraordinary proclamation of God's best intentions for us?...

Upon our eyes there seems to have fallen a strange dimness.

Within our ears there seems to have fallen a strange dullness.

In our minds there is a stupor, and in our hearts, I am afraid, there is a great callousness.

It is a wonder, and a terrible responsibility, that we should have this message from the heart of God in our possession and be so little stirred up about it!...

Some think that we are spiritual people and that we belong to spiritual churches. In all frankness, I think many would change their minds if they knew how little response there is, how little sensitivity to the Spirit, how little urgency of the heart in spiritual matters....

I believe that our attitudes must be a great grief to God himself, as He tries to move us to praise and delight and devotion.

John 3:17; Romans 11:33-36; Ephesians 3:20-21; 1 Timothy 1:17
Christ the Eternal Son, 101,102,104,106.

25. Apathy; Holy Spirit: filling; Holiness: conditions for

It is disheartening to those who care, and surely a great grief to the Spirit, to see how many Christians are content to settle for less than the best. Personally I have for years carried a burden of sorrow as I have moved among evangelical Christians who somewhere in their past have managed to strike a base compromise with their heart's holier longings and have settled down to a lukewarm, mediocre kind of Christianity utterly unworthy of themselves and of the Lord they claim to serve. And such are found everywhere....

Every man is as close to God as he wants to be; he is as holy and as full of the Spirit as he wills to be....

Yet we must distinguish wanting from wishing. By "want" I mean wholehearted desire. Certainly there are many who wish they were holy or victorious or joyful but are not willing to meet God's conditions to obtain.

Romans 6:11-14; Ephesians 5:15-18; Ephesians 6:18
That Incredible Christian, 64.

26. Apathy; Jesus Christ: His loveliness

Our problems of spiritual coldness and apathy in the churches would quickly disappear if Christian believers generally would confess their great need for rediscovering the loveliness of Jesus Christ, their Savior.

Song of Solomon 5:16; 2 Corinthians 5:12-15; Revelation 2:4-5
I Talk Back to the Devil, 65.

27. Apathy; Lack of enthusiasm

We live at a fever pitch, and whether we are erecting buildings, laying highways, promoting athletic events, celebrating special days or welcoming returning heroes, we always do it with an exaggerated flourish. Our building will be taller, our highway broader, our athletic contest more colorful, our celebration more elaborate and more expensive than would be true anywhere else on earth. We walk faster, drive faster, earn more, spend more and run higher a blood pressure than any other people in the world.

In only one field of human interest are we slow and apathetic: that is the field of personal religion. There for some strange reason our enthusiasm lags. Church people habitually approach the matter of their personal relation to God in a dull, half-hearted way which is altogether out of keeping with their general temperament and wholly inconsistent with the importance of the subject.

Romans 12:9-13; Colossians 3:23
Of God and Men, 3, 4.

28. Apathy; Lordship of Christ; Jesus Christ: love for

It is rare now to see a transforming conversion. The average convert becomes one by a series of compromises, whereby he surrenders something to gain something and dickers for his salvation like a huckster. The thought of unconditional surrender to the Lordship of Jesus never enters his mind....

The significant words of prophet and apostle were "I saw ... I heard ... the heavens were opened ... I saw the Lord," and other like expressions. Today we try to substitute a pale, waxy "faith" for such vivid encounters. No wonder the Church has taken on the general tone of a convalescent hospital instead of the camp of a victorious army.

[Another] cause of our lack of moral enthusiasm, as I see it, is the absence from our experience of an object for the heart's devotion. The great spiritual souls of other days had such an object. In the Old Testament they were frankly and unashamedly in love with the Most High God, and when He became flesh and dwelt among us He came still nearer to the hearts of His people. Paul's heart exploded into a burning volcano of love for the Lord Jesus.

Acts 26:13-19; Romans 12:1-2; 2 Corinthians 5:17; Philippians 3:4-11
The Price of Neglect, 30, 31.

29. Apostasy; Walk humbly; Church: God's judgment

God can deal ruthlessly with nations and men and men's favorite religions and temples. There is no religious group or church organization in the world that God will not abandon if it ceases to fulfill His divine will. Ecclesiastical robes are not impressive enough or gold crosses heavy enough or titles long enough to save the church once she ceases to fulfill the will of God among sinful men who need the transforming news of Christ's gospel.

The God who raised them up in centuries past will turn away unless they continue to fulfill the gracious will of God, following on to know the Lord, walking humbly and meekly in faith and love. Crowds do not impress the Almighty. Size is not a significant matter with Him. He will turn His blessing to some small mission, to a simple-hearted people somewhere whose greatest possession is the desire to love Him and obey Him.

Isaiah 57:16; Isaiah 66:2; Micah 6:8; 1 John 2:19
Tragedy in the Church: The Missing Gifts, 58.

30. Approval; Pride: human; Boldness

I cannot believe in the spirituality of any Christian man who keeps an eye open for the approval of others, whoever they may be. The man after God's own heart must be dead to the opinion of his friends as well as his enemies. He must be as willing to cross important persons as obscure ones. He must be ready to rebuke his superior as quickly as those who may be beneath him on the ecclesiastical ladder. To reprove one man in order to gain the favor of another is no evidence of moral courage. It is done in the world all the time.

We'll never be where we should be in our spiritual lives until we are so devoted to Christ that we ask no other approbation than His smile. When we are wholly lost in Him the frantic effort to please men will come to an end. The circle of persons we struggle to please will be narrowed to One. Then we will know true freedom, but not a moment before.

John 15:18-21; Galatians 1:9-10;
1 Thessalonians 2:4-6; 2 Timothy 3:12; 2 Timothy 4:1-5
The Price of Neglect, 141.

31. Atheism; Defiance; Man: rebellion against God

Man has no say about the time or the place of his birth; God determines that without consulting the man himself. One day the little man finds himself in consciousness and accepts the fact that he is. There his volitional life begins. *Before* that he had nothing to say about anything. *After* that he struts and boasts and utters his defiant proclamations of individual freedom, and encouraged by the sound of his own voice he may declare his independence of God and call himself an "atheist" or an "agnostic." Have your fun, little man; you are only chattering in the interim between *first* and *last*; you had no voice at the first and you will have none at the last. God reserves the right to take up at the last where He began at the first, and you are in the hands of God whether you will or not.

Psalm 2; Isaiah 64:8; Romans 9:19-21
The Root of the Righteous, 158, 159.

32. Authors; Writing

Christian literature, to be accepted and approved by evangelical leaders of our times, must follow very closely the same train of thought, a kind of "party line" from which it is scarcely safe to depart. A half-century of this in America has made us smug and content. We imitate each other with slavish devotion. Our most strenuous efforts are put forth to try to say the same thing that everyone around us is saying—and yet to find an excuse for saying it, some little safe variation on the approved theme or, if no more, at least a new illustration.

Ecclesiastes 12:12
The Pursuit of God, 84.

B

33. Balance; Mysticism; Communion with God

. . . every real Christian, however practical, is in some degree a mystic, his mysticism lying on the upper side of his life. He prays, meditates on spiritual things and communes with God and the invisible world. Also, every Christian, however he may be dedicated to the holy art of prayer and worship, must of necessity descend to work and eat and sleep and pay his taxes and get on somehow with the hard world around him. And if he follows on to know the Lord he must serve in every useful way outlined for him in the Scriptures of truth. To be a Christian it is necessary that he serve his generation as well as his God.

The big problem is to keep the two elements of the Christian life in proper balance. Martha and Mary are sisters and we need both.

Joshua 1:7-8; Psalm 1:1-3; Luke 10:38-42; 2 Thessalonians 3:10
The Price of Neglect, 45, 46.

34. Beatitudes; Sermon on the Mount; Man: sinfulness of

A fairly accurate description of the human race might be furnished to one unacquainted with it by taking the Beatitudes, turning them wrong side out and saying, "Here is your human race." For the exact opposite of the virtues in the Beatitudes are the very qualities which distinguish human life and conduct.

In the world of men we find nothing approaching the virtues of which Jesus spoke in the opening words of the famous Sermon on the Mount. Instead of poverty of spirit we find the rankest kind of pride; instead of mourners we find pleasure seekers; instead of meekness, arrogance; instead of hunger after righteousness we hear men saying, "I am rich and increased with goods and have need of nothing"; instead of mercy we find cruelty; instead of purity of heart, corrupt imaginings; instead of peacemakers we find men quarrelsome and resentful; instead of rejoicing in mistreatment we find them fighting back with every weapon at their command.

Of this kind of moral stuff civilized society is composed.

Jeremiah 17:9; Matthew 5:3-12; Revelation 3:15-17
The Pursuit of God, 101, 102.

35. Bible: apparent contradictions; Mystery: acceptance of

The beginner in Christ will not have read long in the Scriptures till he comes upon passages that appear to contradict each other. . . .

Far better than the attempt to understand is the humility that admits its ignorance and waits quietly on God for His own light to appear in His own time. We will be better able to understand when we have accepted the humbling truth that there are many things in heaven and earth that we shall never be able to understand. It will be good for us to accept the universe and take our place in the mighty web of God's creation, so perfectly known to Him and so slightly known to even the wisest of men. "The meek will he guide in judgment: and the meek will he teach his way." . . .

No one should be ashamed to admit that he does not know, and no Christian should fear the effect of such a confession in the realm of things spiritual. Indeed the very power of the cross lies in the fact that it is the wisdom of God and not the wisdom of man. The day we manage to explain everything spiritual will be the day that we have (for ourselves) destroyed everything divine.

Psalm 25:9; Isaiah 40:12-15; Romans 11:33-36; 1 Corinthians 2:6-8
The Root of the Righteous, 77,78,79,80.

36. Bible: authority of

The scholar has a vitally important task to perform within a carefully prescribed precinct. His task is to guarantee the purity of the text, to get as close as possible to the Word as originally given. He may compare Scripture with Scripture until he has discovered the true meaning of the text. But right there his authority ends. He *must never sit in judgment upon what is written.* He dare not bring the *meaning* of the Word before the bar of his reason. He dare not commend or condemn the Word as reasonable or unreasonable, scientific or unscientific. After the meaning is discovered, that meaning judges him; never does he judge it.

John 5:36-40; 2 Timothy 3:16-17; 2 Peter 1:20-21
The Knowledge of the Holy, 31.

37. Bible: authority of

God has given us the Book, brother, and the Book comes first. If it can't be shown in the Book, then I don't want anyone coming to me all aquiver and trying to tell me anything. The Book—you must give me the Word!

1 Thessalonians 2:13; 2 Timothy 3:16-17; Hebrews 4:12
The Counselor, 114.

38. Bible: authority of; Skeptics; Bible: inspiration of

Let a man question the inspiration of the Scriptures and a curious, even monstrous, inversion takes place: thereafter he judges the Word instead of letting the Word judge him; he determines what the Word should teach instead of permitting it to determine what he should believe; he edits, amends, strikes out, adds at his pleasure; but always he sits above the Word and makes it amenable to him instead of kneeling before God and becoming amenable to the Word.

2 Timothy 3:16-17; Revelation 22:18-19
Man: The Dwelling Place of God, 109.

39. Bible: difficult passages; Cults; False teaching

If I do not know what a difficult passage means, I can at least know what it does not mean. . . .

Let us take a homemade illustration. I am trying to identify a piece of fruit I have just pulled from a tree. It is purple in color, egg-shaped, contains one large pit at its center, has a series of sharp spikes growing all over its surface, has the fragrance of a rose and the taste of watermelon. I shake my head and admit I do not know what it is. Immediately an eager-faced helper appears and says, "If you do not know what it is, I can help you. It is a banana. Now that I have given you the light, come and follow me. I know a lot more things just as wonderful as this."

But I am not so easily fooled. My answer is, "No, my friend, I will not follow you. True, I do not know what this fruit is, *but I surely know what it is not. It is not a banana.*" That will dispose of my little helper most effectively, especially if I can produce a real banana for comparison.

Now what does all this add up to? Simply this—the fact that I may not be able to explain a passage does not obligate me to accept from another an explanation that is obviously phony. *I do not know what it means, but I do know what it does not mean.*

1 Thessalonians 5:20-21; 2 Peter 3:14-18; 1 John 4:1
This World: Playground or Battleground?, 98, 99.

40. Bible: difficult passages; False teaching

Scores of books have been written by people who have taken

opposite sides on some of these difficult passages of Scripture. I have read and studied many of these books.

In this context, I recall a friend's story. He told me that he had discovered a woodworking shop where all varieties of wooden products, like clothes pins and chair legs, were made and sold. There was a rather startling sign in front of the shop. It read: "All Kinds of Twisting and Turning Done Here." When I have read the narrow, partisan arguments set forth in some of these books I mention, I have felt they too could use the words as an overall title: *All Kinds of Twisting and Turning Done Here!*

2 Peter 2:12-15; 2 Peter 3:16; Jude 14-15
Jesus, Author of Our Faith, 100.

41. Bible: meditation

Let's practice the art of Bible meditation. But please don't grab that phrase and go out and form a club—we are organized to death already. Just meditate. Let us just be plain, thoughtful Christians. Let us open our Bibles, spread them out on a chair and meditate on the Word of God. It will open itself to us, and the Spirit of God will come and brood over it.

I do challenge you to meditate, quietly, reverently, prayerfully, for a month. Put away questions and answers and the filling in of the blank lines in the portions you haven't been able to understand. Put all of the cheap trash away and take the Bible, get on your knees, and in faith, say, "Father, here I am. Begin to teach me!"

Joshua 1:7-8; Psalm 1; Psalm 119
The Counselor, 137.

42. Bible: meditation

What is the word when we come to the Bible? It is *meditate*. We are to come to the Bible and meditate. That is what the old saints did. They meditated. They laid the Bible on the old-fashioned handmade chair, got down on the old, scrubbed board floor and meditated on the Word. As they meditated, faith mounted. The Spirit and faith illuminated. They had nothing but a Bible with fine print and narrow margins and poor paper, but they knew their Bible better than some of us with all of our helps. Let's practice the art of Bible meditation.

Joshua 1:7-8; Psalm 1; Psalm 119:97
How to Be Filled With the Holy Spirit, 56, 57.

43. Bible: meditation; Knowledge of God: in the Bible

Every problem that touches us is answered in the Book—stay by the Word! I want to preach the Word, love the Word and make the Word the most important element in my Christian life.

Read it much, read it often, brood over it, think over it, meditate over it—meditate on the Word of God day and night. When you are awake at night, think of a helpful verse. When you get up in the morning, no matter how you feel, think of a verse and make the Word of God the important element in your day. The Holy Spirit wrote the Word, and if you make much of the Word, He will make much of you. It is through the Word that He reveals Himself. Between those covers is a living Book. God wrote it and it is still vital and effective and alive. God is in this Book, the Holy Spirit is in this Book, and if you want to find Him, go into this Book.

Joshua 1:7-8; Psalm 1; Psalm 5:3; Psalm 63:5-6
The Counselor, 136.

44. Bible: meditation; Listening to God

Whoever will listen will hear the speaking Heaven. This is definitely not the hour when men take kindly to an exhortation to listen, for listening is not today a part of popular religion. We are at the opposite end of the pole from there. Religion has accepted the monstrous heresy that noise, size, activity and bluster make a man dear to God. But we may take heart. To a people caught in the tempest of the last great conflict God says, "Be still, and know that I am God" (Psalm 46:10), and still He says it, as if He means to tell us that our strength and safety lie not in noise but in silence.

It is important that we get still to wait on God. And it is best that we get alone, preferably with our Bible outspread before us. Then if we will we may draw near to God and begin to hear Him speak to us in our hearts.

Psalm 46:10; Isaiah 30:15; Matthew 6:6
The Pursuit of God, 73, 74.

45. Bible: memorization of; Bible: study of; Holy Spirit: power of God

That is why I believe we ought to memorize Scripture. That is why we ought to get to know the Word, why we ought to fill our minds with the great hymns and songs of the church. They will mean little to us until the Holy Spirit comes. But when He comes He will have fuel to use. Fire without fuel will not burn, but fuel without fire is dead. And the Holy Spirit will not come on a church where there is no biblical body of truth. The Holy Spirit never comes into a vacuum, but where the Word of God is, there is fuel, and the fire falls and burns up the sacrifice.

Psalm 119:9-11; John 14:26; 2 Timothy 2:14-15
Faith Beyond Reason, 28, 29.

46. Bible: misapplication of; Politics

Of all the books in the world, the one most quoted, most misunderstood and most misapplied is the Bible. . . .

Adlai Stevenson, former governor of Illinois, when going through the throes of deciding whether or not he should let his name stand for nomination for the presidency, reportedly had a deep indisposition for the office. He was quoted as having repeated the words of Christ in the garden of Gethsemane, "My Father, if it is possible, may this cup be taken from me. Yet not as I will, but as you will."

Now it is remotely possible that a true saint of God, in a moment of awful and heart-searching prayer, might in hushed reverence quote these words of the Savior and apply them to his or her own case. But their use at a political convention came as a dash of cold water in the face of some who heard. In the midst of endless billows of hoarse shouting, grandiose and unsupported claims of achievements, bitter and abusive denunciating of others who did not agree with them, senseless and moronic acts of childish demonstrating, "snake dancing" and horn blowing, obsequious flattering and downright lying, it is hard to see how the spirit of our Lord's solemn and tender words could have a place. All political conventions are alike, regardless of party, and should Christ appear at one of them and demand that His Lordship be acknowledged and His commandments be obeyed, He would be forthright shouted down and led from the room by the sergeant at arms. Yet His words are quoted as if they had a place there—surely a painful misapplication of Scripture.

Matthew 26:39; Acts 2:46-47
This World: Playground or Battleground?, 43, 44, 45.

47. Bible: neglect of; Meditation; Distractions

The present neglect of the inspired Scriptures by civilized man is a shame and a scandal; for those same Scriptures tell him all he wants to know, or should want to know, about God, his own soul and human destiny....

Whatever keeps me from the Bible is my enemy, however harmless it may appear to be. Whatever engages my attention when I should be meditating on God and things eternal does injury to my soul. Let the cares of life crowd out the Scriptures from my mind and I have suffered loss where I can least afford it. Let me accept anything else instead of the Scriptures and I have been cheated and robbed to my eternal confusion.

Joshua 1:8; Psalm 1:1-3; Psalm 119:97
That Incredible Christian, 81, 82.

48. Bible: obedience to

The threefold purpose of the Bible is to inform, to inspire faith and to secure obedience. Whenever it is used for any other purpose, it is used wrongly and may do actual injury. The Holy Scriptures will do us good only as we present an open mind to be taught, a tender heart to believe and a surrendered will to obey.

Psalm 119:9-11; 2 Timothy 3:16-17; James 1:22-25
The Next Chapter After the Last, 93.

49. Bible: obedience to

The boast that the Bible is the world's best seller sounds a little hollow when the character and purpose of the Bible are understood.

It is not how many Bibles are sold that counts, nor even how many people read them; what matters is how many actually believe what they read and surrender themselves in faith to live by the truth. Short of this the Bible can have no real value for any of us....

God's Word is not to be enjoyed as one might enjoy a Beethoven symphony or a poem by Wordsworth. It demands immediate action, faith, surrender, committal. Until it has secured these it has done nothing positive for the reader, but it has increased his responsibility and deepened the judgment that must follow.

Matthew 7:24-27; James 1:22-25
The Set of the Sail, 165, 166.

50. Bible: obedience to

In a time of disaster such as earthquake or flood first-aid information and the instructions of the medical authorities are often matters of life or death. What would we think of a man if we found him at such a time comfortably reclined reading this material for its literary beauty? He might feel an aesthetic thrill at the terse, concise language and still die of typhoid, for his life depends not upon his admiration of the words of the official directives but upon his obedience to them.

As preposterous as such conduct would be, yet something like it is practiced constantly in a sphere where the consequences are far more weighty. Men who have but a little while to prepare themselves for the eternal world read the only book that can tell them how—not to learn how, but to enjoy the literary beauty of the book. Only the blindness of heart occasioned by sin would permit men so to do.

John 6:63-65; James 1:22-25
The Set of the Sail, 166, 167.

51. Bible: reading of

When religion loses its sovereign character and becomes mere form, this spontaneity is lost also, and in its place come precedent, propriety, system—and the file-card mentality. . . .

Here's how the file card works when it gets into the Christian life and begins to create mental habits: It divides the Bible into sections fitted to the days of the year, and compels the Christian to read according to rule. No matter what the Holy Spirit may be trying to say to a man, still he goes on reading where the card tells him, dutifully checking it off each day.

Every Spirit-led saint knows that there are times when he is held by an inward pressure to one chapter, or even one verse, for days at a time while he wrestles with God till some truth does its work within him. To leave that present passage to follow a prearranged reading schedule is for him wholly impossible. He is in the hand of the free Spirit, and reality is appearing before him to break and humble and lift and liberate and cheer. But only the free soul can know the glory of this. To this the heart bound by system will be forever a stranger.

Psalm 119:20,24
Of God and Men, 79, 80.

52. Bible: reading of; Bible: meditation; Prayer: necessity of

To think God's thoughts requires much prayer. If you do not

learn to know the place of faith in our relation to God. If it points us to the moon and the stars, it is that we may know how frail we are. If it talks about the birds, it is to teach us to trust our Heavenly Father without fear or doubting. It tells us about hell not to satisfy our morbid curiosity, but that we may steer our feet far from its terrors. It tells us about heaven that we may be prepared to enter there. It writes the history of human disgrace that we may learn the value of divine grace. It warns in order that it may turn our feet away from the paths that go down to the path of destruction. It rebukes in order that we may see our own faults and be delivered from them. . . .

Sir Walter Scott, when he was dying, called for "the book." A servant inquired which of his thousands of volumes he meant, and the great man replied, "The Bible, of course. For a dying man there can be no other book."

Genesis 9:13; Psalm 8:1,9; Proverbs 14:12-13; Luke 12:24; John 6:63-65; Hebrews 11:8-10
We Travel an Appointed Way, 7, 8.

58. Biography: Biblical

Next to the Holy Scriptures the greatest aid to the life of faith may be Christian biography. It is indeed notable that a large part of the Bible itself is given over to the life and labors of prophets, patriarchs and kings—who they were, what they did and said, how they prayed and toiled and suffered and how they triumphed at last. Sometimes this is given in brief outline—a quick candid shot and no more—but often there is much fullness of detail covering page after page of the Sacred Word.

These favored ones whose names appear on the roll of the spiritually great have been adopted by succeeding generations of pilgrims as guides and teachers in the holy way. We have all felt their presence. We have stood with Abraham as he shielded his eyes and peered down the centuries to see by faith the fulfillment of the promise. We have sat with David under pale light of the stars as, accompanied by his homemade lyre, he tried out some verses that were later to become immortal. Who among us has not been made wiser and better by knowing Elijah or Daniel or Paul? And who has not thanked God that their story was written down for us to read?

1 Corinthians 10:6,11; Hebrews 11
Let My People Go: The Life of Robert A. Jaffray, 1.

59. Biography: humanness in

"Leave the warts in," said Lincoln when about to sit for his portrait, and to the everlasting credit of the artist he had the courage to do it. . . .

George Washington has the misfortune to be respected by everybody and loved by nobody. Parson Weems saw to that. He wrote a life of Washington that fixed a great gulf between him and every downright American from that day forward. The pretty boy with the cherry cheeks, the innocent little hatchet and the sententious manner of speech which Weems gave to the world can never excite the affections of sincere men and women. But I wonder whether Lincoln's warts and his uncurried hair may not have created a secret bond of sympathy between him and two generations of American boys. No one wants a hero who is too perfect.

1 Timothy 1:12-15
Wingspread; A.B. Simpson: A Study in Spiritual Altitude, 8.

60. Biography: interpretation of

Biography may be either a help or a hindrance, depending upon how we interpret and apply it. The biographer usually accents the high, stirring moments in the life of his subject and of necessity passes over the days and years when nothing out of the ordinary happened. Yet without the thousands of common days there could have been no continuity between the uncommon ones to bind the life together. In reading the lives of great men we must beware that we do not become dissatisfied with our tame existence and hold lightly the countless treasures which through the mercy of God we all possess. A life that lasted 50 or 70 or 90 years must be condensed into a few pages with the result that the terrain is shoved together and the view distorted. From this out-of-focus picture we are likely to draw three erroneous conclusions: one, that the subject was greater than he actually was; two, that by contrast we are smaller than we really are, and three, that God respects persons and distributes His favors unevenly among His children.

Acts 10:34-35; Romans 2:11; Galatians 2:6; James 2:1-5
The Price of Neglect, 131.

61. Blessings: remembrance of

Bernard of Clairvaux speaks somewhere of a "perfume compounded of the remembered benefits of God." Such fragrance is too rare. Every follower of Christ should be redolent of such perfume; for have we not all received more from God's kindness than our imagination could have conceived before we knew Him and discovered for ourselves how rich and how generous He is?

That we have received of His fullness grace for grace no one will deny; but the fragrance comes not from the receiving; it comes from the remembering, which is something quite different indeed. Ten lepers received their health; that was the benefit. One came back to thank his benefactor; that was the perfume. Unremembered benefits, like dead flies, may cause the ointment to give forth a stinking savor.

Psalm 103:1-2; Luke 17:17; John 1:16
Of God and Men, 154.

62. Boards: lack of vision; Faith: confidence in God; Church: finances

Here in the New Testament was Philip the Calculator—Philip the Mathematician, Philip the Clerk. There was need for a miracle, and Philip set out to calculate the odds. Probably every Christian group has at least one person with a calculator. I have sat on boards for many years, and rarely is there a board without a Philip the Calculator among its members. When you suggest something, out comes the calculator to prove that it cannot be done. . . .

As I say, I have been sitting on these boards for many years, and there are always two kinds of board members: those who can see the miracle and those who can only see their calculators and their strings of calculations. . . .

The people with the calculators have seen the problem, but they have not seen God. They have figured things out, but they have not figured God in.

Philip the Calculator. He can be a dangerous man in the church of our Lord Jesus Christ. Every suggestion made in the direction of progress gets a negative vote from this man.

Matthew 6:25-34; Matthew 16:8; John 6:5-7
Faith Beyond Reason, 137, 138, 139.

63. Body of Christ; Unity

I feel that we evangelicals are making two serious mistakes. One is insisting upon union where it should not be, and the other is creating divisions artificially where there is no justification for them.

One blessed fact to be kept ever in mind is the organic unity of all true believers in Christ. However ill taught God's children may be on this subject and however widely separated by artificial barriers, they are nonetheless all members of Christ and as surely one as a man's hands and feet and eyes and ears are one by being members of his body. Unity in Christ is not something to be achieved; it is something to be recognized.

Acts 2:42-44; 1 Corinthians 12; Ephesians 4:1-6
God Tells the Man Who Cares, 54, 55.

64. Boldness; America: sinfulness

We stand in desperate need of a few men like Elijah who will dare to face up to the brazen sinners who dictate our every way of life. Sin in the full proportions of a revolution or a plague has all but destroyed our civilization while church people have played like children in the marketplace.

What has happened to the spirit of the American Christian? Has our gold become dim? Have we lost the spirit of discernment till we can no longer recognize our captors? How much longer will we hide in caves while Ahab and Jezebel continue to pollute the temple and ravage the land? Surely we should give this some serious thought and prayer before it is too late—if indeed it is not too late already.

1 Kings 18:18; 1 Kings 19:9-10
The Next Chapter After the Last, 18, 19.

65. Boldness; Courage; Defensiveness

Why don't we have the courage that belongs to our sound Christian faith? I cannot understand all of this ignoble apologizing and the whipped-dog attitude of so many professing Christians! . . .

But many Christians spend a lot of time and energy in making excuses, because they have never broken through into a real offensive for God by the unlimited power of the Holy Spirit! The world has nothing that we want—for we are believers in a faith that is as well authenticated as any solid fact of life. The truths we believe and the links in the chain of evidence are clear and rational. I contend that the church has a right to rejoice and that this is no time in the world's history for Christian believers to settle for a defensive holding action!

Romans 1:14-16; 2 Timothy 1:7,12; 2 Timothy 4:1-5; 1 Peter 1:3-5
I Call It Heresy!, 30.

66. Boldness; Satisfaction

Elijah had gone far beyond philosophy and its uncertainties. He had found God! It was not a religious theory that Elijah had found. He had found the very key to life and eternity.

God the Creator made us for Himself. Our hearts and beings will never be satisfied until we find our satisfaction in God Himself. Long before Elijah stood in Ahab's presence, Elijah had met God. That was what made his salutation to Ahab so significant: "I stand before God. God is here with me. I stand really in His presence, not yours."

1 Kings 17:1; Psalm 95:6-7
Men Who Met God, 94, 95.

67. Books: evil; False teaching; Reading: dangers of

History will show that bad books have ruined not only individuals but whole nations as well. What the writings of Voltaire and Rousseau did to France is too well-known to need further mention here. Again, it would not be difficult to establish a cause and effect relationship between the philosophy of Friedrich Nietzsche and the bloody career of Adolph Hitler. Certainly the doctrines of Nietzsche appeared again in the mouthings of Adolf Hitler and soon became the official party line for the Nazi propagandists. And it is hardly conceivable that Russian Communism could have come into being apart from the writings of Karl Marx. . . .

Just what part evil literature has played in the present moral breakdown throughout the world will never be known till men are called forth to answer to a holy God for their unholy deeds, but it must be very great indeed. For thousands of young people the first doubt about God and the Bible came with the reading of some evil book. We must respect the power of ideas. And printed ideas are as powerful as spoken ones; they may have a longer fuse but their explosive power is just as great.

2 Corinthians 10:5; Ephesians 5:6; Colossians 2:8-9
Of God and Men, 88, 89.

68. Books: evil; Reading: dangers of

Just what part evil literature has played in this present moral breakdown throughout our land will never be known till men are called forth to answer to a holy God for their unholy deeds. For thousands of young people, the first doubt about God and the Bible came with the reading of some evil book. We must respect the power of ideas. Printed ideas are as powerful as spoken ones—they may have a longer fuse, but their explosive power is just as great.

What all this adds up to is that we Christians are bound in all conscience to discourage the reading of subversive literature and to promote as fully as possible the circulation of good books and magazines. Our Christian faith teaches us to expect to answer for every idle word—how much more severely shall we be held to account for every evil word, whether printed or spoken. . . .

The desire to appear broad-minded is not easy to overcome, because it is rooted in our ego and is simply a none-too-subtle form of pride. In the name of broad-mindedness many a Christian home has been opened to literature that sprang not from a broad mind but from a little mind, dirty and polluted with evil.

We require our children to wipe their feet before entering the house. Dare we demand less of the literature that comes into our home?

Matthew 12:34-37; 2 Corinthians 10:5; Ephesians 5:6; Colossians 2:8-9
This World: Playground or Battleground?, 32, 33.

69. Books: value of; Reading: limitations of

Perhaps a word of warning would not be amiss here: It is that we beware the common habit of putting confidence in books, as such. It takes a determined effort of the mind to break free from the error of making books and teachers ends in themselves. The worst thing a book can do for a Christian is to leave him with the impression that he has received from it anything really good; the best it can do is to point the way to the Good he is seeking. The function of a good book is to stand like a signpost directing the reader toward the Truth and the Life. That book serves best which early makes itself unnecessary, just as a signpost serves best after it is forgotten, after the traveler has arrived safely at his desired haven. The work of a good book is to incite the reader to moral action, to turn his eyes toward God and urge him forward. Beyond that it cannot go.

John 14:6
The Pursuit of Man, xv.

70. Books: value of; Reading: limitations of

A book is a reservoir in which the raw material of thought is stored; or, otherwise viewed, a channel through which ideas are piped from one mind to another. It is therefore not an end but a means only. In itself it is but a few ounces of paper and cloth and ink, the sum of which can be bought anywhere for a few cents. . . .

The Greek moral philosopher, Epictetus, understood well the difference between means and end, and exhorted his listeners constantly to beware mistaking the one for the other. The wise old Stoic looked for results in the life and was not impressed by the number of books his students had read. "Show me then your progress in this point," he demanded. "As if I should say to a wrestler, 'Show me your muscle' and he should answer, 'See my dumbbells.' Your dumbbells are your own affair. I desire to see the *effect* of them."

The Size of the Soul, 36, 37.

71. Boredom: from overstimulation

Today more than ever we Christians need to learn how to sanctify the ordinary. This is a blasé generation. People have been overstimulated to the place where their nerves are jaded and their tastes corrupted. Natural things have been rejected to make room for things artificial. The sacred has been secularized, the holy vulgarized and worship converted into a form of entertainment. A dopey, blear-eyed generation seeks constantly for some new excitement powerful enough to bring a thrill to its worn-out and benumbed sensibilities. So many wonders have been discovered or invented that nothing on earth is any longer wonderful. Everything is common and almost everything boring. . . .

When the whole moral and psychological atmosphere is secular and common how can we escape its deadly effects? How can we sanctify the ordinary and find true spiritual meaning in the common things of life? The answer has already been suggested. It is to consecrate the whole of life to Christ and begin to do everything in His name and for His sake.

1 Corinthians 10:31; Colossians 3:16-18; 1 Peter 4:11
Born After Midnight, 68, 69.

72. Boredom: religious

In other words, we are bored with God Almighty. We chuckle at Pogo and laugh at Dear Abby, but we are bored with God.

Isaiah 43:15,22
Rut, Rot or Revival: The Condition of the Church, 159.

73. Boredom: religious; Church: boredom

It does not speak too well for our Christian testimony when God tells us that He has sent His Son to be His final revelation in this world—and we act bored about it! . . .

That must be the key to our boredom with Christianity: We have not been keeping in very close touch with our Man in glory. We have been doing in our churches all those churchly things that we do. We have done them with our own understanding and in our own energy. But without a bright and conscious confirmation of God's presence, a church service can be very deadly and dull.

We go to church and we look bored—even when we are supposed to be singing God's praises. We look bored because we *are* bored. If the truth were known, we are bored with God, but we are too pious to admit it. I think God would love it if some honest soul would begin his or her prayer by admitting, "God, I am praying because I know I should, but the truth is I do not want to pray. I am bored with the whole thing!"

I doubt if the Lord would be angry at such candor. Rather, I believe He would think, "Well, there is hope for that person. That person is being truthful with Me. Most people are bored with Me and will not admit it."

John 1:14; Hebrews 1:1-2
Jesus, Our Man in Glory, 15, 16.

74. Boredom: religious; Preaching: experiencing God; Jesus Christ: His loveliness

I for one admit that I am weary of the familiar religious pep talk. I am tired of being whipped into line, of being urged to work harder, to pray more, to give more generously, when the speaker does not show me Christ. This is sure to lead to a point of diminishing return and leave us exhausted and a little bored with it all. . . .

I have spent many uncomfortable hours in prayer meetings listening to my brethren begging for blessings, but all prayer is comfortable when the heart is having fellowship with God and the inner eyes are looking upon His blessed face. I have suffered through many a dull and tedious sermon, but no sermon is poor or long when the preacher is showing me the beauty of Jesus. A sight of His face will inspire love and zeal and a longing to grow in grace and in the knowledge of God.

The sum of all this is that nothing can preserve the sweet savor of our first experience except to be preoccupied with God Himself. Our little rill is sure to run dry unless we keep it replenished from the fountain.

John 12:21; 2 Peter 3:14-18; Revelation 2:4-5
God Tells the Man Who Cares, 128, 129.

75. Bride of Christ; Blood of Christ

Just as He had done with Adam, God put Jesus on the cross in a deep sleep and opened His side. Out from His side flowed not a rib but water and blood. From that water and blood God is washing, cleansing and preparing a bride worthy of Jesus. God did not create Eve from nothing as He had Adam, but He created her from the wounded side of Adam. Even so, the Lord is not creating a race that does not now exist to be His church. He takes the race that now exists—certain members of it—and washes it in the blood that came from the wounded side. By the Holy Spirit, He gives the nature of Christ to the bride, so she will be worthy of Him. . . .

A theologian once noted that God took the bone that made the woman not from Adam's head, that she might lord it over him; not from his feet, that he might lord it over her; but from his heart, that she might understand him, and he might love her. That is what the church is—the bride of Christ.

Genesis 2:21-22; Ephesians 5:25-29; 1 John 1:6-9
Rut, Rot or Revival: The Condition of the Church, 129.

76. Burdens; Trials: attitude toward

Unnecessary burdens are crushing the life out of people every day. Mental institutions are overflowing and psychiatrists are doing a rushing business because the burden of living is getting to be more than we can bear. Civilization has not made our lot easier except in things pertaining to the body; the burdens of the heart are growing more numerous, and science has found no remedy. The silky voice of the practitioner may soothe the mind for a time, but the disease is too deep to yield itself to such inadequate measures.

Surely we could live longer and better and be far happier and more useful if we could learn to cast our burdens upon the Lord. Then it would not matter how heavy they were, for He would carry them for us.

Psalm 55:22; Matthew 11:28-30; Philippians 4:6-7
We Travel an Appointed Way, 40.

C

77. Call of Christ; Honors

To be called to follow Christ is a high honor; higher indeed than any honor men can bestow upon each other.

Were all the nations of the earth to unite in one great federation and call a man to head that federation, that man would be honored above any other man that ever lived. Yet the humblest man who heeds the call to follow Christ has an honor far above such a man; for the nations of the earth can bestow only such honor as they possess, while the honor of Christ is supreme over all. God has given Him a name that is above every name.

Matthew 4:19; Luke 9:23-25; John 12:24-26; Philippians 2:9-11
Man: The Dwelling Place of God, 11, 12.

78. Call of Christ; Pastoral ministry: significance

One thing is certain: the call of Christ is always a promotion. Were Christ to call a king from his throne to preach the gospel to some tribe of aborigines, that king would be elevated above anything he had known before. Any movement toward Christ is ascent, and any direction away from Him is down.

Acts 9:15-16; 1 Timothy 1:12-15
Man: The Dwelling Place of God, 14.

79. Call of God; God: His voice

I say that we have not been given up. That is plain from the Book of Genesis. Recall that the sound of God's gentle voice was heard saying, "Adam, where art thou?"—and that voice has never died out!

The echo of that voice sounding down through the years has never ceased to reverberate, to echo and re-echo from peak to peak, from generation to generation, from race to race, continent to continent, and off to the islands and back to continents again.

The voice of God is entreating us. With everything inside of my beating heart, chastened and criticized by everything inside of my mind, I believe in the voice of God sounding in this world, calling men!

Genesis 3:9; Isaiah 55:1-2; Revelation 22:17
The Tozer Pulpit, Volume 1, Book 1, 16, 17.

80. Call of God; Salvation: invitation to

The gospel invitation is offered to one and all, but many are too preoccupied to hear or heed. They never allow God's call to become a reason for decision. Their relationship with God never becomes a personal encounter. As a result, they live out their entire lives insisting that they never heard any call from God.

The answer to that is plain. God has been trying to get through to them, but their line is always busy! They are engrossed in a host of worldly pursuits.

Isaiah 55:1; 2 Corinthians 4:4; 2 Corinthians 6:2; Revelation 22:17
Jesus, Author of Our Faith, 45.

81. Call of God; Salvation: invitation to

Although the human mind stubbornly resists and resents the suggestion that it is a sick, fallen planet upon which we ride, everything within our consciousness, our innermost spirit, confirms that the voice of God is sounding in this world—the voice of God calling, seeking, beckoning to lost men and women! . . .

Sacred revelation declares plainly that the inhabitants of the earth are lost. They are lost by a mighty calamitous visitation of woe which came upon them somewhere in that distant past and is still upon them.

But it also reveals a glorious fact—that this lost race has not been given up!

There is a divine voice that continues to call. It is the voice of the Creator, God, and it is entreating them. Just as the shepherd went everywhere searching for his sheep, just as the woman in the parable went everywhere searching for her coins, so there is a divine search with many variations of the voice that entreats us, calling us back. . . .

Think of the Genesis account: Adam fleeing from the face of God, hiding among the trees of the garden. It was then that the sound of God's gentle voice was heard, saying "Adam, where are you?" (Genesis 3:9).

I would remind you that His seeking voice has never died out. The echo of that voice is sounding throughout the widening years. It has never ceased to echo and reecho from peak to peak, from generation to generation, from race to race, and continent to continent, and off to islands and back to the continent again. Throughout all of man's years, "Adam, where are you?" has been the faithful call.

Genesis 3:9; Isaiah 55:1-2; Luke 15:3-10
Echoes from Eden, 3, 8.

82. Carelessness

I'll tell you this—if some women kept house like they keep their soul, they'd be in for a divorce. Their husbands wouldn't stay around. If some people kept their business the way they keep their souls, they'd go bankrupt.

Proverbs 4:23; Matthew 26:40-41; Ephesians 6:18
Success and the Christian, 32.

83. Carnality

The Apostle Paul talked about the carnal Christians of Corinth, and he labored and prayed and wept over the carnality of those Christians. This describes most evangelicals today: carnal, immature, without miracles, without wonders, lacking a wonderful sense of the presence of the Lord, held together by social activities and nothing else.

1 Corinthians 3:1-3; 2 Corinthians 2:4; 2 Corinthians 12:20-21
Rut, Rot or Revival: The Condition of the Church, 97, 98.

84. Carnality; Holy Spirit: revelation of God

I believe that it might be well for us if we just stopped all of our business and got quiet and worshiped God and waited on Him. It doesn't make me popular when I remind you that we are a carnal bunch, but it is true, nevertheless, that the body of Christians is carnal. The Lord's people ought to be a sanctified, pure, clean people, but we are a carnal crowd. We are carnal in our attitudes, in our tastes and carnal in many things. Our young people often are not reverent in our Christian services. We have so degraded our religious tastes that our Christian service is largely exhibitionism. We desperately need a divine visitation—for our situation will never be cured by sermons! It will never be cured until the Church of Christ has suddenly been confronted with what one man called the *mysterium tremendium*—the fearful mystery that is God, the fearful majesty that is God. This is what the Holy Spirit does. He brings the wonderful mystery that is God to us, and presents Him to the human spirit.

Psalm 8:1,9; Psalm 46:10; John 17:15-18
The Counselor, 66, 67.

85. Carnality; New believer

The true Christian is a child of two worlds. He lives among fallen men, receives all of his earlier concepts from them and develops a fallen view of life along with everyone from Adam on. When he is regenerated and inducted into the new creation he is called to live according to the laws and principles that underlie the new kingdom, but all his training and his thinking have been according to the old. So he may, unless he is very wise and prayerful, find himself trying to live a heavenly life after an earthly pattern. This is what Paul called "carnal" living. The issues of the new Christian life are influenced by the automatic responses of the old life and confusion results.

Romans 7:15-25; 1 Corinthians 3:1-3; 2 Corinthians 5:17; Ephesians 4:14-16
Born After Midnight, 97, 98.

86. Carnality; Sin: victory over

God is love and His kindness is unbounded, but He has no sympathy with the carnal mind. He remembers that we are dust, indeed, but He refuses to tolerate the doings of the flesh. He has given us His word; He has promised that we would never be tempted above what we were able to bear; He has placed Himself at our disposal in response to believing prayer; He has made available to us the infinite moral power of His Holy Spirit to enable us to do His will here on earth. There is no excuse for our acting like timid weaklings.

Psalm 103:13-14; 1 Corinthians 10:13; 1 John 4:16
That Incredible Christian, 106.

87. Celebrities; Testimonials

A system of literature has grown up around the notion that Christianity may be proven by the fact that great men believe in Christ. If we can just get the story of a politician who believes in Christ, we spread it all over our magazines, "Senator So-and-so believes in Christ." The implication is that if he believes in Christ, then Christ must be all right. When did Jesus Christ have to ride in on the coattail of a senator?

No, no, my brother! Jesus Christ stands alone, unique and supreme, self-validating, and the Holy Spirit declares Him to be God's eternal Son. Let all the presidents and all the kings and queens, the senators, and the lords and ladies of the world, along with the great athletes and great actors—let them kneel at His feet and cry, "Holy, holy, holy is the Lord God Almighty!" (Revelation 4:8b).

Only the Holy Spirit can do this, my brethren. For that reason, I don't bow down to great men. I bow down to the Great Man, and if you have learned to worship the Son of Man, you won't worship other men.

1 Corinthians 1:26-29; 1 Corinthians 12:1-11; Revelation 4:8
The Counselor, 32, 33.

88. Change; Status quo

The problem is change, which disturbs many people. They have accepted the status quo as being the very tablets given by God on the mountain. Most people, if they happen to be in any church anywhere, accept the status quo without knowing or caring to inquire how it came to be. In other words, they do not ask, "Oh God, is this of You, is this divine, is this out of the Bible?" Because it was done and is being done, and because a lot of people are doing it, they assume it is all right....

Today we need people who dare to question the status quo and say, "Wait a minute here. Where do you find this in the Bible?"

Isaiah 1:16-18
Rut, Rot or Revival: The Condition of the Church, 95, 96.

89. Character; Virtue

Because this is a moral universe, character, which is the excellence of moral beings, is naturally paramount. As the excellence of steel is strength and the excellence of art is beauty, so the excellence of mankind is moral character. "An honest man is the noblest work of God," an apothegm usually attributed to John Wesley, may sound at first rather extreme, but if we allow the word "honest" to stand for all the moral virtues we may be able to understand the apothegm and possibly to agree with it. A saint should be not only a man of intense spiritual devotion but a man of symmetrical virtues and perfectly balanced character.

Philippians 4:8; Colossians 1:9-11; 2 Peter 1:5-7
The Set of the Sail, 122.

90. Children; Child dedication

When our little girl came to us, we dedicated her to the Lord in a morning service, but that was nothing. My own personal dedication of that child was a prolonged, terrible, sweaty thing. I finally said to God, "Yes, Lord, you can have her." I knew that God wasn't going to let her die, for I had learned that lesson years before with her two older brothers.

But the thing was this—I didn't know what He wanted, and it was a struggle to give up, to yield.

Later, in giving a testimony in our church, I said, "The dearest thing we have in the world is our little girl, but God knows that He can have her whenever He wants her."

After the service someone came and said, "Mr. Tozer, aren't you afraid to talk like that about your little girl?"

"Afraid?" I said, "Why, I have put her in the hands of perfect love and love cannot wound anyone and love cannot hurt anyone. I am perfectly content that she is shielded in the life of Jesus Christ, His name being love and His hands being strong and His face shining like the beauty of the sun and His heart being the tender heart of God in compassion and lovingkindness."

1 Samuel 3:18; 1 John 4:18
I Talk Back to the Devil, 87.

91. Choices; Commitment; Ambition

Who wins when it's a choice between God and money, between God and ambition? A lot of young people turn to the Lord when they're in their teens and are doing fine—and then they become ambitious. They have some talent and develop it, and the world finds out and sends for them. Then they have to make a choice between following that ambition, which will take them to the world and away from the church, or following the Lord. And I think a clean 97 percent of them will follow their ambition.

Who wins when it's a question of fleshly enjoyment or doing the will of God? Out in the world God would never get a vote, but in the Church it would seem to me that God ought to get all the votes there are. And yet when it's a choice between fleshly enjoyments and God, the Church usually votes on the side of fleshly enjoyments—provided we can somehow strike a compromise and have God too.

Who wins when it's a choice between marriage and God's will? I have known or read of a few instances where men and women separate because one or the other is not a Christian.... Now that happens once in a blue moon. But it doesn't happen very often. Usually, a young man or woman follows the Lord blissfully and happily along. They're the first one to young people's service and the last one out. They're the first one to take part and witness and to testify and all, until they meet someone. And then God gets shunted aside while they decide whether they are to marry and who to marry. And if it's a choice between God and marriage, they marry.

Matthew 6:24,33; Romans 6:19; 2 Corinthians 6:14-15
Success and the Christian, 134, 135.

92. Choices; Priorities; Values

The important thing about a man is not where he goes when he is compelled to go, but where he goes when he is free to go where he will....

A man is absent from church Sunday morning. Where is he? If he is in a hospital having his appendix removed his absence tells us nothing about him except that he is ill; but if he is out on the golf course, that tells us a lot. To go to the hospital is compulsory; to go to the golf course, voluntary. The man is free to choose and he chooses to play instead of to pray. His choice reveals what kind of man he is. Choices always do....

I think it might be well for us to check our spiritual condition occasionally by the simple test of compatibility. When we are free to go, where do we go? In what company do we feel most at home? Where do our thoughts turn when they are free to turn where they will? When the pressure of work or business or school has temporarily lifted and we are able to think of what we will instead of what we must, what do we think of then?

The answer to these questions may tell us more about ourselves than we can comfortably accept. But we had better face up to things. We haven't too much time at the most.

Joshua 24:14-15; 1 Kings 18:21; Acts 4:23; Philippians 4:8
Man: The Dwelling Place of God, 158, 159, 160, 161.

93. Christian life; Obedience: need for

There is an evil which I have seen under the sun and which in its effect upon the Christian religion may be more destructive than Communism, Romanism and Liberalism combined. It is the glaring disparity between theology and practice among professing Christians.

So wide is the gulf that separates theory from practice in the church that an inquiring stranger who chances upon both would scarcely dream that there was any relation between them. An intelligent observer of our human scene who heard the Sunday morning sermon and later watched the Sunday afternoon conduct of those who had heard it would conclude that he had been examining two distinct and contrary religions.

It appears that too many Christians want to enjoy the thrill of feeling right but are not willing to endure the inconvenience of being right. So the divorce between theory and practice becomes permanent in fact, though in word the union is declared to be eternal. Truth sits forsaken and grieves till her professed followers come home for a brief visit, but she sees them depart again when the bills become due. They protest great and undying love for her but they will not let their love cost them anything.

Matthew 7:24-27; Romans 2:13; James 1:22-25; James 2:14-20
The Root of the Righteous, 51, 52, 53.

94. Christians: contradictions

Note the contradictions: . . .

The Christian soon learns that if he would be victorious as a son of heaven among men on earth he must not follow the common pattern of mankind, but rather the contrary. That he may be safe he puts himself in jeopardy; he loses his life to save it and is in danger of losing it if he attempts to preserve it. He goes down to get up. If he refuses to go down he is already down, but when he starts down he is on his way up.

He is strongest when he is weakest and weakest when he is strong. Though poor he has the power to make others rich, but when he becomes rich his ability to enrich others vanishes. He has most after he has given most away and has least when he possesses most.

He may be and often is highest when he feels lowest and most sinless when he is most conscious of sin. He is wisest when he knows that he knows not and knows least when he has acquired the greatest amount of knowledge. He sometimes does most by doing nothing and goes furthest when standing still. In heaviness he manages to rejoice and keeps his heart glad even in sorrow. . . .

He loves supremely One whom he has never seen, and though himself poor and lowly he talks familiarly with One who is King of all kings and Lord of all lords, and is aware of no incongruity in so doing. He feels that he is in his own right altogether less than nothing, yet he believes without question that he is the apple of God's eye and that for him the Eternal Son became flesh and died on the cross of shame.

Matthew 16:24-26; 1 Corinthians 1:26-29; 2 Corinthians 8:2,9; 2 Corinthians 12:9-10
That Incredible Christian, 12, 13.

95. Christians: contradictions

A real Christian is an odd number anyway. He feels supreme love for One whom he has never seen, talks familiarly every day to Someone he cannot see, expects to go to heaven on the virtue of Another, empties himself in order to be full, admits he is wrong so he can be declared right, goes down in order to get up, is strongest when he is weakest, richest when he is poorest, and happiest when he feels worst. He dies so he can live, forsakes in order to have, gives away so he can keep, sees the invisible, hears the inaudible, and knows that which passeth knowledge.

Romans 6:4-7; Ephesians 3:9; Titus 3:4-7; 1 Peter 1:6-9, 13
The Root of the Righteous, 156.

96. Christians: fools for Christ; Respectability

. . . some are fearful that they will lose their reputation as sober and conservative and traditional Christians. In other words, they have never been willing to be a fool for Jesus' sake!

It is amazing that genuine Christians are not willing to stand up wherever they are and give a good word for the Lord. There are great political ideologies sweeping the world now whose members will make double-eyed, long-eared donkeys of themselves for the sake of the party and the cause. There are religious sects whose witnesses are willing to go to jail, to be pushed around, to be lampooned for the sake of a miserable, twisted doctrine! But in our Christian ranks, we prefer to be respectable and smooth, and we have a reputation for being very solemn Christian believers.

I can only conclude from my experience that many solemn, professing Christians will never make any spiritual progress and will never really be happy in the Lord until God finds some way to shake them out of their deadly respectability!

Acts 26:24; Romans 1:14-16; 1 Corinthians 4:10-13
I Talk Back to the Devil, 9.

97. Christians: in the world

God fully expects the church of Jesus Christ to prove itself a miraculous group in the very midst of a hostile world. Christians of necessity must be in contact with the world but in being and spirit ought to be separated from the world—and as such, we should be the most amazing people in the world.

John 15:18-21; 2 Corinthians 6:17-18; Colossians 4:5,6
I Call It Heresy!, 37.

98. Christians: in the world; Christlikeness

The man who refers to one or another act as being "unfair" to him is not a victorious man. He is inwardly defeated, and in self-defense he is appealing to the referee to note that he has been fouled. This gives him an alibi when they carry him out on a stretcher and saves his face while his bruises heal. He can always blame his defeat on the fact that he was treated unfairly by others.

Christians who understand the true meaning of the cross will never whine about being treated unfairly. Whether or not they are given fair treatment will never enter their heads. They know they have been called to follow Christ, and certainly Christ did not receive anything remotely approaching fair treatment from mankind. Right there lies the glory of the cross—that a Man suffered unfairly, was abused and maligned and crucified by people unworthy to breathe the same air with Him. Yet He did not open His mouth. Though reviled He did not return the hatred, and when He suffered, He did not threaten anyone. The thought of His shouting for fair play simply cannot be entertained by the reverent heart.

Isaiah 53:7; Matthew 5:10-12; John 15:18-20; 1 Corinthians 4:10-13
This World: Playground or Battleground?, 79.

99. Christians: in the world; Opposition; Persecution

The man whom Christ illuminates with His message has eyes, and that resolves the old difficulty of blindness; but he must use his new eyes in a blind world, and that creates another problem. The world in its blindness resents his claim to sight and will go to any lengths to discredit the claim. The truth of Christ brings assurance and so removes the former problem of fear and uncertainty, but that assurance will be interpreted as bigotry by the fear-ridden multitudes. And sooner or later this misunderstanding will get the man of God into trouble. And so with many other of the blessed benefits of the gospel. As long as we remain in this twisted world, these benefits will create their own problems. We cannot escape them.

John 16:33; 2 Corinthians 4:4; 2 Timothy 1:7,12
We Travel an Appointed Way, 35.

100. Christians: in the world; Opposition; Persecution; Christlikeness

Sometimes we Christians are opposed and persecuted for reasons other than our godliness. We like to think it is our spirituality that irritates people, when in reality, it may be our personality. . . .

It might be a shock to some of us if we could know why we are disliked and why our testimony is rejected so violently. Could it be that we are guilty of a deep sinfulness of disposition that we just cannot keep hidden? Arrogance, lack of charity, contempt, self-righteousness, religious snobbery, fault-finding—and all this kept under careful restraint and disguised by a pious smile and synthetic good humor. This sort of thing is felt rather than understood by those who touch us in everyday life. They do not know why they cannot stand us, but we are sure that the reason is our exalted state of spirituality! Perilous comfort. Deep heart searching and prolonged repentance would be better.

1 Corinthians 13:1-3; 1 Thessalonians 4:11-12; 1 Peter 3:16-17; 1 Peter 4:15-16
We Travel an Appointed Way, 36, 37.

101. Christians: peculiar people

The result of Christ's purifying work is the perfecting of God's very own people, referred to in this passage from the King James version as "a peculiar people."

Many of us know all too well that this word *peculiar* has been often used to cloak religious conduct both strange and irrational. People have been known to do rather weird things and then grin a self-conscious grin and say in half-hearted apology: "Well, we are a peculiar people!"

Anyone with a serious and honest concern for scriptural admonition and instruction could quickly learn that this English word *peculiar* in the language of 1611 describing the redeemed people of God had no connotation of queerness, ridiculousness nor foolishness.

The same word was first used in Exodus 19:5 when God said that Israel "shall be a peculiar treasure unto me above all people" (KJV). It was God's way of emphasizing that His people would be to Him a treasure above all other treasures. In the etymological sense, it means "shut up to me as my special jewel."

Every loving mother and father has a good idea of what God meant. There are babies in houses up and down every street, as you can tell by the baby clothes hanging on the lines on a summer day.

But in the house where you live, there is one little infant in particular, and he is a peculiar treasure unto you above all others. It does not mean necessarily that he is prettier, but it does mean that he is the treasure above all other treasures and you would not trade him for any other child in the whole world. He is a *peculiar* treasure!

This gives us some idea, at least, of what we are—God's special jewels marked out for Him!

Exodus 19:5; Titus 2:11-14; 1 Peter 2:9
Who Put Jesus on the Cross?, 182, 183.

102. Christians: relationship with Christ

A Christian is not one who has been baptized, necessarily, though a Christian is likely to be baptized. A Christian is not one who receives Communion, though a Christian may receive Communion, and if he's been properly taught, he will. But that is not a Christian necessarily. A Christian is not one who has been born into a Christian home, though the chances are more likely that he will be a Christian if he has a good Christian background. A Christian is not one who has memorized the New Testament, or is a great lover of Christian music, or who goes to hear the Apollo Club sing "The Messiah" every year. A Christian may do all of those things and I think it might be fine if he did; but that doesn't make one a Christian. A Christian is one who sustains a right relationship to Jesus Christ.

John 1:11-13; Ephesians 2:8-10; 2 Timothy 1:9; Titus 3:4-7; Hebrews 6:1
Success and the Christian, 66.

103. Christ-like thinking; Sin: hatred of

By the intellectual, I mean we should think the way Jesus Christ thinks; that we should think scripturally, that we should see things the way the Lord Jesus sees them, that we should learn to feel the way the Lord Jesus feels about anything or anybody, that we should love what He loves and hate what He hates. . . .

It is a psychological impossibility to love anything without hating its opposite. If I love holiness, I hate sin. If I love truth, I hate lies. If I love honesty, I hate dishonesty. If I love purity, I hate filth. Hate is only bad when it is aimed against people made in the image of God or when it springs out of some unworthy or low motive like jealousy or envy or anger. We should learn to hate what Jesus hates. I'm sure that if we had the mind of Christ intellectually, so that we judged things the way He judges them, there would be less need for preaching separation from the world than there is today among Christians. . . .

I believe that is what the Holy Spirit wants to do for us. I believe that He wants our intellectual relationship to Jesus Christ to become so close, so intimate, so all-embracing that we'll think as Jesus thought, and love as He loved and hate what He hated and value what He valued and have the mind of Christ in us.

Matthew 11:28-30; Philippians 2:5; 1 Peter 4:1-2
Success and the Christian, 71, 72, 73.

104. Christmas: true meaning

So completely are we carried away by the excitement of this midwinter festival that we are apt to forget that its romantic appeal is the least significant thing about it. The theology of Christmas too easily gets lost under the gay wrappings, yet apart from the theological meaning it really has none at all. A half dozen doctrinally sound carols serve to keep alive the great deep truth of the Incarnation, but aside from these, popular Christmas music is void of any real lasting truth. The English mouse that was not even stirring, the German Tannenbaum so fair and lovely and the American red-nosed reindeer that has nothing to recommend it have pretty well taken over in Christmas poetry and song. These along with merry old St. Nicholas have about displaced Christian theology. . . .

It does seem strange that so many persons become excited about Christmas and so few stop to inquire into its meaning; but I suppose this odd phenomenon is quite in harmony with our unfortunate human habit of magnifying trivialities and ignoring matters of greatest import. . . .

The Christmas message, when stripped of its pagan overtones, is relatively simple: God is come to earth in the form of man.

John 1:14; Galatians 4:4-5; 1 Timothy 3:16
The Warfare of the Spirit, 96, 97, 98.

105. Christmas: worldly celebration

In these latter-years of the twentieth century no other season of the year reveals so much religion and so little godliness as the Christmas season. . . .

How far have we come in the corruption of our tastes from the reverence of the simple shepherds, the chant of the angels and the beauty of the heavenly host! The Star of Bethlehem could not lead a wise man to Christ today; it could not be distinguished amid the millions of artificial lights hung aloft on Main Street by the Merchants Association. No angels could sing loudly enough to make themselves heard above the raucous, earsplitting rendition of "Silent Night" meant to draw customers to the neighborhood stores.

In our mad materialism we have turned beauty into ashes, prostituted every normal emotion and made merchandise of the holiest gift the world ever knew. Christ came to bring peace and we celebrate His coming by making peace impossible for six weeks of each year. Not peace but tension, fatigue and irritation rule the Christmas season. He came to free us of debt and many respond by going deep into debt each year to buy enervating luxuries for people who do not appreciate them. He came to help the poor and we heap gifts upon those who do not need them. The simple token given out of love has been displaced by expensive presents given because we have been caught in a squeeze and don't know how to back out of it. Not the beauty of the Lord our God is found in such a situation, but the ugliness and deformity of human sin.

Matthew 2:1-11; Luke 2:8-20; Luke 4:18-19
The Warfare of the Spirit, 58, 60-61.

106. Church: activities

Every activity now being carried on in the name of Christ must meet the last supreme test: Does it have biblical authority back of it? Is it according to the letter and the spirit of the Scripture? Is its spiritual content divinely given? That it succeeds proves nothing. That it is popular proves less. Where are the proofs of its heavenly birth? Where are its scriptural credentials? What assurance does it give that it represents the operation of the Holy Spirit in the divine plan of the ages? These questions demand satisfactory answers.

Matthew 7:24-27
The Price of Neglect, 88.

107. Church: activities; Activity: religious; Busyness

In an effort to get the work of the Lord done we often lose contact with the Lord of the work and quite literally wear our people out as well. I have heard more than one pastor boast that his church was a "live" one, pointing to the printed calender as a proof—something on every night and several meetings during the day. Of course this proves nothing except that the pastor and the church are being guided by a bad spiritual philosophy. A great many of these time-consuming activities are useless and others plain ridiculous. "But," say the eager beavers who run the religious squirrel cages, "they provide fellowship and they hold our people together."

To this I reply that what they provide is not fellowship at all, and if that is the best thing the church has to offer to hold the people together it is not a Christian church in the New Testament meaning of that word. The center of attraction in a true church is the Lord Jesus Christ. . . .

If the many activities engaged in by the average church led to the salvation of sinners or the perfecting of believers they would justify themselves easily and triumphantly; but they do not. *My observations have led me to the belief that many, perhaps most, of the activities engaged in by the average church do not contribute in any way to the accomplishing of the true work of Christ on earth. I hope I am wrong, but I am afraid I am right.*

Acts 2:42-44; Colossians 1:28-29; 1 Timothy 4:13-16; 2 Timothy 2:14-16
That Incredible Christian, 136, 137.

108. Church: activities; Worship: meaningless; Knowledge of God: Church's need; Simplicity

Every age has its own characteristics. Right now we are in an age of religious complexity. The simplicity which is in Christ is rarely found among us. In its stead are programs, methods, organizations and a world of nervous activities which occupy time and attention but can never satisfy the longing of the heart. The shallowness of our inner experience, the hollowness of our worship, and that servile imitation of the world which marks our promotional methods all testify that we, in this day, know God only imperfectly, and the peace of God scarcely at all.

If we would find God amid all the religious externals, we must first determine to find Him, and then proceed in the way of simplicity.

Matthew 6:24, 33; Philippians 3:10-14; Colossians 3:1-4
The Pursuit of God, 17.

109. Church: apathy; Church: activities

Were some watcher or holy one from the bright world above to come among us for a time with the power to diagnose the spiritual ills of church people, there is one entry which I am quite sure would appear on the vast majority of his reports: *Definite evidence of chronic spiritual lassitude; level of moral enthusiasm extremely low.* . . .

It is true that there is a lot of religious activity among us: inter-church basketball tournaments, religious splash parties followed by devotions, weekend camping trips with a Bible quiz around the fire. Sunday school picnics, building fund drives and ministerial breakfasts are with us in unbelievable numbers, and they are carried on with typical American gusto. It is when we enter the sacred precincts of the heart's personal religion that we suddenly lose all enthusiasm.

So we find this strange and contradictory situation: a world of noisy, headlong religious activity carried on without moral energy or spiritual fervor.

Colossians 3:23; 1 Timothy 4:13-16; 2 Timothy 1:6-7
Of God and Men, 3, 4.

110. Church: apathy; Church: separation; Worldliness

The church, generally speaking, is afflicted with a dread, lingering illness that shows itself daily in the apathy and spiritual paralysis of its members. How can it be otherwise when 20th-century Christians refuse to acknowledge the sharp moral antithesis that God Himself has set between the church, as the body of Christ, and this present world with its own human systems?

The differences between the churchly world and the followers of the Lamb are so basic that they can never be reconciled and they can never be negotiated. God never promised His believing people that they would become a popular majority in this earthly scene....

This revelation of what God expects of the New Testament church makes me fall down before the Lord. I find myself crying in faith and determination: "Jesus, I will trust You and follow You in this present evil age. I will trust You to be my very life and sufficiency in the fellowship and joy of the body of believers, Your church!"

Matthew 10:22; John 15:18-21; John 17:14-16; 2 Corinthians 6:17-18
Jesus, Author of Our Faith, 109, 110, 111.

111. Church: apathy; Church: spiritual condition

Let me show you the progressive stages.

I begin with what I will call the *rote.* This is repetition without feeling.... We repeat without feeling, we repeat without meaning, we sing without wonder, and we listen without surprise. That is my description of the rote.

We go one step further and come to what I will call the *rut,* which is bondage to the rote. When we are unable to see and sense bondage to the rote, we are in a rut. . . .

There is a third word, and I do not particularly like to use it, but the history of the church is filled with it. The word is *rot*. The church is afflicted by dry rot. This is best explained when the psychology of nonexpectation takes over and spiritual rigidity sets in, which is an inability to visualize anything better, a lack of desire for improvement.

Rut, Rot or Revival: The Condition of the Church, 7, 8.

112. Church: apathy; Church: spiritual condition; New believer

What is the present condition of the evangelical church? The bulk of Christians are asleep. . . .

The present condition is that we are asleep. These sleeping Christians do two things that God must grieve over. One is that they control church affairs. We are democratic, and if we do not like a pastor we give him the bounce or pray that he will get another call. Then when the time comes we vote in whom we want and vote out whom we do not want. Church people control church affairs because they are intellectually, mentally and physically awake, but they may be morally and spiritually asleep. That is, they are so far down in the rut that they do not see up. . . .

The second thing sleeping Christians do is set the standards for new Christians. When you bring in a newly converted Christian, he or she automatically takes on the coloration, general mood and temperature of the solemn seats around him or her. Pretty soon he or she is where they are, and once again there are no good examples of the Christian life.

Romans 13:11-14; 1 Corinthians 11:1; 1 Thessalonians 1:6-8; Hebrews 13:17
Rut, Rot or Revival: The Condition of the Church, 29, 30, 31.

113. Church: apathy; Current conditions: shallowness; Spiritual growth

There are Christians who grow up and have no relish for anything spiritually advanced. They're preoccupied with their first lessons. The average church is a school with only one grade and that is the first one. These Christians never expect to get beyond that and they don't want to hear a man very long who wants to take them beyond that. If their pastor insists they do their homework and get ready for the next grade, they begin to pray that the Lord will call "our dear brother" somewhere else. The more they hate him the more they bear down on the words "our dear brother." All he's trying to do is prepare them for another grade, but that church is dedicated to the first grade, and the first grade is where it's going to remain.

Paul said some of them went up into the second grade and gave it up, and said, "It's too hard here," and they went back to the first.

"How long have you been in the first grade, Junior?"

"Twelve years."

Well, how long have you been listening to the same truth and hearing the same doctrine? You must be born again and there's a judgment and so on. While that is true and we must not leave that, we must use that to advance. But we don't do it. Whole generations of Christians grow up in the first grade. They learn to read their Bible in the light of this. To them, nothing in the Bible ever means anything beyond this elementary stage. They have Bible conferences dedicated to the first grade in the Christian life, Bible schools dedicated to the continuance of the first grade. For my part, I feel that I want a little ambition, a little spiritual ambition. Paul said, "Forgetting what is behind . . . I press on toward the goal" (Philippians 3:13b-14a). There was a man not satisfied with the first grade.

Philippians 3:13-14; Hebrews 5:11-12
Success and the Christian, 4, 5.

114. Church: apathy; Evangelism: urgency of

In our churches we have fairly well programmed ourselves into deadness and apathy. Think of this woman running to testify the good news brimming over in her soul. If someone had halted her by grasping her garment as she ran and had said, "Sister, we are glad to see the new light in your face and we would like to have you third on the program," she would have died along with those scribes, other Samaritans and all the rest. But she went bouncing along, eager to share the new revelation that had come to her heart. She wanted to tell the men she knew that she had found the Master, the one who had told her everything she had ever done and known.

John 4:28-29
Faith Beyond Reason, 108, 109.

115. Church: authority

The present position of Christ in the gospel churches may be likened to that of a king in a limited, constitutional monarchy. The king (sometimes depersonalized by the term "the Crown") is in such a country no more than a traditional rallying point, a pleasant symbol of unity and loyalty much like a flag or a national anthem. He is lauded, feted and supported, but his real authority is small. Nominally he is head over all, but in every crisis someone else makes the decisions. On formal occasions he appears in his royal attire to deliver the tame, colorless speech put into his mouth by the real rulers of the country. The whole thing may be no more than good-natured make-believe, but it is rooted in antiquity, it is a lot of fun and no one wants to give it up.

Among the gospel churches Christ is now in fact little more than a beloved symbol. "All Hail the Power of Jesus' Name" is the church's national anthem and the cross is her official flag, but in the week-by-week services of the church and the day-by-day conduct of her members someone else, not Christ, makes the decisions. Under proper circumstances Christ is allowed to say "Come to me, all you who are weary and burdened" or "Do not let your hearts be troubled," but when the speech is finished someone else takes over. Those in actual authority decide the moral standards of the church, as well as all objectives and all methods employed to achieve them. Because of long and meticulous organization it is now possible for the youngest pastor just out of seminary to have more actual authority in a church than Jesus Christ has.

Matthew 11:28-30; John 14:1; Ephesians 1:22-23; Ephesians 5:23-24; Colossians 1:18
God Tells the Man Who Cares, 206, 207.

116. Church: authority; Boards: lack of dependence on God

What church board consults our Lord's words to decide matters under discussion? Let anyone reading this who has had experience on a church board try to recall the times or time when any board member read from the Scriptures to make a point, or when any chairman suggested that the brethren should see what instructions the Lord had for them on a particular question. Board meetings are habitually opened with a formal prayer or "a season of prayer"; after that the Head of the Church is respectfully silent while the real rulers take over. Let anyone who denies this bring forth evidence to refute it. I for one will be glad to hear it.

God Tells the Man Who Cares, 209.

117. Church: boredom; Church: entertainment

Without Biblical authority, or any other right under the sun, carnal religious leaders have introduced a host of attractions that serve no purpose except to provide entertainment for the retarded saints.

It is now common practice in most evangelical churches to offer the people, especially the young people, a maximum of entertainment and a minimum of serious instruction. It is scarcely possible in most places to get anyone to attend a meeting where the only attraction is God. One can only conclude that God's professed children are bored with Him, for they must be wooed to meeting with a stick of striped candy in the form of religious movies, games and refreshments.

This has influenced the whole pattern of church life, and even brought into being a new type of church architecture, designed to house the golden calf.

So we have the strange anomaly of orthodoxy in creed and heterodoxy in practice. The striped- candy technique has been so fully integrated into our present religious thinking that it is simply taken for granted. Its victims never dream that it is not a part of the teachings of Christ and His apostles.

Acts 2:42-44; Ephesians 6:4; Colossians 4:2
Man: The Dwelling Place of God, 135, 136.

118. Church: boredom; Church: entertainment

A religious mentality characterized by timidity and lack of moral courage has given us today a flabby Christianity, intellectually impoverished, dull, repetitious and to a great many persons just plain boring. This is peddled as the very faith of our fathers in direct lineal descent from Christ and the apostles. We spoon-feed this insipid pablum to our inquiring youth and, to make it palatable, spice it up with carnal amusements filched from the unbelieving world. It is easier to entertain than to instruct, it is easier to follow degenerate public taste than to think for oneself, so too many of our evangelical leaders let their minds atrophy while they keep their fingers nimble operating religious gimmicks to bring in the curious crowds.

Ephesians 4:14-16; 2 Timothy 1:6-7
The Set of the Sail, 67, 68.

119. Church: business meetings

Throughout the New Testament after Pentecost one marked

characteristic of all Christian meetings was the believers' preoccupation with their risen Lord. Even the first Church Council (which might be called a "business" meeting if such a thing really existed in Bible times) was conducted in an atmosphere of great dignity and deep reverence. They talked of God and Christ and the Holy Ghost and the Scriptures and consecrated men who had hazarded their lives for the name of Jesus. They conferred for a while, then drew up a letter of instruction and sent it to the Gentile churches by the hand of Judas and Silas. It is of course unthinkable that such a meeting could have been held without some kind of agenda. Someone had to know what they had gathered to discuss. The important point to be noticed, however, is that proceedings were carried on in an atmosphere of Christian worship. They lost sight of the program in the greater glory of a Presence.

Acts 15
The Root of the Righteous, 93, 94.

120. Church: competition; Selfishness; Body of Christ

It is too bad that anything so obvious should need to be said at this late date, but from all appearances, we Christians have about forgotten the lesson so carefully taught by Paul: God's servants are not to be competitors, but co-workers.

In any religious work there are two interests, either of which may be served: the spiritual interest or the natural; the divine or the human; our own or God's. And it is altogether possible to serve our own interests with poured-out devotion. It is possible to serve the flesh even while engaged in the most intense sort of religious activities. The very fact that our activities are religious will sometimes disguise the presence of the rankest kind of selfishness. . . .

A local church, as long as it is indwelt by the Holy Spirit, cannot entertain the psychology of competition. When it begins to compete with another church, it is a true church of God no longer; it has voided its character and gone down onto a lower level. The Spirit that indwells it is no longer divine; it is human merely, and its activities are pitched on the plane of the natural. . . .

The Holy Spirit always cooperates with Himself in His members. The Spirit-directed body does not tear itself apart by competition. The ambitions of the various members are submerged in the glory of the Head, and whatever brings honor to the Head meets with the most eager approval of the members.

We should cultivate the idea that we are co-workers rather than competitors. We should ask God to give us the psychology of cooperation. We should learn to think of ourselves as being members in particular of one and the same body, and we should reject with indignation every suggestion of the enemy designed to divide our efforts.

Matthew 20:20-28; 1 Corinthians 12; 2 Timothy 2:24-26; 1 Peter 5:1-4
The Next Chapter After the Last, 56, 57.

121. Church: concept of God

Always the most revealing thing about the Church is her idea of God, just as her most significant message is what she says about Him or leaves unsaid, for her silence is often more eloquent than her speech. She can never escape the self-disclosure of her witness concerning God. . . .

So necessary to the Church is a lofty concept of God that when that concept in any measure declines, the Church with her worship and her moral standards declines along with it. The first step down for any church is taken when it surrenders its high opinion of God. . . .

The heaviest obligation lying upon the Christian Church today is to purify and elevate her concept of God until it is once more worthy of Him—and of her.

2 Chronicles 6:14; Psalm 95:1-7; Philippians 2:9-11
The Knowledge of the Holy, 2, 6.

122. Church: concept of God; Worship: adoration

Often enough we have been warned that the morality of any nation or civilization will follow its concepts of God. A parallel truth is less often heard: When a church begins to think impurely and inadequately about God, decline sets in.

We must think nobly and speak worthily of God. Our God is sovereign. We would do well to follow our old-fashioned forebears who knew what it was to kneel in breathless, wondering adoration in the presence of the God who is willing to claim us as His own through grace.

Psalm 8; Psalm 96:1-6; Psalm 111:1-4
Jesus, Our Man in Glory, 43.

123. Church: conflict

Chestnut Street Church belonged to the Presbyterian Church North, which, a traveler from another planet might be shocked to learn, means this: that years after the Civil War had been lost and won, and Grant had clicked his heels and handed back to Lee his officer's sword as a generous gesture toward a gallant but defeated foe . . . after Lincoln had gone down in blood to the immense sorrow of a whole united people; after the gray-clad soldiers had put down their guns and gone back to raising sweet potatoes on the river bottoms of Georgia and Tennessee; after the senators from down south were back in Washington holding forth on the glory of southern manhood and the virtues of southern fried chicken, and getting applause from the galleries, and the country was getting back to normal again, *the churches were still fighting the Civil War.* The world fights and forgets; God's people fight and remember.

Wingspread; A.B. Simpson: A Study in Spiritual Altitude, 44, 45.

124. Church: conflict; Satan; Opposition

Show me an individual or a congregation committed to spiritual progress with the Lord, interested in what the Bible teaches about spiritual perfection and victory, and I will show you where there is strong and immediate defiance by the devil!

Matthew 16:18; 1 Peter 5:8-9
I Talk Back to the Devil, 4.

125. Church: cultural impact; Truth: bold proclamation of; Boldness

The mission of the church is to declare, to proclaim, to witness. She has been left on earth to be a witness to certain great eternal truths which she received from God and which the world could not possibly know unless she told it.

"Therefore go and make disciples of all nations" (Matthew 28:19), said Jesus to the infant church. The church was to teach and the world was to listen. . . .

But always the world was on the receiving end. The church spake and the world heard. Thus it was as Christ said it must be.

But hear, O ye heavens, and be astonished, O earth, for a mighty derangement has occurred in the relative position of the church and the world, a transposition so radical and so grotesque as would not have been believed if it had been foretold but a few years ago.

The church has lost her testimony. She has no longer anything to say to the world. Her once robust shout of assurance has faded away to an apologetic whisper. She who one time went out to declare now goes out to inquire. Her dogmatic declaration has become a respectful suggestion, a word of religious advice, given with the understanding that it is after all only an opinion and not meant to sound bigoted. . . .

The Christian must not allow himself to be entrapped by current vogues in religion, and above all he must never go to the world for his message. He is a man of heaven sent to give witness on earth. As he shall give account to the Lord that bought him, let him see to his commission.

Matthew 28:18-20; 1 Timothy 4:13-16; 2 Timothy 4:1-5
God Tells the Man Who Cares, 34, 36, 42.

126. Church: current condition

Over the last few years the world has gone on to woo the Church (about like water woos a duck!) and has won her heart and hand in what seems to be a case of true love. The honeymoon is still on and the church is now the pampered bride of the world. And what a dowry she has brought to her sensuous and drooling lover! An impenitent and unregenerate populace buys religious books by the millions, to the delight of the profit-hungry publishers. Movie stars now write our hymns; the holy name of Christ sounds out from the gaudy jukebox at the corner pool hall, and in all-night stomp sessions hysterical young people rock and roll to the glory of the Lord.

Today dark-browed Pessimism has gone out of vogue and her happy and responsible sister Optimism has come in to take her place. Christianity is now conceived as fun and the only cross is the one on which Jesus died several hundred years ago. Christ's yoke is not only easy, it is downright thrilling. His burden is not only light, it is jaunty. The church goes along with everything and stands against nothing—until she is convinced that it is the safe and popular thing to do; then she passes her courageous resolutions and issues her world-shaking manifestoes—all in accord with the world's newest social venture, whatever it may be.

Matthew 11:28-30; 2 Corinthians 6:17-18; 1 John 2:15-17
The Size of the Soul, 137.

127. Church: current condition

The church as announced by Christ, seen in the book of Acts and explained by Paul is a thing of great simplicity and rare beauty.

The church as we see it today is unsymmetrical, highly complex and anything but beautiful. Indeed I think that if some angel of God were made familiar with the church as it appears in the New Testament and then sent to the earth to try to locate it, it would be extremely doubtful whether the heavenly messenger would recognize anything now existing in the field of religion as the church he was looking for. So far have we departed from the pattern shown us in the mount.

Matthew 16:18; Acts 2:42-47; Ephesians 4:3-6
The Set of the Sail, 145.

128. Church: current condition; Adjustment; Christians: in the world

The . . . tragedy is that the gospel churches are confused and intimidated by numbers. They accept the belief that there has been change and that Christians must adjust to the change. The word used is adjustment. We must get adjusted, forgetting that the world has always been blessed by the people who were not adjusted. The poor people who get adjusted cannot do much anyhow. They are not worth having around.

In every field of human endeavor progress has been made by those who stood up and said, "I will not adjust to the world." The classical composers, poets and architects were people who would not adjust. Today society insists that if you do not adjust you will get a complex. If you do not get adjusted, you will have to go to a psychiatrist.

Jesus was among the most maladjusted people in His generation. He never pretended to adjust to the world. He came to die for the world and to call the world to Himself, and the adjustment had to be on the other side.

Isaiah 11:2-4; Zechariah 4:6; Colossians 4:5-6
Rut, Rot or Revival: The Condition of the Church, 103, 104.

129. Church: current condition; Celebrities

Why do we build our churches upon human flesh? Why do we set such store by that which the Lord has long ago repudiated, and despise those things which God holds in such high esteem? For we teach men not to die with Christ but to live in the strength of their dying manhood. We boast not in our weakness but in our strength. Values which Christ has declared to be false are brought back into evangelical favor and promoted as the very life and substance of the Christian way. How eagerly do we seek the approval of this or that man of worldly reputation. How shamefully do we exploit the converted celebrity. Anyone will do to take away the reproach of obscurity from our publicity-hungry leaders: famous athletes, congressmen, world travelers, rich industrialists; before such we bow with obsequious smiles and honor them in our public meetings and in the religious press. Thus we glorify men to enhance the standing of the Church of God, and the glory of the Prince of Life is made to hang upon the transient fame of a man who shall die.

Jeremiah 9:23-24; 1 Corinthians 2:1-5; 2 Corinthians 12:9-10; Galatians 6:14; 1 Thessalonians 2:4-6
The Pursuit of Man, 50-51.

130. Church: current condition; Leaders: spiritual need

Within the circles of evangelical Christianity itself there has arisen in the last few years dangerous and dismaying trends away from true Bible Christianity. A spirit has been introduced which is surely not the Spirit of Christ, methods employed which are wholly carnal, objectives adopted which have not one line of Scripture to support them, a level of conduct accepted which is practically identical with that of the world—and yet scarcely one voice has been raised in opposition. And this in spite of the fact that the Bible-honoring followers of Christ lament among themselves the dangerous, wobbly course things are taking. . . .

The times call for a Spirit-baptized and articulate orthodoxy. They whose souls have been illuminated by the Holy Ghost must arise and under God assume leadership. There are those among us whose hearts can discern between the true and the false, whose spiritual sense of smell enables them to detect the spurious afar off, who have the blessed gift of knowing. Let such as these arise and be heard. Who knows but the Lord may return and leave a blessing behind Him?

Acts 20:28-31; 2 Timothy 3:1-7; 2 Timothy 4:1-5; 1 John 4:1
The Price of Neglect, 6, 7.

131. Church: current condition; Preaching: watered down

This is one of the marks of our modern time—that many are guilty of merely "nibbling" at the truth of the Christian gospel.

I wonder if you realize that in many ways the preaching of the Word of God is being pulled down to the level of the ignorant and spiritually obtuse; that we must tell stories and jokes and entertain and amuse in order to have a few people in the audience? We do these things that we may have some reputation and that there may be money in the treasury to meet the church bills. . . .

In many churches Christianity has been watered down until the solution is so weak that if it were poison it would not hurt anyone, and if it were medicine it would not cure anyone!

Galatians 1:9-10; 1 Thessalonians 2:3-9; 2 Timothy 4:1-5
I Talk Back to the Devil, 30, 31.

132. Church: current condition; Revival: need for; Worldliness

Evangelical Christianity is now tragically below the New Testament standard. Worldliness is an accepted part of our way of life. Our religious mood is social instead of spiritual. We have lost the art of worship. We are not producing saints. Our models are successful businessmen, celebrated athletes and theatrical personalities. We carry on our religious activities after the methods of the modern advertiser. Our homes have been turned into theaters. Our literature is shallow and our hymnody borders on sacrilege. And scarcely anyone appears to care.

We must have a better kind of Christian soon or within another half century we may have no true Christianity at all. Increased numbers of demi-Christians is not enough. We must have a reformation.

Matthew 5:14-16; Philippians 2:15; 2 Timothy 2:21,22
Of God and Men, 38.

133. Church: entertainment

These people who have to have truckloads of gadgets to get their religion going, what will they do when they don't have anything like that? The truck can't get where they're going.

I heard a man boast this afternoon on the radio to come to his place because they were going to bring in equipment from Pennsylvania and Ohio to serve the Lord with. What equipment do you need to serve the Lord with, brother? Why, the dear old camp meeting ladies used to say, "See, this is my harp with ten strings and I praise the Lord!" And they'd clap their little old wrinkled hands with shining faces. What claptrap do you need? Do you need a bushel basket full of stuff to serve the Lord with?

Success and the Christian, 30.

134. Church: entertainment; Church: presence of God

You know, the Church started out with a Bible, then it got a hymnbook, and for years that was it—a Bible and a hymnbook. The average church now certainly wouldn't be able to operate on just a hymnbook and the Bible. Now we have to have all kinds of truck. A lot of people couldn't serve God at all without at least a vanload of equipment to keep them happy.

Some of these attractions that we have to win people and keep them coming may be fine or they may be cheap. They may be elevated or they may be degrading. They may be artistic or they may be coarse—it all depends upon who is running the show! But the Holy Spirit is not the center of attraction, and the Lord is not the one who is in charge. We bring in all sorts of antiscriptural and unscriptural claptrap to keep the people happy and keep them coming.

As I see it, the great woe is not the presence of these religious toys and trifles—but the fact that they have become a necessity, and the presence of the Eternal Spirit is not in our midst!

The Counselor, 41.

135. Church: family; Fellowship: need for; Body of Christ

A community of believers must be composed of persons who have each one met God in individual experience. No matter how large the family, each child must be born individually. Even twins or triplets are born one at a time. So it is in the local church. Each member must be born of the Spirit individually.

It will not escape the discerning reader that while each child is born separate from the rest it is born into a family, and after that must live in the fellowship of the rest of the household. And the man who comes to Christ in the loneliness of personal repentance and faith is also born into a family. The church is called the household of God, and it is the ideal place to rear young Christians. Just as a child will not grow up to be a normal adult if forced to live alone, so the Christian who withdraws from the fellowship of other Christians will suffer great soul injury as a result. Such a one can never hope to develop normally. He'll get too much of himself and not enough of other people; and that is not good....

No one is wise enough to live alone, nor good enough nor strong enough. God has made us to a large degree dependent upon each other. From our brethren we can learn how to do things and sometimes also we can learn how not to do them....

Next to God Himself we need each other most. We are His sheep and it is our nature to live with the flock. And too, it might be well to remember that should we for a moment lose sight of the Shepherd we only have to go where His flock is to find Him again. The Shepherd always stays with His flock.

Acts 2:42-47; Galatians 6:10; Ephesians 2:19-20
Born After Midnight, 113, 114.

136. Church: finances

Somebody else came in with a machine that takes wastepaper and crushes it into a bale. He said, "You announce to your audiences, 'Bring all your wastepaper to church.' We'll bale it and you can sell it and have money to pay the preacher and keep the church and your missionary program going."

I said, "Mister, over there's the door. I want you to get to that door just as fast as you can. I don't want my board to know that I even talked to you. If they even found out that I'd let you even make a proposition like this to me, they'd be on my neck. In this church, we go down in our pants pocket, pull the money up, take it out and put it silently in the plate. That's how we get our offerings. We don't bale wastepaper."

Can you imagine when God sent His only begotten Son, the best He had, and His Son gave His blood, the best He had, and the apostles gave their lives, the best they had, we'd bring God our wastepaper?

1 Samuel 2:17; Proverbs 3:9-10; Malachi 3:10; Luke 6:20-38; 2 Corinthians 9:7-8
Success and the Christian, 123, 124.

137. Church: finances

An economic interest in religion is deadly. As soon as a man becomes thus entangled in the snare of economic interest he is a true prophet no longer, but a son of mammon. His heart degenerates and his spirit begins to die. Let him perform a religious duty, do a moral act, advocate a reform, or preach a doctrine because he must do so to guarantee his income, and he is no true shepherd now, but a hireling....

A grave obligation lies upon the church to keep the minister financially free to teach what he from the heart believes. The economic boycott is a weapon sometimes used against the man who insists upon preaching unwelcome truth, and pity the man who is caught in it. Pity more, however, the church that would stoop to exercise it.

Deuteronomy 12:19; 1 Corinthians 9:14; 1 Timothy 5:17-18
The Price of Neglect, 48, 49.

138. Church: finances

We in the churches seem unable to rise above the fiscal philosophy which rules the business world; so we introduce into our church finances the psychology of the great secular institutions so familiar to us all and judge a church by its financial report much as we judge a bank or a department store.

A look into history will quickly convince any interested person that the true church has almost always suffered more from prosperity than from poverty. Her times of greatest spiritual power have usually coincided with her periods of indigence and rejection; with wealth came weakness and backsliding. If this cannot be explained, neither apparently can it be escaped....

The point I am trying to make here is that while money has a proper place in the total life of the church militant, the tendency is to attach to it an importance that is far greater than is biblically sound or morally right. The average church has so established itself organizationally and financially that God is simply not necessary to it. So entrenched is its authority and so stable are the religious habits of its members that God could withdraw Himself completely from it and it could run on for years on its own momentum.

2 Corinthians 8:1-3
The Warfare of the Spirit, 9, 10, 11.

139. Church: finances

The treasury will be full if the people are holy; or if the people are generous but poor, then the Holy Spirit will give them fruit out of all proportion to their financial report. The fruit of the church agrees with its basic spirituality, never upon the state of its exchequer.

Exodus 36:4-7; 2 Chronicles 31:9-10; 2 Corinthians 8:3-5
The Warfare of the Spirit, 11.

140. Church: finances; Church treasurer

Church finances are a good and proper part of church life, but there is an ever-present danger that they will grow too important in the thinking of the church officers and slowly crowd out more vital things. In our local assemblies and other evangelical organizations there are signs that should disturb us greatly, signs of degeneration and decay that can only lead to spiritual death if the infection is not discovered and checked.

To be specific, some of our religious leaders appear to have developed mercantile minds and have come to judge all things by their effect upon the church finances. What a church can or cannot do is decided by the state of the treasury. Its spiritual outgo is determined by its financial income, with no margin for miracle and no recognition of a spiritual ministry unrelated to money. Such evil practice results from an erroneous attitude toward the whole financial question as it relates to religion.

It is an ominous thing in any church when the treasurer begins to exercise power. Since he may be presumed to be a man of God he should have a place equal to that of any other member, and if he is a man of gifts and virtues he will naturally have certain influences among the brethren. This is right and normal as long as he exercises his influences as a man of God and not as a treasurer. The moment he becomes important *because* he is treasurer, the Spirit will be grieved and His manifestations will begin to diminish.

Proverbs 11:24; 2 Corinthians 9:8-11; Philippians 4:18-19
The Warfare of the Spirit, 7, 8.

141. Church: focus

Christless Christianity sounds contradictory but it exists as a real phenomenon in our day. Much that is being done in Christ's name is false to Christ in that it is conceived by the flesh, incorporates fleshly methods, and seeks fleshly ends. Christ is mentioned from time to time in the same way and for the same reason that a self-seeking politician mentions Lincoln and the flag, to provide a sacred front for carnal activities and to deceive the simplehearted listeners. This giveaway is that Christ is not central: He is not all and in all.

Ephesians 1:22-23; Colossians 1:18
Man: The Dwelling Place of God, 124.

142. Church: focus

The business of the Church is God. She is purest when most engaged with God and she is astray just so far as she follows other interests, no matter how "religious" or humanitarian they may be.

Acts 6:3-7
The Set of the Sail, 80.

143. Church: focus; Church: power of God; Pastoral ministry: dependence on God

The kind of Christianity that relies upon the influence of its own human and earthly power makes God sick, for the church of Jesus Christ is a heavenly institution.

For myself, if I could not have the divine power of God, I would walk out and quit the whole religious business. . . .

We must keep our little field of God's planting healthy, and there is only one way to do that: keep true to the Word of God! We must constantly go back to the grass roots and get the Word into the church.

Zechariah 4:6; Ephesians 3:20-21; 2 Timothy 4:1-5; Hebrews 4:12
Renewed Day by Day, Volume 1, Feb. 13.

144. Church: focus; Church: spiritual condition; Spiritual victory

The men who pioneered our great North American continent took over a wilderness and conquered it. They went out with their axes, cutting down trees, building houses and then planting corn, potatoes, other vegetables and grain. You know, when they planted, they didn't go to bed and sleep until time for the harvest. They fought encroachment from the wilderness from the day they planted their corn and the rest of their crops until they harvested them and had them safely in their log barns.

The wilderness encroaches on the fruitful field, and unless there is constant fighting off of this encroachment, there will be little or no harvest.

I think it is exactly the same with the Church. . . .

This is to remind us that we must fight for what we have. Our little field of God's planting must have the necessary weapons and plenty of watchmen out there to drive off the crows and all sorts of creatures, to say nothing of the little insects that destroy the crops. We have to keep after them. We must keep our field healthy, and there is only one way to do that, and that is to keep true to the Word of God. We must constantly go back to the grass roots and get the Word into the Church.

Nehemiah 4:16-17; Ephesians 6:10-18; Revelation 3:15-17
The Counselor, 5, 6.

145. Church: focus; Church: success

I am not preaching a gloomy religion to you. I am only telling you there must be a new direction set. We must seek the Lord. One glimpse of His face will take away all our carnal desires for anything less than that.

Then the hungry-hearted, the thirsty, the disillusioned, the disappointed and the sick will come our way. They will come because they will want to come, and they will know why they are coming. They will not come because a person invited them but because of Christ Jesus. The church will begin to grow. It will grow in power, in grace, in numbers, in usefulness, in prestige and in influence. Everybody will know it is the church that the Lord has blessed.

Matthew 5:6; Luke 4:18-19; John 12:21; Hebrews 12:1-2
Rut, Rot or Revival: The Condition of the Church, 149, 150.

146. Church: focus; Eternal perspective

We must live to gear ourselves into things eternal and to live the life of heaven here upon the earth. We must put loyalty to Christ first at any cost. Anything less than that really isn't a Christian church. I would rather be a member of a group that meets in a little room on a side street than to be part of a great going activity that is not New Testament in its doctrine, in its spirit, in its living, in its holiness, in all of its texture and tenor. We need not expect to be popular in such a church, but certain fruits will follow if we make a church that kind of a church.

Acts 2:33; Galatians 1:9-10; 1 Thessalonians 2:2-4
The Counselor, 7.

147. Church: Holy Spirit's work

When the Holy Spirit is ignored or rejected, religious people are forced either to do their own creating or to fossilize completely. A few churches accept fossilization as the will of God and settle down to the work of preserving their past—as if it needed preserving. Others seek to appear modern, and imitate the current activities of the world with the mistaken idea that they are being creative. And after a fashion they are, but the creatures of their creative skill are sure to be toys and trifles, mere imitations of the world and altogether lacking in the qualities of eternity—holiness and spiritual dignity. The hallmark of the Holy Spirit is not there.

All religious leaders should remember that they will either let the Holy Spirit work through them or their work will be in vain.

Psalm 127:1-5; 1 Corinthians 15:58; Ephesians 5:15-18
This World: Playground or Battleground?, 36, 37.

148. Church: Holy Spirit's work

I say this because it is possible to run a church and all of its activity without the Holy Spirit. You can organize it, get a board together, call a pastor, form a choir, launch a Sunday school and a ladies' aid society. You get it all organized—and the organization part is not bad. I'm for it. But I'm warning about getting organized, getting a pastor and turning the crank—some people think that's all there is to it, you know.

The Holy Spirit can be absent and the pastor goes on turning the crank, and nobody finds it out for years and years. What a tragedy, my brethren, what a tragedy that this can happen in a Christian church! But it doesn't have to be that way! "He who has an ear, let him hear what the Spirit says to the churches" (Revelation 3:22). . . .

If you could increase the attendance of your church until there is no more room, if you could provide everything they have in churches that men want and love and value, and yet you didn't have the Holy Spirit, you might as well have nothing at all. For it is "'Not by might nor by power, but by my Spirit,' says the Lord Almighty" (Zechariah 4:6). Not by the eloquence of a man, not by good music, not by good preaching, but it is by the Spirit that God works His mighty works.

Isaiah 30:1; Zechariah 4:6; John 14:15-17,26; Revelation 3:22
The Counselor, 38, 39.

149. Church: Holy Spirit's work

I think there can be no doubt that the need above all other needs in the Church of God at this moment is the power of the Holy Spirit. More education, better organization, finer equipment, more advanced methods—all are unavailing. It is like bringing a better Pulmotor after the patient is dead. Good as these things are they can never give life. "It is the Spirit that quickeneth." Good as they are they can never bring power. "Power belongeth unto God." Protestantism is on the wrong road when it tries to win merely by means of a "united front." It is not organizational unity we need most; the great need is power. The headstones in the cemetery present a united front, but they stand mute and helpless while the world passes by.

Psalm 62:11; John 6:63-65; Acts 1:8
The Pursuit of Man, 93.

150. Church: Holy Spirit's work; Evangelism: difficult task

The greatest event in history was the coming of Jesus Christ into the world to live and to die for mankind. The next greatest event was the going forth of the Church to embody the life of Christ and to spread the knowledge of His salvation throughout the earth.

It was not an easy task which the Church faced when she came down from that upper room. To carry on the work of a man who was known to have died—to have died as criminals die—and more than that, to persuade others that this man had risen again from the dead and that He was the Son of God and Saviour: this mission was, in the nature of it, doomed to failure from the start. Who would credit such a fantastic story? Who would put faith in one whom society had condemned and crucified?

Acts 1:8; Romans 1:14-16; 1 Corinthians 1:18,20-21
Paths to Power, 7.

151. Church: Holy Spirit's work; Holy Spirit: spiritual gifts

I find three basic requirements God makes of the body of Christ if it is to do His final work—His eternal work. . . .

Actually, it will be such prayer and the meeting of God's conditions that bring us to the third requirement if God is to fulfill His ordained accomplishments through the church. I speak of the Christian's dependence on the Holy Spirit and our willingness to exercise the Spirit's gifts. . . .

A true work of revival cannot be brought in by airplane or by freightliner. God's presence and blessing cannot be humanly induced.

Such revival wonders can take place only as the Holy Spirit energizes the Word of God as it is preached. Genuine blessing cannot come unless the Holy Spirit energizes, convinces and stirs the people of God.

Acts 1:8; Romans 12:3-8; 2 Timothy 4:1-5
Tragedy in the Church: The Missing Gifts, 4, 5, 8, 9.

152. Church: Holy Spirit's work; Prayer: necessity of

I find three basic requirements God makes of the body of Christ if it is to do His final work—His eternal work. . . .

A second important requirement if the believing church is to be used in God's ministry is prayer and the response God makes to our prayers uttered in true faith. . . . No matter what our stature or status, we have the authority in the family of God to pray the prayer of faith. The prayer of faith engages the heart of God, meeting God's conditions of spiritual life and victory.

Our consideration of the power and efficacy of prayer enters into the question of why we are part of a Christian congregation and what that congregation is striving to be and do. We have to consider whether we are just going around and around—like a religious merry-go-round. Are we simply holding on to the painted mane of the painted horse, repeating a trip of very insignificant circles to a pleasing musical accompaniment? . . .

All of the advertising we can do will never equal the interest and participation in the things of God resulting from the gracious answers to the prayers of faith generated by the Holy Spirit.

Acts 2:42-44; 1 Timothy 2:1-8; James 5:16
Tragedy in the Church: The Missing Gifts, 4, 5, 7, 8.

153. Church: Holy Spirit's work; Servanthood; Celebrities

I find three basic requirements God makes of the body of Christ if it is to do His final work—His eternal work.

First, Christian believers and Christian congregations must be thoroughly consecrated to Christ's glory alone. This means absolutely turning their backs on the contemporary insistence on human glory and recognition. I have done everything I can to keep "performers" out of my pulpit. I was not called to recognize "performers." I am confident our Lord never meant for the Christian church to provide a kind of religious stage where performers proudly take their bows, seeking personal recognition. That is not God's way to an eternal work. He has never indicated that proclamation of the gospel is to be dependent on human performances.

Instead, it is important to note how much the Bible has to say about the common people—the plain people. The Word of God speaks with such appreciation of the common people that I am inclined to believe they are especially dear to Him. Jesus was always surrounded by the common people. He had a few "stars," but largely

His helpers were from the common people—the good people and, surely, not always the most brilliant. . . .

To please God, a person must be just an instrument for God to use. . . .

Many people preach and teach. Many take part in the music. Certain ones try to administer God's work. But if the power of God's Spirit does not have freedom to energize all they do, these workers might just as well stay home.

Natural gifts are not enough in God's work. . . .

You can write it down as a fact: no matter what a man does, no matter how successful he seems to be in any field, if the Holy Spirit is not the chief energizer of his activity, it will all fall apart when he dies.

1 Corinthians 1:26-29; Ephesians 1:12-14; Colossians 1:18
Tragedy in the Church: The Missing Gifts, 4, 5, 6, 7.

154. Church: ineffectiveness; Church: spiritual condition; Sin: consequences of

Dispositional sins are fully as injurious to the Christian cause as the more overt acts of wickedness. These sins are as many as the various facets of human nature. Just so there may be no misunderstanding let us list a few of them: sensitiveness, irritability, churlishness, faultfinding, peevishness, temper, resentfulness, cruelty, uncharitable attitudes; and of course there are many more. These kill the spirit of the church and slow down any progress which the gospel may be making in the community. Many persons who had been secretly longing to find Christ have been turned away and embittered by manifestations of ugly dispositional flaws in the lives of the very persons who were trying to win them. . . .

Unsaintly saints are the tragedy of Christianity. People of the world usually pass through the circle of disciples to reach Christ, and if they find those disciples severe and sharp-tongued they can hardly be blamed if they sigh and turn away from Him. . . .

The low state of religion in our day is largely due to the lack of public confidence in religious people.

John 13:34-35; Romans 12:9-16; Ephesians 4:25-32; Colossians 3:5-11
Of God and Men, 84, 85.

155. Church: ineffectiveness; Prayer: unanswered; Hypocrisy

Unquestionably there is not another institution in the world that talks as much and does as little as the church. Any factory that required as much raw material for so small a finished product would go bankrupt in six months. I have often thought that if one-tenth of one per cent of the prayers made in the churches of any ordinary American village on one Sunday were answered the country would be transformed overnight.

But that is just our trouble. We pour out millions of words and never notice that the prayers are not answered. . . .

We settle for words in religion because deeds are too costly. It is easier to pray, "Lord, help me to carry my cross daily" than to pick up the cross and carry it; but since the mere request for help to do something we do not actually intend to do has a certain degree of religious comfort, we are content with repetition of the words.

Luke 9:23-25; James 1:22-25; 1 John 3:17-19
Born After Midnight, 34.

156. Church: ineffectiveness; Sartre, Jean-Paul

Did you know that the often-quoted Jean-Paul Sartre describes his turning to philosophy and hopelessness as a turning away from a secularistic church? He says, "I did not recognize in the fashionable God who was taught me, Him who was waiting for my soul. I needed a Creator; I was given a big businessman!"

None of us is as concerned as we should be about the image we really project to the community around us. At least not when we profess to belong to Jesus Christ and still fail to show forth His love and compassion as we should.

John 13:34,35; Colossians 2:8-9; 1 Thessalonians 1:6-8; Revelation 3:17-19
Whatever Happened to Worship?, 10.

157. Church: ineffectiveness; World: imitation of; Celebrities

A great deal can be learned about people by observing whom and what they imitate. The weak, for instance, imitate the strong; never the reverse. The poor imitate the rich. The self-assured are imitated by the timid and uncertain, the genuine is imitated by the counterfeit, and people all tend to imitate what they admire.

By this definition power today lies with the world, not with the church, for it is the world that initiates and the church that imitates what she has initiated. By this definition the church admires the world. The church is uncertain and looks to the world for assurance. A weak church is aping a strong world to the amusement of intelligent sinners and to her own everlasting shame. . . .

Secularized fundamentalism is a horrible thing, a very horrible thing, much worse in my opinion than honest modernism or outright atheism. It is all a kind of heart heterodoxy existing along with creedal orthodoxy. Its true master may be discovered by noting whom it admires and imitates. The test is, *Whom do these Christians want to be like? Who excites them and makes their eyes shine with pleasure? Whom go they forth to see? Whose techniques do they borrow?* Never the meek soul, never the godly saint, never the self-effacing, cross-carrying follower of Jesus. Always the big wheel, the celebrity, the star, the VIP—provided of course that these persons have given a "testimony" in favor of Christ somewhere in the midst of the fleshly, vain world of artificial lights and synthetic sounds which they inhabit.

1 Corinthians 4:16; 1 Corinthians 11:1; Philippians 3:17; Philippians 4:9; 1 Thessalonians 1:6-8
The Size of the Soul, 64, 66, 67.

158. Church: invincibility

Let me say that those who would come forward to bury the faith of our fathers have reckoned without the host. Just as Jesus Christ was once buried away with the full expectation that He had been gotten rid of, so His church has been laid to rest times without number; and as He disconcerted His enemies by rising from the dead so the church has confounded hers by springing again to vigorous life after all the obsequies had been performed over her coffin and the crocodile tears had been shed at her grave!

Hebrews 12:22-24
Renewed Day by Day, Volume 1, Apr. 1.

159. Church: invincibility; Trials: storms; Second coming: hope for

So it is today in the church of Jesus Christ. There are still disagreements among the people of God. There were in Paul's day, and there are now. There are many imperfections among us. There are existing conditions that ought not to be there—but they are. On the sea that night long ago, the disciples were tired, weary, sleepy, homesick—sailing for Capernaum and home. Their situation was not ideal. They were still in human circumstances. But they were the apple of our Lord's eye. He loved them, and He prayed for them. . . .

As the wind rose and the tempest in its fury tossed their ship, no doubt the disciples on the Sea of Galilee cried out, "Where are you, Lord?" And the church of Jesus Christ, caught in a moral tempest that threatens to tear it apart, makes the same plea. Thank God, we have Christ's assurance that "the gates of Hades will not overcome" His church. Churches may die, but the church still lives. The church of Jesus Christ, composed of all the people of God, shall never perish! . . .

And just as He left the mountain at the proper time, miraculously walking on the water to join His struggling disciples, so He will return from heaven to gather us up and bring us home. He is not here yet, but He is coming! We do not know when He will come within hailing distance, but we know He will come at just the right time. His love and His keen interest in His people will not permit Him to remain away longer than necessary.

Matthew 16:18; John 6:16-21; 1 Thessalonians 4:13-18
Faith Beyond Reason, 158, 159.

160. Church: leadership; Celebrities

The Church in America suffered a greater loss than she has since discovered when she rejected the example of good men and chose for her pattern the celebrity of the hour.

1 Timothy 4:12; Titus 2:7; 3 John 9
The Set of the Sail, 17.

161. Church: leadership; Church: government

You cannot deny that the life and vitality of the Christian church lie in the spiritual leadership of men anointed of the Holy Ghost. I dare to tell you that there is danger in too much democracy in the life of the church.

I am sure that some of you with a strong Baptist background will curl up like a burning leaf in the autumn to hear me say this, but that is all right: I am half Baptist myself!

But I do not believe that God expects the Christian church to thrive and mature and grow just on plain democratic principles. If you will check around you will find that even those who hold to democracy in their church policy never get beyond first base unless they have leaders within the denomination who are anointed men, strongly spiritual in leadership.

1 Corinthians 16:16; 1 Thessalonians 5:12-13; 1 Timothy 5:17-18; Hebrews 13:17; 1 Peter 5:1-4
Christ the Eternal Son, 127.

162. Church: leadership; Church: government; Leaders: spiritual need

I believe that it might be accepted as a fairly reliable rule of thumb that the man who is ambitious to lead is disqualified as a leader. The Church of the Firstborn is no place for the demagogue or the petty religious dictator. The true leader will have no wish to lord it over God's heritage, but will be humble, gentle, self-sacrificing and altogether as ready to follow as to lead when the Spirit makes it plain to him that a wiser and more gifted man than himself has appeared.

It is undoubtedly true, as I have said so often, that the church is languishing not for leaders but for the right kind of leaders; for the wrong kind is worse than none at all. Better to stand still than to follow a blind man over a precipice. History will show that the church has prospered most when blessed with strong leaders and suffered the greatest decline when her leaders were weak and time serving. The sheep rarely go much farther than the Shepherd.

That is why unqualified democracy is not good for a church unless every voting member is full of the Holy Spirit and wisdom. To put the work of the church in the hands of the group is to exchange one leader for many; and if the group is composed of carnal professors it is to exchange one weak leader for a number of bad ones. One hundred blind men cannot see any better than one.

Ezekiel 34:2-4; Acts 6:3-7; 1 Peter 5:1-4
The Warfare of the Spirit, 191, 192.

163. Church: leadership; Leaders: spiritual need; Worship: missing in churches

Well, we have great churches and we have beautiful sanctuaries and we join in the chorus, "We have need of nothing." But there is every indication that we are in need of worshipers.

We have a lot of men willing to sit on our church boards who have no desire for spiritual joy and radiance and who never show up for the church prayer meeting. These are the men who often make the decisions about the church budget and the church expenses and where the frills will go in the new edifice.

They are the fellows who run the church, but you cannot get them to the prayer meeting because they are not worshipers. . . .

It seems to me that it has always been a frightful incongruity that men who do not pray and do not worship are nevertheless actually running many of the churches and ultimately determining the direction they will take

It hits very close to our own situations, perhaps, but we should confess that in many "good" churches, we let the women do the praying and let the men do the voting.

Because we are not truly worshipers, we spend a lot of time in the churches just spinning our wheels, burning the gasoline, making a noise but not getting anywhere.

Acts 6:3-7; Acts 12:5; Revelation 3:17-19
Whatever Happened to Worship?, 16, 17.

164. Church: modeling

I would like to see a church become so godly, so Spirit-filled that it would have a spiritual influence on all of the churches in the entire area. Paul told some of his people, "you became a model to all the believers" and "your faith in God has become known everywhere" (1 Thessalonians 1:7,8).

It is entirely right that I should hope this of you. I could hope that we might become so Spirit-filled, walking with God, learning to worship, living so clean and so separated that everybody would know it, and the other churches in our area would be blessed on account of it. . . .

There is no reason why we could not be a people so filled with the Spirit, so joyfully singing His praises and living so clean in our business and home and school that the people and other churches would know it and recognize it.

Ephesians 5:18-19; Colossians 3:16-18; 1 Thessalonians 1:6-8
The Counselor, 9, 10.

165. Church: necessity of

All else being equal, the individual Christian will find in the communion of a local church the most perfect atmosphere for the fullest development of his spiritual life. There also he will find the best arena for the largest exercise of those gifts and powers with which God may have endowed him.

The religious solitary may gain on a few points, and he may escape some of the irritations of the crowd, but he is a half-man, nevertheless, and worse, he is a half-Christian. Every solitary experience, if we would realize its beneficial effects, should be followed immediately by a return to our own company. There will be found the faith of Christ in its most perfect present manifestation. . . .

That Christian is a happy one who has found a company of true believers in whose heavenly fellowship he can live and love and labor. And nothing else on earth should be as dear to him nor command from him such a degree of loyalty and devotion.

Acts 2:42-44; 1 Corinthians 12:25-27; Hebrews 10:24-25
The Set of the Sail, 22, 23.

166. Church: numbers

To God quality is vastly important and size matters little. When set in opposition to size, quality is everything and size nothing. . . .

Man's moral fall has clouded his vision, confused his thinking and rendered him subject to delusion. One evidence of this is his all but incurable proneness to confuse values and put size before quality in his appraisal of things. The Christian faith reverses this order, but even Christians tend to judge things by the old Adamic rule. How big? How much? and How many? are the questions oftenest asked by religious persons when trying to evaluate Christian things. . . .

The Church is dedicated to things that matter. Quality matters. Let's not be led astray by the size of things.

1 Samuel 16:7; Matthew 20:20-28; Luke 16:15
Born After Midnight, 72, 73, 75.

167. Church: numbers

This brings to light a most wonderful truth. In the body of Christ there are no insignificant congregations. Each has His Name and each is honored by His Presence. . . .

Large or small, the church must be an assembly of believers brought together through a Name to worship a Presence. The blessed thing is that God does not ask whether it is a big church or a little church.

But people do insist on asking questions about size and number of people because they are carnal. I know all about such human judgments. "This is a very little church," or, "That is a poor, unknown church." Meanwhile, God is saying, "It is My church—they are all My churches, and each has every right to all I bestow!"

Matthew 16:18; Matthew 18:20
Tragedy in the Church: The Missing Gifts, 39.

168. Church: numbers; Growth emphasis

The emphasis today in Christian circles appears to be on quantity, with a corresponding lack of emphasis on quality. Numbers, size and amount seem to be very nearly all that matters even among evangelicals. The size of the crowd, the number of converts, the size of the budget, the amount of the weekly collections: if these look good the church is prospering and the pastor is thought to be a success. The church that can show an impressive quantitative growth is frankly envied and imitated by other ambitious churches.

This is the age of the Laodiceans. The great goddess Numbers is worshiped with fervent devotion and all things religious are brought before her for examination. Her Old Testament is the financial report and her New Testament is the membership roll. To these she appeals as arbiters of all questions, the test of spiritual growth and the proof of success or failure in every Christian endeavor.

A little acquaintance with the Bible should show this up for the heresy it is. To judge anything spiritual by statistics is to judge by another than scriptural judgment. It is to admit the validity of externalism and to deny the value our Lord places upon the soul as over against the body. It is to mistake the old creation for the new and to confuse things eternal with things temporal. Yet it is being done every day by ministers, church boards and denominational leaders. And hardly anyone notices the deep and dangerous error.

1 Corinthians 3:12-14; Revelation 3:14-22
The Set of the Sail, 153, 154.

169. Church: numbers; Growth emphasis; Pastoral ministry: expectations

Time may show that one of the greatest weaknesses in our modern civilization has been the acceptance of quantity rather than quality as the goal after which to strive. . . .

Christianity is resting under the blight of degraded values. And it all stems from a too-eager desire to impress, to gain fleeting attention, to appear well in comparison with some world-beater who happens for the time to have the ear or the eye of the public.

This is so foreign to the Scriptures that we wonder how Bible-loving Christians can be deceived by it. The Word of God ignores size and quantity and lays all its stress upon quality. Christ, more than any other man, was followed by the crowds, yet after giving them such help as they were able to receive, He quietly turned from them and deposited His enduring truths in the breasts of His chosen 12. . . .

Pastors and churches in our hectic times are harassed by the temptation to seek size at any cost and to secure by inflation what they cannot gain by legitimate growth. The mixed multitude cries for quantity and will not forgive a minister who insists upon solid values and permanence. Many a man of God is being subjected to cruel pressure by the ill-taught members of his flock who scorn his slow methods and demand quick results and a popular following regardless of quality.

The Next Chapter After the Last, 7, 8.

170. Church: numbers; Growth emphasis; Preaching: watered down

The devotees of this doctrine ["we must get the message out" regardless of how we go about it] appear to be more concerned with quantity than with quality. They seem burned up with desire to "bring the people in" even if they have not much to offer them after they are in. They take inexcusable liberties both with message and with method. The Scriptures are used rather than expounded and the Lordship of Christ almost completely ignored. . . .

The crowds-at-any-price mania has taken a firm grip on American Christianity and is the motivating power back of a shockingly high percentage of all religious activity. Men and churches compete for the attention of the paying multitudes who are brought in by means of any currently popular gadget or gimmick ostensibly to have their souls saved, but, if the truth were told, often for reasons not so praiseworthy as this. . . .

Our constant effort should be to reach as many persons as possible with the Christian message, and for that reason numbers are critically important. But our first responsibility is not to make converts but to uphold the honor of God in a world given over to the glory of fallen man. No matter how many persons we touch with the gospel we have failed unless, along with the message of invitation, we have boldly declared the exceeding sinfulness of man and the transcendent holiness of the Most High God. They who degrade or compromise the truth in order to reach larger numbers, dishonor God and deeply injure the souls of men.

The temptation to modify the teachings of Christ with the hope that larger numbers may "accept" Him is cruelly strong in this day of speed, size, noise and crowds. But if we know what is good for us, we'll resist it with every power at our command.

1 Timothy 6:20-21; 2 Timothy 1:13-14; 2 Timothy 4:1-5
The Size of the Soul, 116, 117, 118, 119.

171. Church: numbers; Preaching: watered down

I just want to make the observation that many of the preachers in our day are adept with the old-fashioned custom of the pacifier, the sugar nipple. They think it will result in more people coming to their churches. They think it will result in bigger offerings. They think that they will be more likely to be successful.

If there has to be some kind of compromise or pacifier to be crowded out, then they can go right on past as far as I am concerned.

God Almighty never said, "Young fellow, get yourself a pocketful of sugar nipples and go out and feed them to the carnal public."

What He did say was, "Preach My Word. . . ."

Acts 20:18-21,27; 2 Timothy 4:1-5
Christ the Eternal Son, 62.

172. Church: objectives; Church: focus

There are few things as frustrating as to work without knowing what we are trying to accomplish; that is, to be lost in the means and ignorant of the end.

Examples of this are found in "parts" factories where men spend years making small articles that have no significance in themselves and can have satisfying meaning only when related to hundreds of other and dissimilar articles and to the completed object of which each one is a small part.

Since the human mind is designed to deal with ends and wholes, this enforced preoccupation with parts and means is particularly disconcerting. The urge to plan and to create according to plan is strong in us, and we feel fenced in and defeated when we are compelled to spend our days in toil that attains no visible objective. It is this rather than the work itself that makes so many jobs dull and boresome.

I have wondered whether the flat tedium found in most

churches cannot be explained at least in part as the psychological consequence of numbers of persons meeting together at stated times without quite knowing why they have met....

Some persons, for instance, find church intolerable because there is no objective toward which pastor and people are moving, aside possibly from the limited one of trying to enlist eight more women and 10 more men to chaperon the annual youth cookout or reaching the building fund quota for the month....

It was the knowledge that they were part of an eternal plan that imparted unquenchable enthusiasm to the early Christians. They burned with holy zeal for Christ and felt that they were part of an army which the Lord was leading to ultimate conquest over all the powers of darkness. That was enough to fill them with perpetual enthusiasm.

Matthew 28:18-20; 1 Corinthians 9:16; 2 Corinthians 5:12-15; Ephesians 3:10-11; Ephesians 4:11-16
The Set of the Sail, 90, 91.

173. Church: power of God

The Church must be a witness to powers beyond the earthly and the human; and because I know this, it is a source of great grief to me that the church is trying to run on its human powers....

Now, a plain word here about the Christian Church trying to carry on in its own power: that kind of Christianity makes God sick, for it is trying to run a heavenly institution after an earthly manner.

For myself, if I couldn't have the divine power of God, I would quit the whole business. The church that wants God's power will have something to offer besides social clubs, knitting societies, the Boy Scout troops and all of the other side issues.

Zechariah 4:6; Acts 2:14; Acts 3:10; Acts 4:31-33
The Counselor, 4, 5.

174. Church: power of God; Church: apathy; Revival: conditions for

Look around today and see where the miracles of power are taking place. Never in the seminary where each thought is prepared for the student, to be received painlessly and at second hand; never in the religious institution where tradition and habit have long ago made faith unnecessary; never in the old church where memorial tablets plastered over the furniture bear silent testimony to a glory that once was.

Invariably where daring faith is struggling to advance against hopeless odds, there is God sending "help from the sanctuary.". . .

Look at that church where plentiful fruit was once the regular and expected thing, but now there is little or no fruit, and the power of God seems to be in abeyance. What is the trouble? God has not changed, nor has His purpose for that church changed in the slightest measure. No, the church itself has changed.

A little self-examination will reveal that it and its members have become fallow. It has lived through its early travails and has now come to accept an easier way of life. It is content to carry on its painless program with enough money to pay its bills and a membership large enough to assure its future. Its members now look to it for security rather than for guidance in the battle between good and evil. It has become a school instead of a barracks. Its members are students, not soldiers. They study the experiences of others instead of seeking new experiences of their own.

The only way to power for such a church is to come out of hiding and once more take the danger-encircled path of obedience. Its security is its deadliest foe. The church that fears the plow writes its own epitaph: the church that uses the plow walks in the way of revival.

Psalm 20:2; Hosea 10:12; 2 Timothy 2:3-4
Paths to Power, 36, 37, 38.

175. Church: presence of Christ; Jesus Christ: His preeminence; Christians: in the world

I long for every believer in the church of our Lord to join me in a clear-cut manifesto to our times. I want it to be a declaration of our intentions to restore Christ to the place that is rightfully His in our personal lives, in our family situations and in the fellowship of the churches that bear His name. . . .

The need today is for men and women of faith and courage and daring. The need is for Christians who are so concerned for the presence of Jesus Christ in their midst that they will demonstrate the standards of godliness and biblical holiness as a rebuke to this wicked and perverse generation.

Ephesians 1:22-23; Colossians 1:18; Titus 2:11-14; Hebrews 12:1,2
Jesus, Author of Our Faith, 109.

176. Church: presence of God

... I mean that heavenly quality which marks the Church as a divine thing. The greatest proof of our weakness these days is that there is no longer anything terrible or mysterious about us. The Church has been explained—the surest evidence of her fall. We now have little that cannot be accounted for by psychology and statistics. In that early Church they met together on Solomon's porch, and so great was the sense of God's presence that "no man durst join himself to them." The world saw fire in that bush and stood back in fear; but no one is afraid of ashes. Today they dare come as close as they please. They even slap the professed bride of Christ on the back and get coarsely familiar. If we ever again impress unsaved men with a wholesome fear of the supernatural we must have once more the dignity of the Holy Spirit; we must know again that awe-inspiring mystery which comes upon men and churches when they are full of the power of God.

Acts 2:42-44; Acts 3:11; Acts 4:31-33
Paths to Power, 10, 11.

177. Church: presence of God; Church: services; Church: boredom

The Bible teaches plainly enough the doctrine of the divine omnipresence, but for the masses of professed Christians this is the era of the Absentee God. Most Christians speak of God in the manner usually reserved for a departed loved one, rarely as of one present; but they do not often speak to Him. . . .

At the far end of the spectrum are the conventional churches. I think it is the deep-seated notion that God is absent that makes so many of our church services so insufferably dull. When true believers gather around a present Christ it is all but impossible to have a poor meeting. The drabbest sermon may be endured cheerfully when the sweet fragrance of Christ's presence fills the room. But nothing can save a meeting held in the name of an Absentee God.

Exodus 33:14-16; Psalm 95:1-2; Matthew 18:20
God Tells the Man Who Cares, 76, 79.

178. Church: presence of God; Longing for God; God: His glory

The world is evil, the times are waxing late, and the glory of God has departed from the church as the fiery cloud once lifted from the door of the Temple in the sight of Ezekiel the prophet.

The God of Abraham has withdrawn His conscious Presence from us, and another God whom our fathers knew not is making himself at home among us. This God we have made and because we have made him we can understand him; because we have created him he can never surprise us, never overwhelm us, nor astonish us, nor transcend us.

The God of glory sometimes revealed Himself like a sun to warm and bless, indeed, but often to astonish, overwhelm, and blind before He healed and bestowed permanent sight. This God of our fathers wills to be the God of their succeeding race. We have only to prepare Him a habitation in love and faith and humility. We have but to want Him badly enough, and He will come and manifest Himself to us.

Ezekiel 10:18-19; Hosea 5:6; 2 Timothy 3:1-7
The Knowledge of the Holy, 67, 68.

179. Church: presence of God; Revival: need for; Knowledge of God: church's need

When viewed from the perspective of eternity, the most critical need of this hour may well be that the Church should be brought back from her long Babylonian captivity and the name of God be glorified in her again as of old. Yet we must not think of the Church as an anonymous body, a mystical religious abstraction. We Christians are the Church and whatever we do is what the Church is doing. The matter, therefore, is for each of us a personal one. Any forward step in the Church must begin with the individual.

What can we plain Christians do to bring back the departed glory? Is there some secret we may learn? Is there a formula for personal revival we can apply to the present situation, to our own situation? The answer to these questions is *yes.* . . .

The secret is an open one which the wayfaring man may read. It is simply the old and ever-new counsel: *Acquaint thyself with God.* To regain her lost power the Church must see heaven opened and have a transforming vision of God.

Exodus 24:9-18; Isaiah 6:1-8; John 1:51; Revelation 19:11-16
The Knowledge of the Holy, 179, 180.

180. Church: problems; Church: conflict; Church: unity; Body of Christ

Because the church is a society of human beings, the problems that plague families and nations are found in the church, too. If Christians stand alone, their only problems are personal, but as soon as other Christians join them, they have social problems as well. True, the members of the church are redeemed human beings, but that fact does not make them any less human. Differences of taste, temperament, opinion, moral energy and speed of action among religious people in close association create a certain amount of friction in the group. Wise Christian leaders will anticipate this and will know what to do when it develops. . . .

The church is a body of moving parts, a society of many members. The problems arising in any church will be in direct proportion to the zeal, the activity and the energy of its members. This is inevitable and should be taken in stride.

Some misguided Christian leaders feel that they must preserve harmony at any cost, so they do everything possible to reduce friction. They should remember that there is no friction in a machine that has been shut down for the night. Turn off the power, and you will have no problem with moving parts. Also remember that there is a human society where there are no problems—the cemetery. The dead have no differences of opinion. They generate no heat, because they have no energy and no motion. But their penalty is sterility and complete lack of achievement.

What then is the conclusion of the matter? That problems are the price of progress, that friction is the concomitant of motion, that a live and expanding church will have a certain quota of difficulties as a result of its life and activity. A Spirit-filled church will invite the anger of the enemy.

1 Corinthians 12:25-27; Ephesians 6:10-12; 1 Peter 5:8-9
This World: Playground or Battleground?, 111, 112, 113.

181. Church: problems; Church: spiritual condition

The tragedy that happened to Rome on the inside is the same kind of threat that can harm and endanger a complacent and worldly church on the inside. It is hard for a proud, unconcerned church to function as a spiritual, mature and worshiping church. There is always the imminent danger of failure before God.

Many people loyal to the church and to forms and traditions deny that Christianity is showing any injury in our day. But it is the *internal* bleeding that brings death and decay. We may be defeated in the hour when we bleed too much within.

Matthew 7:15-16; Acts 20:28-31; 2 Timothy 3:1-7
Whatever Happened to Worship?, 96.

182. Church: proper place of

Faithfulness to the local church is also a good thing. The true Christian will, by a kind of spiritual instinct, find a body of believers somewhere, identify himself with it and try by every proper means to promote its growth and prosperity. And that, we repeat, is good. But when the church becomes so large and important that it hides God from our eyes it is no longer for us a good thing. Or better say that it is a good thing wrongly used. For the church was never intended to substitute for God. Let us understand that every local church embraces *el-beth-el* and the right balance will be found and maintained: God first and His house second. . . .

We may judge our spiritual growth pretty accurately by observing the total emphasis of our heart. Where is the primary interest? Is it Beth-el or El-beth-el? Is it my church or my Lord? Is it my ministry or my God? My creed or my Christ? We are spiritual or carnal just as we are concerned with the house or with the God of the house.

Genesis 28:19; Genesis 35:7
Of God and Men, 134, 135.

183. Church: pulpit committee; Pastoral ministry: expectations

When considering a pastor the average church asks in effect, "Is this man worthy to speak to us?" I suppose such a question is valid, but there is another one more in keeping with the circumstances; it is, "Are we worthy to hear this man?" An attitude of humility on the part of the hearers would secure for them a great deal more light from whatever sized candle the Lord might be pleased to send them.

1 Thessalonians 5:12-13; 1 Timothy 5:17-18; Hebrews 13:17
The Root of the Righteous, 21.

184. Church: religious game; Religion: emptiness of

By observing the ways of men at play I have been able to understand better the ways of men at prayer. Most men, indeed, play at religion as they play at games, religion itself being of all games the one most universally played. The various sports have their rules and their balls and their players; the game excites interest, gives pleasure and consumes time, and when it is over the competing teams laugh and leave the field.... The whole thing is arbitrary. It consists in solving artificial problems and attacking difficulties which have been deliberately created for the sake of the game. It has no moral roots and is not supposed to have. No one is the better for his self-imposed toil. It is all but a pleasant activity which changes nothing and settles nothing at last.

If the conditions we describe were confined to the ball park we might pass it over without further thought, but what are we to say when this same spirit enters the sanctuary and decides the attitude of men toward God and religion? For the Church has also its fields and its rules and its equipment for playing the game of pious words. It has its devotees, both laymen and professionals, who support the game with their money and encourage it with their presence, but who are no different in life or character from many who take in religion no interest at all.

As an athlete uses a ball so do many of us use words: words spoken and words sung, words written and words uttered in prayer. We throw them swiftly across the field; we learn to handle them with dexterity and grace; we build reputations upon our word-skill and gain as our reward the applause of those who have enjoyed the game. But the emptiness of it is apparent from the fact that after the pleasant religious game *no one is basically any different from what he had been before.* The bases of life remain unchanged, the same old principles govern, the same old Adam rules.

Matthew 23:23-24; Acts 20:18-21,24; 2 Timothy 2:24-26
The Pursuit of Man, 18-19.

185. Church: routine; Church: current condition

The treacherous enemy facing the church of Jesus Christ today is the dictatorship of the routine, when the routine becomes "lord" in the life of the church. Programs are organized and the prevailing conditions are accepted as normal. Anyone can predict next Sunday's service and what will happen. This seems to be the most deadly threat in the church today. When we come to the place where everything can be predicted and nobody expects anything unusual from God, we are in a rut. The routine dictates, and we can tell not only what will happen next Sunday, but what will occur next month and, if things do not improve, what will take place next year. Then we have reached the place where what has been determines what is, and what is determines what will be.

That would be perfectly all right and proper for a cemetery. Nobody expects a cemetery to do anything but conform. The greatest conformists in the world today are those who sleep out in the community cemetery. They do not bother anyone. They just lie there, and it is perfectly all right for them to do so. You can predict what everyone will do in a cemetery from the deceased right down to the people who attend a funeral there. Everyone and everything in a cemetery has accepted the routine. Nobody expects anything out of those buried in the cemetery. But the church is not a cemetery and we should expect much from it, because what has been should not be lord to tell us what is, and what is should not be ruler to tell us what will be. God's people are supposed to grow.

Ephesians 4:14-16; 1 Peter 2:1-2; 2 Peter 3:18
Rut, Rot or Revival: The Condition of the Church, 5, 6.

186. Church: separation

The church's mightiest influence is felt when she is different from the world in which she lives. Her power lies in her being different, rises with the degree in which she differs and sinks as the difference diminishes.

This is so fully and clearly taught in the Scriptures and so well illustrated in Church history that it is hard to see how we can miss it. But miss it we do, for we hear constantly that the Church must try to be as much like the world as possible, excepting, of course, where the world is too, too sinful. . . .

Let us plant ourselves on the hill of Zion and invite the world to come over to us, but never under any circumstances will we go over to them. The cross is the symbol of Christianity, and the cross speaks of death and separation, never of compromise. No one ever compromised with a cross. The cross separated between the dead and the living. The timid and the fearful will cry "Extreme!" and they will be right. The cross is the essence of all that is extreme and final. The message of Christ is a call across a gulf from death to life, from sin to righteousness and from Satan to God.

1 Corinthians 1:18; 2 Corinthians 6:17-18; Ephesians 4:17-24
The Set of the Sail, 35, 36.

187. Church: separation

It is no more than a religious platitude to say that the trouble with us today is that we have tried to bridge the gulf between two opposites, the world and the Church, and have performed an illicit marriage for which there is no biblical authority. Actually no real union between the world and the Church is possible. When the Church joins up with the world it is the true Church no longer but only a pitiful hybrid thing, an object of smiling contempt to the world and an abomination to the Lord.

1 Corinthians 10:21; 2 Corinthians 6:14-15; Ephesians 5:7-8,11
The Pursuit of Man, 115-116.

188. Church: separation

I for one am determined that we will not capitulate to the times in which we live! There is such a thing as just getting tough about this. In the power of the Spirit we must say, "I am not yielding and I will not yield to the time in which I live!" We can say that to our Lord, to ourselves and, betimes, maybe, over our shoulders to the devil!

The faithful body of Christ will not give up to the ways of the world or even to the more common ways of religion that are all about us. Faithful believers will not succumb to the temptation to judge themselves by what others are doing. Neither will they allow their assemblies to be judged, or their spiritual body life affected, by the attitudes of others. They will be happy and continue to rejoice in the fact that they have taken the New Testament standard as their standard.

2 Corinthians 6:17-18; 1 John 2:15-17; Revelation 18:4
Tragedy in the Church: The Missing Gifts, 56.

189. Church: separation; Revival: need for

This has been an honest effort to understand the religious situation in the present critical hour. It is not meant as a denunciation, but as an appraisal. Surely there are a few names even today who have not defiled their garments and they shall walk with God in white, for they are worthy. Possibly we are coming near to a time when those who are on the Lord's side may be forced to withdraw from the religious hodgepodge and form a company of believers that will insist upon New Testament doctrine and New Testament practice. The temple waits to be cleansed. We should pray day and night till that happy event takes place.

Exodus 32:26; Matthew 21:12-13; Revelation 3:4
The Price of Neglect, 101.

190. Church: separation; Worldliness

The most pressing need just now is that we who call ourselves Christians should frankly acknowledge to each other and to God that we are astray; that we should confess that we are worldly, that our moral standards are low and we are spiritually cold. We need to cease our multitude of unscriptural activities, stop running when and where we have not been sent, and cease trying to sanctify carnal projects by professing that we are promoting them "in the name of the Lord" and "for the glory of God." We need to return to the message, methods and objectives of the New Testament. We need boldly and indignantly to cleanse the temple of all that sell cattle in the holy place, and overthrow the tables of the money-changers. *And this must be done in our own lives first and then in the churches of which we are a part.*

Matthew 21:12-13; Acts 2:42-47; Ephesians 4:11-16
The Size of the Soul, 132, 133.

191. Church: services; Church: presence of Christ

When we compare our present carefully programed meetings with the New Testament we are reminded of the remark of a famous literary critic after he had read Alexander Pope's translation of Homer's Odyssey: "It is a beautiful poem, but it is not Homer." So the fast-paced, highly spiced, entertaining service of today may be a beautiful example of masterful programing—but it is not a Christian service. The two are leagues apart in almost every essential. About the only thing they have in common is the presence of a number of persons in one room. There the similarity ends and glaring dissimilarities begin. . . .

The point we make here is that in our times the program has been substituted for the Presence. The program rather than the Lord of glory is the center of attraction. So the most popular gospel church in any city is likely to be the one that offers the most interesting program; that is, the church that can present the most and best features for the enjoyment of the public....

We'll do our churches a lot of good if we each one seek to cultivate the blessed Presence in our services. If we make Christ the supreme and constant object of devotion the program will take its place as a gentle aid to order in the public worship of God. If we fail to do this the program will finally obscure the Light entirely. And no church can afford that.

Colossians 1:18; Hebrews 12:1-2; Revelation 2:4-5
The Root of the Righteous, 92-93, 95, 96.

192. Church: services; Hymnody

I suppose it is not of vast importance that the third stanza is so often omitted in the singing of a hymn, but just for the record let it be said that the worshipers are deprived of the blessing of the hymn by that omission if, as is often true, the hymn develops a great Christian truth in sermonic outline. To omit a stanza is to lose one link in a golden chain and greatly to reduce the value of the whole hymn.

The significant thing, however, is not what the omission actually does, but what it suggests, viz., a nervous impatience and a desire to get the service over with. We are, for instance, singing "When I Survey the Wondrous Cross." We long to forget the big noisy world and let our hearts go out in reverent worship of that Prince of Glory who died for us, but our sad sweet longing is killed in the bud by the brisk, unemotional voice of the director ordering us to "omit the third verse." We wonder vaguely whether the brother is hungry or has to catch an early train or just why he is so anxious to get through with the hymn. Since all standard hymns have been edited to delete inferior stanzas and since any stanza of the average hymn can be sung in less than one minute... and since many of our best hymns have already been shortened as much as good taste will allow, we are forced to conclude that the habit of omitting the third stanza reveals religious boredom, pure and simple, and it would do our souls good if we would admit it.

The Price of Neglect, 123, 124.

193. Church: services; Non-expectation

One characteristic that marks the average church today is lack of anticipation. Christians when they meet do not expect anything unusual to happen; consequently only the usual happens, and that usual is as predictable as the setting of the sun. . . .

We need today a fresh spirit of anticipation that springs out of the promises of God. We must declare war on the mood of nonexpectation, and come together with childlike faith. Only then can we know again the beauty and wonder of the Lord's presence among us.

Psalm 95:1-7; Psalm 98:1-6; Psalm 100
God Tells the Man Who Cares, 168, 170.

194. Church: services; Pastors: prophetic ministry

Within the last quarter of a century we have actually seen a major shift in the beliefs and practices of the evangelical wing of the church so radical as to amount to a complete sellout; and all this behind the cloak of fervent orthodoxy. With Bibles under their arms and bundles of tracts in their pockets, religious persons now meet to carry on "services" so carnal, so pagan, that they can hardly be distinguished from the old vaudeville shows of earlier days. And for a preacher or a writer to challenge this heresy is to invite ridicule and abuse from every quarter.

Our only hope is that renewed spiritual pressure will be exerted increasingly by self-effacing and courageous men who desire nothing but the glory of God and the purity of the church. May God send us many of them. They are long overdue.

2 Timothy 4:1-5
Of God and Men, 17.

195. Church: services; Worship: meaningless

In the light of this it will be seen how empty and meaningless is the average church service today. All the means are in evidence; the one ominous weakness is the absence of the Spirit's power. The form of godliness is there, and often the form is perfected till it is an aesthetic triumph. Music and poetry, art and oratory, symbolic vesture and solemn tones combine to charm the mind of the worshiper, but too often the supernatural afflatus is not there. The power from on high is neither known nor desired by pastor or people. This is nothing less than tragic, and all the more so because it falls within the field of religion where the eternal destinies of men are involved.

Luke 24:49; Acts 1:8; 2 Timothy 3:1-7; 1 John 2:20
The Pursuit of Man, 91.

196. Church: social club; Church: focus

The average local church is to a large extent a social organization where well-intentioned people get together and know each other. They are drawn together by coffee, tea, friendship, skating parties and things like that. Those things are harmless. But when we know what the church really is, we will understand that while these things are all right on the margin of the church, they are not the purpose of it.

Meeting, shaking hands and drinking coffee are perfectly legitimate if we do not need them—they are not what holds us together. But when those activities are what hold us together, we do not have a church; we have something else. Unfortunately, we might as well admit it: That is often all that the churches have. . . .

We want a separated-from-the-world, heads-up, knees-bent, living church! Sure we can have our skating parties, gatherings and coffees. Nothing is wrong with that, provided we know that we do not need it. These activities are something on the side so we can relax. Jesus Christ is our center (, and so the way to get in is by faith and confession.)

Acts 2:42-47
Rut, Rot or Revival: The Condition of the Church, 125, 126, 136.

197. Church: social club; Church: presence of God

First, the fellowship of the Church has degenerated into a social fellowship with a mild religious flavor.

In that regard, I want you to know where I stand—it is important and I want to say it plainly. I want the presence of God Himself, or I don't want anything at all to do with religion. You would never get me interested in the old maids' social club with a little bit of Christianity thrown in to give it respectability. I want all that God has, or I don't want any.

Exodus 33:14-16; Revelation 3:15-17
The Counselor, 40.

198. Church: spiritual condition

I believe that a pastor who is content with a vineyard that is not at its best is not a good husbandman. It is my prayer that we may be a healthy and fruitful vineyard and that we may be an honor to the Well Beloved, Jesus Christ the Lord, that He might go before the Father and say, "These are mine for whom I pray, and they have heard the Word and have believed on Me." I pray that we might fit into the high priestly prayer of John 17, that we would be a church after Christ's own heart so that in us He might see the travail of His soul and be satisfied.

John 17; Acts 20:28-31; 2 Timothy 4:1-5
Rut, Rot or Revival: The Condition of the Church, 112.

199. Church: spiritual condition

Now suppose we are ready to admit that we are in a rut. You say, "Well, what is the church doing?" I don't know, because it is the individual that matters. You see, the church is composed of this fellow that lives out here a little way and those two people who live out there in Scarboro and the five who live in Rexdale and the seven who live up in Willowdale and the 14 who live out east. That is the church. What the church does is what the individuals do. How well or how sick the church is depends on how well or how sick the individuals are. In other words, it depends upon how you are.

Matthew 5:3-12; 1 Corinthians 12:25-27; Ephesians 4:11-13; Colossians 1:28-29
Rut, Rot or Revival: The Condition of the Church, 17, 18.

200. Church: spiritual condition

When you are trying to find out the condition of a church, do not just inquire whether it is evangelical. Ask whether it is an evangelical rationalistic church that says, "The text is enough," or whether it is a church that believes that the text plus the Holy Spirit is enough. . . .

I would rather be part of a small group with inner knowledge than part of a vast group with only intellectual knowledge. In that great day of Christ's coming, all that will matter is whether or not I have been inwardly illuminated, inwardly regenerated, inwardly purified.

Colossians 1:3-4; 1 Thessalonians 1:2-3; 2 Thessalonians 1:3-4
Faith Beyond Reason, 30, 32.

201. Church: spiritual condition; Church: apathy; Fellowship: not the answer

Times are bad in the kingdom and getting worse. The tendency is to settle into a rut, and we must get out of it. . . .

When God sends some preacher to say this to a congregation and the congregation is even half ready to listen to him, they say to themselves, "I think the pastor is right about this. We are in a rut, aren't we? No use fighting it. I think we ought to do something about this." Then 99.99 percent of the time the remedy prescribed will be, "Let's come together and eat something. I know we are in a rut. We don't see each other often enough. We ought to get to know each other better, so let's come together and eat something." I have no objection to fellowship, but it is not the answer to what is wrong with us. . . .

I am quite sure that when the man of God thundered, "You have stayed long enough in this place. You are going around in circles. Get you out and take what is given to you by the hand of your God," nobody got up and said, "Mr. Chairman, let's eat something." Eating probably would not have helped.

Deuteronomy 1:6-8; Deuteronomy 2:3
Rut, Rot or Revival: The Condition of the Church, 13, 14, 15.

202. Church: spiritual condition; Church: cultural impact

Paganism is slowly closing in on the Church, and her only response is an occasional "drive" for one thing or another—usually money—or a noisy but timid campaign to improve the morals of the movies. Such activities amount to little more than a slight twitching of the muscles of a drowsy giant too sleepy to care. These efforts sometimes reach the headlines, but they accomplish little that is lasting, and are soon forgotten. The Church must have power; she must become formidable, a moral force to be reckoned with, if she would regain her lost position of spiritual ascendancy and make her message the revolutionizing, conquering thing it once was.

Matthew 28:18-20; Acts 1:8; Acts 4:31-33; Acts 17:6
Paths to Power, 9.

203. Church: spiritual condition; Revival: need for; Obedience: need for

We must have a reformation within the Church. To beg for a flood of blessing to come upon a backslidden and disobedient Church is to waste time and effort. A new wave of religious interest will do no more than add numbers to the churches that have no intention to own the Lordship of Jesus and come under obedience to His commandments. God is not interested in increasing church attendance unless those who attend amend their ways and begin to live holy lives.

Joshua 7:10-12; 2 Chronicles 7:14; Colossians 1:9-11; James 4:9-10
Keys to the Deeper Life, 24.

204. Church: spiritual condition; Rigidity; Nonexpectation

The church is afflicted by dry rot. This is best explained when the psychology of nonexpectation takes over and spiritual rigidity sets in, which is an inability to visualize anything better, a lack of desire for improvement.

There are many who respond by arguing, "I know lots of evangelical churches that would like to grow, and they do their best to get the crowds in. They want to grow and have contests to make their Sunday school larger." That is true, but they are trying to get people to come and share their rut. They want people to help them celebrate the rote and finally join in the rot. Because the Holy Spirit is not given a chance to work in our services, nobody is repenting, nobody is seeking God, nobody is spending a day in quiet waiting on God with open Bible seeking to mend his or her ways. Nobody is doing it—we just want more people. But more people for what? More people to come and repeat our dead services without feeling, without meaning, without wonder, without surprise? More people to join us in the bondage to the rote? For the most part, spiritual rigidity that cannot bend is too weak to know just how weak it is.

Acts 2:46-47; Acts 6:3-7; James 4:6
Rut, Rot or Revival: The Condition of the Church, 8, 9.

205. Church: spiritual condition; Spiritual discernment; Holy Spirit: need for

For our gospel-believing Christian circles in general, I fear there is an alarming lack of spiritual discernment. Because we have shut out the Holy Spirit in so many ways, we are stumbling along as though we are spiritually blindfolded. Ruling out the discernment and leadership of the Holy Spirit is the only possible explanation for the manner in which Christian churches have yielded to the temptation to entertain.

There is no other explanation for the wave of rationalism that now marks the life of many congregations. And what about the increasing compromise with all of the deadening forces of worldliness? The true, humble and uncompromising church of Christ is harder and harder to find. It is not because leaders and the rank and file within the church are bad. It is only because the Holy Spirit of God has been forcibly shut out and the needful gift of discernment about spiritual things is no longer present.

1 Corinthians 12:1-11; 2 Corinthians 1:12; Ephesians 5:15-18; Titus 1:8-9
Tragedy in the Church: The Missing Gifts, 19.

206. Church: spiritual condition; Spiritual discernment; Worldliness

That Bible religion in our times is suffering rapid decline is so evident as to need no proof; but just what has brought about this decline is not so easy to discover. I can only say that I have observed one significant lack among evangelical Christians which might turn out to be the real cause of most of our spiritual troubles; and of course if that were true, then the supplying of that lack would be our most critical need.

The great deficiency to which I refer is the lack of spiritual discernment, especially among our leaders. . . . If the knowledge of Bible doctrine were any guarantee of godliness, this would without doubt be known in history as the age of sanctity. Instead, it may well be known as the age of the Church's Babylonish captivity, or the age of worldliness, when the professed Bride of Christ allowed herself to be successfully courted by the fallen sons of men in unbelievable numbers. The body of evangelical believers, under evil influences, has during the last twenty-five years gone over to the world in complete and abject surrender, avoiding only a few of the grosser sins such as drunkenness and sexual promiscuity.

Psalm 119:66; Philippians 1:9-11; Revelation 3:15-17
The Root of the Righteous, 108, 109.

207. Church: spiritual condition; Spiritual disciplines; Activity: religious

The absence of spiritual devotion today is an omen and a portent. The modern church is all but contemptuous of the sober virtues—meekness, modesty, humility, quietness, obedience, self-effacement, patience. To be accepted now, religion must be in the popular mood. Consequently, much religious activity reeks with pride, display, self-assertion, self-promotion, love of gain and devotion to trivial pleasures.

It behooves us to take all this seriously. Time is running out for all of us. What is done must be done quickly. We have no right to lie idly by and let things take their course. A farmer who neglects his farm will soon lose it; a shepherd who fails to look after his flock will find the wolves looking after it for him. A misbegotten charity that allows the wolves to destroy the flock is not charity at all but indifference, rather, and should be known for what it is and dealt with accordingly.

It is time for Bible-believing Christians to begin to cultivate the sober graces and to live among men like sons of God and heirs of the ages. And this will take more than a bit of doing, for the whole world and a large part of the church is set to prevent it. But if God be for us, who can be against us?

Acts 20:28-31; Romans 8:31; Romans 13:11-14; 2 Corinthians 6:17-18; Colossians 3:12-14
We Travel an Appointed Way, 50, 51.

208. Church: success; Church: current condition; Pragmatism

Much that passes for Christianity today is the brief bright effort of the severed branch to bring forth its fruit in its season. But the deep laws of life are against it. Preoccupation with appearances and a corresponding neglect of the out-of-sight root of the true spiritual life are prophetic signs which go unheeded. Immediate "results" are all that matter, quick proofs of present success without a thought of next week or next year. Religious pragmatism is running wild among the orthodox. Truth is whatever works. If it gets results it is good. There is but one test for the religious leader: success. Everything is forgiven him except failure.

A tree can weather almost any storm if its root is sound, but when the fig tree which our Lord cursed "dried up from the roots" it immediately "withered away." A church that is soundly rooted cannot be destroyed, but nothing can save a church whose root is dried up. No stimulation, no advertising campaigns, no gifts of money and no beautiful edifice can bring back life to the rootless tree.

Matthew 21:6-9; Mark 4:5-6; John 15:1-7
The Root of the Righteous, 8, 9.

209. Church: success; Church: presence of Christ; Status symbols

In our time we have all kinds of status symbols in the Christian church—membership, attendance, pastoral staff, missionary offerings. But there is only one status symbol that should make a Christian congregation genuinely glad. That is to know that our Lord is present, walking in our midst! . . .

No matter the size of the assembly or its other attributes, our Lord wants it to be known by His presence in the midst. I would rather have His presence in the church than anything else in all the wide world.

Hearing the proud manner in which some speak of the high dollar cost of their sanctuaries must lead people to suppose that spirituality can be purchased. But the secret of true spiritual worship is to discern and know the presence of the living Christ in our midst. . . .

The Christian church dares not settle for anything less than the illumination of the Holy Spirit and the presence of our divine Prophet, Priest and King in our midst. Let us never be led into the mistake that so many are making—sighing and saying, "Oh, if we only had bigger, wiser men in our pulpits! Oh, if we only had more important men in places of Christian leadership!"

In John's vision, the sharp, double-edged sword proceeded out of the mouth of the Son of man. All other swords will fail and vanish, but the sharp sword, the Word of the Lord, will prevail. By all means, we had better stay with the sharp sword of His Word.

Hebrews 4:12; Revelation 1:12-18; Revelation 19:11-16
Jesus Is Victor!, 59, 60, 63.

210. Church: success; Pastoral ministry: pride

Knox Church, Hamilton, was one of the finer churches of Canada, very well-to-do and respectable, with more than twenty years of colorful history behind it, having a large congregation, and equipment the best that money could buy. It had a reputation among the churches, and when for any reason its pulpit became vacant the greatest preachers of the Presbyterian ministry were called to fill it. Such are the ways of churches. The ones that have, to them shall be given, and they shall have more abundantly, and the largest churches take it for granted that they should be able to command the biggest preachers. And ministers, being still human, are too often ready to agree with them.

1 Corinthians 4:7; 2 Corinthians 4:5-7; 1 Thessalonians 2:6-7
Wingspread; A.B. Simpson: A Study in Spiritual Altitude, 37.

211. Church: unity

Someone may fear that we are magnifying private religion out of all proportion, that the "us" of the New Testament is being displaced by a selfish "I." Has it ever occurred to you that one hundred pianos all tuned to the same fork are automatically tuned to each other? They are of one accord by being tuned, not to each other, but to another standard to which each one must individually bow. So one hundred worshipers meeting together, each one looking away to Christ, are in heart nearer to each other than they could possibly be were they to become "unity" conscious and turn their eyes away from God to strive for closer fellowship. Social religion is perfected when private religion is purified. The body becomes stronger as its members become healthier. The whole church of God gains when the members that compose it begin to seek a better and a higher life.

John 17:3,20-24; Ephesians 4:11-16; Philippians 3:10
The Pursuit of God, 87, 88.

212. Church: unity; Church: age divisions

Now for the very reason that the church is one body anything that tends to introduce division is an evil, however harmless, or even useful, it may appear to be. Yet the average evangelical church is divided into fragments which live and work separate from, and sometimes in opposition to, each other. In some churches there is simply no time or place for the worship and service of all members unitedly. These churches are organized to make such unity impossible.

Any belief or practice that causes the members of a local church to separate into groups on any pretext whatever is an evil. At first it may seem necessary to form such groups and it may be easy enough to show how many practical advantages follow these divisions; but soon the spirit of separateness unconsciously enters the minds of the persons involved and grows and hardens until it is impossible for them to think of themselves as belonging to the whole church. They may each and all hold the *doctrine* of unity, but the damage has been done; they *think* and *feel* themselves to be separated nevertheless.

One place where the evil manifests itself is in the practice of dividing the church into age groups. . . .

This age-youth division has gone so far in some churches that the old and the young glare at each other from different parts of the church and can have no spiritual fellowship whatsoever. If all are true Christians the basic unity has not been destroyed, but the *spirit* of unity has, with the result that the Lord is grieved and the church weakened. Yet much current religious education aids and abets division.

Acts 2:42-47; 1 Corinthians 12:12-27; Ephesians 4:1-6; Colossians 3:12-14
God Tells the Man Who Cares, 55, 56.

213. Church: unity; Church: presence of Christ

It is amazing that many people regard the Christian church as just another institution and the observance of Communion as just one of its periodic rituals. Any genuine, New Testament church actually *is* communion. It is not an institution. The Bible makes that plain. . . .

Blessed is the congregation that has found the spiritual maturity and understanding to honestly confess, "Our congregation is so keenly aware of the presence of Jesus in our midst that our entire fellowship is an unceasing communion!" What a joyful experience it is for us in this church age to be part of a congregation drawn together by the desire to know God's presence, to sense His nearness.

John 17:20-24; 1 Corinthians 11:23-29; Colossians 1:3-4
Tragedy in the Church: The Missing Gifts, 105, 106.

214. Church: unity; Tolerance/Intolerance; Pastoral ministry: convictions

Then I don't mean the oneness of passivity and compromise. In order to stay one, some churches have the oneness of passivity. Nobody cares much anyway and so they just compromise. That is the beautiful unity of the dead. I suppose there isn't anything more united than a cemetery. Everybody there, whether they were Democrats, Republicans, Tories or Patriots while they lived, all lie there calmly together because they're dead.

When you go into a church where the pastor is afraid of hurting somebody who has a large checkbook, who is careful to say nothing at all and take no position, everybody gathers around him. He is dead and he gathers a lot of dead people around him and they call that a church. It's not a church at all; it is simply a conglomeration of dead men, afraid to have an opinion. It is the beautiful tolerance of the dead.

Matthew 18:15-17; 1 Corinthians 5:11; Galatians 1:9-10
Success and the Christian, 94.

215. Circumstances; Blessings: spiritual

As Christians we look at everything differently....

People of the world, for instance, hope for life, health, financial prosperity, international peace and a set of favorable circumstances. These are their resources—upon them they rest. They look to them as a child looks to its nursing mother.

Christians do not despise these temporal blessings, and if they come to them, they sanctify them by receiving them with prayers of outpoured gratitude to God. But they know their everlasting welfare is not dependent upon them. These blessings may come or go, but true Christians abide in God where no evil can touch them and where they are rich beyond all the power of their minds to conceive—and this altogether apart from earthly circumstances....

The world's resources are good in their way, but they have this fatal defect—they are uncertain and transitory. Today we have them, tomorrow they are gone....

If the world's foundations crumble we still have God, and in Him we have everything essential to our ransomed beings forever. We have Christ, who also died for us and who now sits at the right hand of the Majesty in the heavens making constant and effective intercession for us. We have the Scriptures, which can never fail. We have the Holy Spirit to interpret the Scriptures to our inner lives and to be to us a Guide and a Comforter. We have prayer and we have faith, and these bring heaven to earth and turn even bitter Marah sweet. And if worse comes to worst here below, we have our Father's house and our Father's welcome.

Exodus 15:23-25; Matthew 6:25-34; John 14:1-3; John 16:13-15; Romans 8:34; Philippians 4:11-12
This World: Playground or Battleground?, 23, 24, 25.

216. Claims of Christ

Frankly, the claims that He made brand Him immediately as being God—or an idiot! The authoritative claims He made outstrip the claims of all other religious teachers in the world.

Of His own body He said, "Destroy this temple and I will raise it again in three days" (John 2:19).

He told His hearers, "I saw Satan fall like lightning from heaven" (Luke 10:18).

He declared with authority, "Before Abraham was born, I am" (John 8:58).

He predicted that "When the Son of Man comes in his glory, and all the angels with him, he will sit on his throne in heavenly glory. All the nations will be gathered before him, and he will separate the people one from another as a shepherd separates the sheep from the goats" (Matthew 25:31-33).

No one else has ever been able to say, "Do not be amazed at this, for a time is coming when all who are in their graves will hear [my] voice and come out" (John 5:28-29).

No one else has ever talked like that!

Matthew 25:31-32; Luke 10:18; John 2:19; John 5:28-29; John 8:58
Echoes from Eden, 26, 27.

217. Commitment; Burning bush

Why did the Almighty God use a scrubby bush to reveal His presence and glory? It would seem that the bush was just a common acacia plant. It had no intrinsic worth. It was in itself completely helpless. And it could not back out. It was caught there, indwelt by the presence of God and fire.

Like the bush, we will never know God until we are helpless in His hands. We will never be of worth to Him until there is no escape. As long as we can run, as long as we know we can depend upon our avenues of escape, we are not really in God's hands....

Let me tell you with assurance that the happy Christian is the one who has been caught—captured by the Lord. He or she no longer wants to escape or go back. The happy Christian has met the Lord personally and found Him an all-sufficient Savior and Lord. He or she has burned all the bridges in every direction.

Some of God's children are dabbling with surrender and victory. They have never reached that place of spiritual commitment which is final and complete and satisfying. They still retain their escape routes. . . .

I thank God for the little bush! It was caught, it was helpless. But it was radiant and useful and enduring in the presence and hands of the living God.

Exodus 3; Luke 9:23-25; Philippians 3:7-16
Men Who Met God, 72, 73, 74.

218. Commitment; Church: cultural impact; Prayers

There is no limit to what God could do in our world if we would dare to surrender before Him with a commitment like this:

"Oh God, I hereby give myself to You. I give my family. I give my business. I give all I possess. Take all of it, Lord—and take me! I give myself in such measure that if it is necessary that I lose everything for your sake, let me lose it. I will not ask what the price is. I will ask only that I may be all that I ought to be as a follower and disciple of Jesus Christ, my Lord. Amen."

If even 300 of God's people became that serious, our world would never hear the last of it! They would influence the news. Their message would go everywhere like birds on the wing. They would set off a great revival of New Testament faith and witness.

Matthew 16:24-26; Acts 17:6; Revelation 7:14-17
Jesus Is Victor!, 116.

219. Commitment; Discipleship

I would . . . make a few recommendations to anyone seeking a more satisfying and more God-possessed life than he now enjoys.

First, determine to take the whole thing in dead earnest. Too many of us play at Christianity. We wear salvation as a kind of convention badge admitting us into the circle of the elect, but rarely stop to focus our whole lives seriously on God's claims upon us.

Second, throw yourself out recklessly upon God. Give up everything and prepare yourself to surrender even unto death all of your ambitions, plans and possessions. And I mean this quite literally. You should not be satisfied with the mere technical aspect of surrender but press your case upon God in determined prayer until a crisis has taken place within your life and there has been an actual transfer of everything from yourself to God.

Third, take a solemn vow never to claim any honor or glory or praise for anything you are or have or do. See to it that God gets all honor, all the time.

Fourth, determine not to defend yourself against detractors and persecutors. Put your reputation in God's hands and leave it there.

Fifth, mortify the flesh with the affections and lusts. Every believer has been judicially put to death with Christ, but this is not enough for present victory. Freedom from the power of the flesh will come only when we have by faith and self-discipline made such death an actuality. Real death to self is a painful thing and tends to reduce a man in his own eyes and humble him into the dust. Not many follow this rugged way, but those who do are the exemplary Christians.

Matthew 22:37-39; Acts 20:24; Romans 6:11-14; Romans 8:13; 2 Corinthians 12:19; Ephesians 3:20-21
Keys to the Deeper Life, 86, 87.

220. Commitment; Following Christ

"Are you sure you want to follow Me?" He asked, and a great many turned away. But Peter said, "Lord, to whom shall we go? thou hast the words of eternal life." And the crowd that wouldn't turn away was the crowd that made history. The crowd that wouldn't turn back was the crowd that was there when the Holy Ghost came and filled all the place where they were sitting. The crowd that turned back never knew what it was all about.

John 6:68; Acts 2:1-4
How to Be Filled With the Holy Spirit, 45, 46.

221. Commitment; Idols

"The dearest idol I have known, Whate'er that idol be, Help me to tear it from Thy throne, And worship only Thee."

We sing this glibly enough, but we cancel out our prayer by our refusal to surrender the very idol of which we sing. To give up our last idol is to plunge ourselves into a state of inward loneliness which no gospel meeting, no fellowship with other Christians, can ever cure. For this reason most Christians play it safe and settle for a life of compromise. They have some of God, to be sure, but not all; and God has some of them, but not all. And so they live their tepid lives and try to disguise with bright smiles and snappy choruses the deep spiritual destitution within them.

Matthew 6:24-33; 1 John 5:21
Keys to the Deeper Life, 54, 55.

222. Commitment; Jesus Christ: response to

There is only one Man whom we can trust to follow. That Man is Jesus Christ. Why is He different from any other person? Why do I refuse to follow other people, and yet follow this Man? Of no other person can it be said, "In the beginning was the Word, and the Word was with God, and the Word was God" (John 1:1). "The Word became flesh and made his dwelling among us. We have seen his glory, the glory of the One and Only, who came from the Father, full of grace and truth" (1:14). Of no other person from Adam to now can it be said, "He will be called Wonderful Counselor, Mighty God, Everlasting Father, Prince of Peace" (Isaiah 9:6). Of no one else can it be said that three days after He had gone into the grave He rose again. . . .

This is the King of glory, this Man; and this Man is the one who says, "Give yourself to me. Surrender to me and concentrate upon me. Be caught in the spell of the irresistible charm."

Isaiah 9:6; John 1:1,14; Acts 1:9-11; Colossians 2:15-17; Revelation 19:11-16
Rut, Rot or Revival: The Condition of the Church, 79, 80.

223. Commitment; Longing for God

In order to get launched into my message let me introduce a little lady who has been dead for about six hundred years. She once lived and loved and prayed and sang in the city of Norwich, England. This little woman hadn't much light and she hadn't any way to get much light, but the beautiful thing about her was that, with what little Biblical light she had, she walked with God so wonderfully close that she became as fragrant as a flower. And long before Reformation times she was in spirit an evangelical. She lived and died and has now been with her Lord nearly six hundred years, but she has left behind her a fragrance of Christ.

England was a better place because this little lady lived. She wrote only one book, a very tiny book that you could slip into your side pocket or your purse, but it's so flavorful, so divine, so heavenly, that it has made a distinct contribution to the great spiritual literature of the world. The lady to whom I refer is the one called the Lady Julian.

Before she blossomed out into this radiant, glorious life which made her famous as a great Christian all over her part of the world, she prayed a prayer and God answered. It is this prayer with which I am concerned tonight. The essence of her prayer was this: "O God, please give me three wounds: the wound of *contrition* and the wound of *compassion* and the wound of *longing after God.*" Then she added this little post-script which I think is one of the most beautiful things I have ever read: "This I ask without condition." She wasn't dickering with God. She wanted three things and they were all for God's glory: "I ask this without condition, Father; do what I ask and then send me the bill. Anything that it costs will be all right with me."

1 Chronicles 4:10; Psalm 42:1-2; Philippians 3:29-30
Man: The Dwelling Place of God, 100, 101.

224. Commitment; Lordship of Christ

What can we do to satisfy the heart of our Father in heaven?

The answer is near thee, even in thy mouth. Vacate the throne room of your heart and enthrone Jesus there. Set Him in the focus of your heart's attention and stop wanting to be a hero. Make Him your all in all and try yourself to become less and less. Dedicate your entire life to His honor alone and shift the motives of your life from self to God. Let the reason back of your daily conduct be Christ and His glory, not yourself, nor your family nor your country nor your church. In all things let Him have the preëminence.

Proverbs 3:5-6; John 3:30; Romans 12:1-2; Colossians 1:18
Born After Midnight, 70.

225. Commitment; Obedience: cost of; Lordship of Christ

It is doubtful whether we can be Christian in anything unless we are Christian in everything. To obey Christ in one or two or ten instances and then in fear of consequences to back away and refuse to obey in another is to cloud our life with the suspicion that we are only fair-weather followers and not true believers at all. To obey when it costs us nothing and refuse when the results are costly is to convict ourselves of moral trifling and gross insincerity....

The Christian businessman when faced with a moral choice must never ask, "How much will this cost me?" The moment he regards consequences, he dethrones Christ as Lord of his life. His only concern should be with the will of God and the moral quality of the proposed act. To consult anything else is to sin against his own soul.

Matthew 6:24-33; Luke 9:57-62; Acts 20:24
The Size of the Soul, 146, 147.

226. Commitment; Persecution; Following Christ; Current conditions: shallowness

In the Book of Acts faith was for each believer a beginning, not an end; it was a journey, not a bed in which to lie while waiting for the day of our Lord's triumph. Believing was not a once-done act; it was more than an act, it was an attitude of heart and mind which inspired and enabled the believer to take up his cross and follow the Lamb whithersoever He went....

Those first believers turned to Christ with the full understanding that they were espousing an unpopular cause that could cost them everything. They knew they would henceforth be members of a hated minority group with life and liberty always in jeopardy.

This is no idle flourish. Shortly after Pentecost some were jailed, many lost all their earthly goods, a few were slain outright and hundreds "scattered abroad."

They could have escaped all this by the simple expedient of denying their faith and turning back to the world; but this they steadfastly refused to do.

Seen thus in comparison with each other, is the Christianity of American evangelicalism today the same as that of the first century? I wonder. But again, I think I know.

Luke 9:23-25; John 15:18-21; Acts 4:3; Acts 5:18,41-42; Acts 7:58; Acts 8:3-4
Born After Midnight, 16, 18.

227. Commitment; Preaching: response to; Life change

Here is what grieves me, and I believe this also grieves the Holy Spirit: My hearers rise to this call emotionally, but they will not confirm it by a corresponding change in their way of life. Their goodness is like the morning clouds—by 9:00 o'clock the sun has burnt off the fog. This is what happens to many people's good intentions. They rise emotionally to an urgent message that we become a New Testament church, that we become a model church, that we have the order of the New Testament and the power of the Holy Spirit in order that we might worship, work and witness. Emotionally they rise to it, but they will not confirm their emotions by corresponding changes in their way of life.

They want to be blessed by God, but they want God to bless them on their terms. They look pensively to God for victory, but they will not bring their giving into line. They will not practice family prayer, rushing off without it. They will not take time for secret prayer and will not forgive those who have wronged them. They will not seek to be reconciled to those with whom they have quarreled. They will not pick up their crosses and say, "Jesus, I my cross have taken, all to leave and follow Thee."

Matthew 5:23-24; Matthew 6:14-16; Matthew 16:24-26; Philippians 2:12,13
Rut, Rot or Revival: The Condition of the Church, 146, 147.

228. Commitment; Priorities

A man of ordinary mind may go on to do marvels in a given field if he has keen enough interest in it, and leave behind many men of finer minds who lack the necessary interest. Sometimes one interest may crowd out another. I wonder how many potential Rubensteins or Heifetzes may have gotten lost in obscurity simply because they could not as boys bring themselves to practice when a ball game was in progress on a corner lot nearby. So worldly interests often crowd out heavenly ones and spiritual receptivity is destroyed as a result.

Romans 12:1-2; Philippians 1:9-11; 1 John 2:15-17
That Incredible Christian, 79.

229. Commitment; Revival: need for; Church: apathy

We need a revival! We need a revival of consecration to death, a revival of happy abandonment to the will of God that will laugh at sacrifice and count it a privilege to bear the cross through the heat and burden of the day. We are too much influenced by the world and too little controlled by the Spirit. We of the deeper life persuasion are not immune to the temptations of ease and we are in grave danger of becoming a generation of pleasure lovers.

Any who disagree with these conclusions are within their rights, and I would be the last to deny them the privilege. But in the name of a thousand struggling churches and disheartended pastors, may I not plead for a little more loyalty to the local church during this season of difficulty?

Amos 6:1; Luke 12:19-21; Philippians 3:6-8
God Tells the Man Who Cares, 159, 160.

230. Commitment; Service: sacrificial

We must offer all our acts to God and believe that He accepts them. Then hold firmly to that position and keep insisting that every act of every hour of the day and night be included in the transaction. Keep reminding God in our times of private prayer that we mean every act for His glory; then supplement those times by a thousand thought-prayers as we go about the job of living. Let us practice the fine art of making every work a priestly ministration. Let us believe that God is in all our simple deeds and learn to find Him there.

1 Corinthians 10:31; Colossians 3:16-18; 1 Peter 4:11
The Pursuit of God, 114.

231. Commitment; Spiritual victory

Let the seeking man reach a place where life and lips join to say continually, "Be thou exalted," and a thousand minor problems will be solved at once. His Christian life ceases to be the complicated thing it had been before and becomes the very essence of simplicity. By the exercise of his will he has set his course, and on that course he will stay as if guided by an automatic pilot. If blown off course for a moment by some adverse wind, he will surely return again as by a secret bent of the soul. The hidden motions of the Spirit are working in his favor, and "the stars in their courses" (Judges 5:20) fight for him. He has met his life problem at its center, and everything else must follow along.

Judges 5:20; Psalm 57:5,11; Philippians 3:13-14
The Pursuit of God, 95.

232. Commitment; Uncertainty; Service: privilege of

But the lives of consecrated people are never their own. To sit back in selfish composure and plan the future is never an option to those who have made the great commitment. They are at the call of Another, and at any time they may receive orders to pick up and move on. This is one of the penalties they must pay for the high privilege of serving God, and if seen from a low point it looks like a hard and unsatisfactory way to live. But the truest appraisal of a way of life is always made at the end of it. Who that have placed themselves at the disposal of God and humanity have ever been sorry at the end of life that they did so? Not one, and that is the best argument for the excellence of the devoted life.

Acts 20:24; 1 Corinthians 6:19-20; 2 Timothy 4:6-8; Hebrews 11:8-10
Let My People Go: The Life of Robert A. Jaffray, 94, 95.

233. Common grace

What have you received of His grace and mercy?

Even though you may still be unconverted and going your own way, you have received much out of the ocean of His fullness. You have received the pulsing life that beats in your bosom. You have received the brilliant mind and brain within the protective covering of your skull. You have received a memory that strings the events you cherish and love as a jeweler strings pearls into a necklace and keeps them for you as long as you live and beyond.

All that you have is out of His grace. Jesus Christ, the eternal Word, who became flesh and dwelt among us, is the open channel through which God moves to provide all the benefits He gives to saints and sinners.

And what about the years, the rest of your existence?

You cannot believe that you have earned it. You cannot believe that it has something to do with whether you are good or bad.

Confess that it is out of His grace, for the entire universe is the beneficiary of God's grace and goodness.

Psalm 139:13-16; Matthew 5:45; John 1:14,16
Christ the Eternal Son, 24.

234. Communion with God

God is a person, and in the deep of His mighty nature He thinks, wills, enjoys, feels, loves, desires, and suffers as any other person may. In making Himself known to us He stays by the familiar pattern of personality. He communicates with us through the avenues of our minds, our wills and our emotions. The continuous and unembarrassed interchange of love and thought between God and the soul of the redeemed man is the throbbing heart of New Testament religion.

Matthew 11:27; Romans 1:19-20; 1 Corinthians 2:11-12
The Pursuit of God, 13.

235. Communion with God

Ransomed men need no longer pause in fear to enter the Holy of Holies. *God wills that we should push on into His presence and live our whole life there.* This is to be known to us in conscious experience. It is more than a doctrine to be held; it is a life to be enjoyed every moment of every day.

Psalm 95:1-2; Hebrews 10:19-23; 1 John 1:1-3
The Pursuit of God, 34.

236. Communion with God; Loneliness

However we may explain this mysterious "ground" within us, we will not have been long in the Christian way until we begin to experience it. We will find that we have within us a secret garden where no one can enter except ourself and God. Not only does no one else enter, no one else can enter. This secret inner chamber is the sacred trysting place for Christ and the believing soul; no one among all our dearest friends has the open sesame that will permit him to enter there. If God is shut out, then there can be only everlasting loneliness and numb despair.

Where God is not known in the inner shrine, the individual must try to compensate for his sense of aloneness in whatever way he can. Most persons rush away to the world to find companionship and surround themselves with every kind of diversionary activity. All devices for killing time, every shallow scheme for entertainment, are born out of this inner loneliness. It is a significant and revealing fact that such things have in these last days grown into billion dollar enterprises! So much will men pay to forget that they are a temple without a God, a garden where no voice is heard in the cool of the day.

Genesis 3:8; Leviticus 26:11-12; 1 Corinthians 6:19-20
The Next Chapter After the Last, 104.

237. Communion with God; Man: rebellion against God

Among the famous sayings of the church fathers, none is better known than Augustine's, "Thou hast formed us for Thyself, and our hearts are restless till they find rest in Thee.". . .

God formed us for His pleasure, and so formed us that we, as well as He, can, in divine communion, enjoy the sweet and mysterious mingling of kindred personalities. He meant us to see Him and live with Him and draw our life from His smile. But we have been guilty of that "foul revolt" of which Milton speaks when describing the rebellion of Satan and his host. We have broken with God. We have ceased to obey Him or love Him, and in guilt and fear have fled as far as possible from His presence.

Jonah 1:3; Hebrews 10:19-23; Revelation 4:8-11
The Pursuit of God, 31, 32.

238. Competition; Spiritual warfare

Nothing spiritual can be gained in competition. . . .

When two men step into a prize ring they know that only one can win, and whoever wins can do so only by forcing the other to lose. When five men line up on the track for a race they know that only one can come in first. Four men must lose that one may win. It is not so in the kingdom of God. Christians do not run against each other. All can win the race. Paul likens a Christian to a fighter, but the Christian's fight is not with other Christians. Each one can win and no one need lose. The man of faith fights against the devil, the flesh and the world. He wins as they lose; but he never wins anything truly spiritual in competition with a fellow believer. In the nature of things he cannot. To think so is to entertain an absurdity.

1 Corinthians 9:24-27; Ephesians 2:1-3; Ephesians 6:10-12; 2 Timothy 2:5
The Price of Neglect, 102, 103.

239. Complacency; Holiness: conditions for

Every man is as holy as he really wants to be. But the want must be all-compelling.

Leviticus 19:2; 2 Corinthians 7:11; 1 Peter 1:14-16; 1 John 3:2-3
Man: The Dwelling Place of God, 40.

240. Complacency; Longing for God

Religious complacency is encountered almost everywhere among Christians these days, and its presence is a sign and a prophecy. For every Christian will become at last what his desires have made him. We are all the sum total of our hungers. The great saints have all had thirsting hearts. Their cry has been "My soul thirsteth for God, for the living God: when shall I come and appear before God?" Their longing after God all but consumed them; it propelled them onward and upward to heights toward which less ardent Christians look with languid eye and entertain no hope of reaching.

Psalm 42:1-2; Psalm 63:1-2; Matthew 5:6
The Root of the Righteous, 55.

241. Complacency; Longing for God

Orthodox Christianity has fallen to its present low estate from lack of spiritual desire. Among the many who profess the Christian faith scarcely one in a thousand reveals any passionate thirst for God.

The Root of the Righteous, 56.

242. Complacency; Spiritual Growth; Longing for God

The complacency of Christians is the scandal of Christianity....

These Christians know, and when pressed will admit, that their finite hearts have explored but a pitifully small part of the infinite riches that are theirs in Christ Jesus. They read the lives of the great saints whose fervent desire after God carried them far up the mountain toward spiritual perfection; and for a brief moment they may yearn to be like these fiery souls whose light and fragrance still linger in the world where they once lived and labored. But the longing soon passes. The world is too much with them and the claims of their earthly lives are too insistent; so they settle back to live their ordinary lives, and accept the customary as normal. After a while they manage to achieve some kind of inner content and that is the last we hear of them.

Romans 9:23-24; Ephesians 1:12-14; Hebrews 3:12-13
Man the Dwelling Place of God, 38, 39.

243. Complaining

Among those sins most exquisitely fitted to injure the soul and destroy the testimony, few can equal the sin of complaining. Yet the habit is so widespread that we hardly notice it among us.

The complaining heart never lacks for occasion. It can always find reason enough to be unhappy. The object of its censure may be almost anything: the weather, the church, the difficulties of the way, other Christians or even God Himself....

... the believer who complains against the difficulties of the way proves that he has never felt or known the sorrows which broke over the head of Christ when He was here among men. After one look at Gethsemane or Calvary, the Christian can never again believe that his own path is a hard one. We dare not compare our trifling pains with the sublime passion endured for our salvation. Any comparison would itself be the supreme argument against our complaints, for what sorrow is like unto His?

Galatians 6:9; Ephesians 4:29; Hebrews 12:3-6; James 3:6-10
The Next Chapter After the Last, 15, 16.

244. Compromise; Current issues: compromise

The rise of a new religious spirit in recent years is marked by disturbing similarities to that earlier "revival" under Constantine. Now as then a quasi-Christianity is achieving acceptance by compromise. It is dickering with the unregenerate world for acceptance and, as someone said recently, it is offering Christ at bargain prices to win customers. The total result is a conglomerate religious mess that cannot but make the reverent Christian sick in his heart. . . .

The sum of all this is that religion today is not transforming the people; rather it is being transformed by the people. It is not raising the moral level of society; it is descending to society's own level and congratulating itself that it has scored a victory because society is smilingly accepting its surrender.

Galatians 1:6-7; 1 Timothy 1:6-7; 1 John 4:1
The Price of Neglect, 95, 96.

245. Compromise; Growth emphasis; Church: numbers

There is a great decision that every denomination has to make sometime in the development of its history. Every church also has to make it either at its beginning or a little later—usually a little later. Eventually every board is faced with the decision and has to keep making it, not by one great decision made once for all, but by a series of little decisions adding up to one great big one. Every pastor has to face it and keep renewing his decision on his knees before God. Finally, every church member, every evangelist, every Christian has to make this decision. It is a matter of judgment upon that denomination, that church, that board, that pastor, that leader and upon their descendants and spiritual children.

The question is this: Shall we modify the truth in doctrine or practice to gain more adherents? Or shall we preserve the truth in doctrine and practice and take the consequences?

2 Timothy 1:13-14; 2 John 8-9; 3 John 4
Rut, Rot or Revival: The Condition of the Church, 165.

246. Compromise; Pastoral ministry: convictions

The question is this: Shall we modify the truth in doctrine or practice to gain more adherents? Or shall we preserve the truth in doctrine and practice and take the consequences? . . .

Actually such a question should never need to be asked. It is like asking, "Should a man be faithful to his wife?" There is only one answer to that question. When we ask, "Shall we preserve the truth and practice of the church, or shall we modify it for immediate and visible results?" we ought to have only one answer. It is not a debatable question, and yet it is one that has to be constantly debated in the secret prayer chamber. It is constantly debated when conferences meet, when boards meet and when a pastor must make a decision.

A commitment to preserving the truth and practice of the church is what separates me from a great many people who are perhaps far greater than I am in ability. This is my conviction, long held and deeply confirmed by a knowledge of the fact that modern gospel churches, almost without exception, have decided to modify the truth and practice a little in order to have more adherents and get along better.

2 Timothy 1:13-14; 2 John 8-9; 3 John 4
Rut, Rot or Revival: The Condition of the Church, 165, 166, 167.

247. Concept of God

. . . the gravest question before the Church is always God Himself, and the most portentous fact about any man is not what he at a given time may say or do, but what he in his deep heart conceives God to be like. We tend by a secret law of the soul to move toward our mental image of God.

Psalm 90:1-2; Isaiah 40:21-31; 1 John 3:2-3
The Knowledge of the Holy, 1.

248. Concept of God; Current conditions: shallowness

A right conception of God is basic not only to systematic theology but to practical Christian living as well. It is to worship what the foundation is to the temple; where it is inadequate or out of plumb the whole structure must sooner or later collapse. I believe there is scarcely an error in doctrine or a failure in applying Christian ethics that cannot be traced finally to imperfect and ignoble thoughts about God.

It is my opinion that the Christian conception of God current in these middle years of the twentieth century is so decadent as to be utterly beneath the dignity of the Most High God and actually to constitute for professed believers something amounting to a moral calamity.

Psalm 19:1-6,14; Isaiah 40:21-31; Romans 1:20-23
The Knowledge of the Holy, 3.

249. Concept of God; God: His love; Communion with God

Satan's first attack upon the human race was his sly effort to destroy Eve's confidence in the kindness of God. Unfortunately for her and for us he succeeded too well. From that day, men have had a false conception of God, and it is exactly this that has cut out from under them the ground of righteousness and driven them to reckless and destructive living.

Nothing twists and deforms the soul more than a low or unworthy conception of God.... The God of the Pharisee was not a God easy to live with, so his religion became grim and hard and loveless. It had to be so, for our notion of God must always determine the quality of our religion....

It is most important to our spiritual welfare that we hold in our minds always a right conception of God. If we think of Him as cold and exacting we shall find it impossible to love Him and our lives will be ridden with servile fear. If, again, we hold Him to be kind and understanding our whole inner life will mirror that idea.

The truth is that God is the most winsome of all beings and His service one of unspeakable pleasure....

The fellowship of God is delightful beyond all telling.

Genesis 3:4-5; Psalm 34:8; Nahum 1:7; Romans 1:20-23
The Root of the Righteous, 13, 14, 15.

250. Concept of God; Man: insignificance of

To be right we must think worthily of God. It is morally imperative that we purge from our minds all ignoble concepts of the Deity and let Him be the God in our minds that He is in His universe. The Christian religion has to do with God and man, but its focal point is God, not man. Man's only claim to importance is that he was created in the divine image; in himself he is nothing. The psalmists and prophets of the Scriptures refer in sad scorn to weak man whose breath is in his nostrils, who grows up like the grass in the morning only to be cut down and wither before the setting of the sun. That God exists for Himself and man for the glory of God is the emphatic teaching of the Bible. The high honor of God is first in heaven as it must yet be in earth.

Genesis 1:26-27; Psalm 8:3-5; Psalm 90:4-6; Isaiah 2:22
The Knowledge of the Holy, 55, 56.

251. Confirmation: need for; Bible: value of; God: His presence

Our shortcoming in spiritual experience is our tendency to believe without confirmation. God Himself does not need to confirm anything within His being. But we are not God. We are humans, and in matters of our faith we need confirmation within ourselves.

Why are so many Christian believers ineffective, anemic, disappointed, discouraged? I think the answer is that we need confirmation within ourselves and we are not getting it.

I have no doubt that God, in love and grace and mercy, awaits to confirm His presence among those who will truly hunger and thirst after righteousness....

Conscious awareness of the presence of God! I defy any theologian or teacher to take that away from the believing church of Jesus Christ!

But be assured they will try. And I refer not just to the liberal teachers. God has given us the Bible for a reason. That reason is so it can lead us to meet God in Jesus Christ in a clear, sharp encounter that will burn on in our hearts forever and ever!

Psalm 34:8; Matthew 5:6; John 5:36-40; 2 Timothy 3:16-17
Men Who Met God, 11, 12.

252. Conscience; Tongue; Profanity

But when a conscience has become seared, when a man has played with the fire and burned his conscience and calloused it until he can handle the hot iron of sin without shrinking, there is no longer any safety for him.

Titus wrote in his epistle about those to whom nothing is pure any longer, "both their minds and consciences are corrupted" (Titus 1:15).

Here Titus speaks of an inward corruption, revealed in impure thoughts and soiled language. I am just as afraid of people with soiled tongues as I am of those with a communicable disease.

Actually, a foul tongue is evidence of a deeper spiritual disease and Titus goes on to tell us that those with defiled consciences become reprobates, something just washed up on the shore, a moral shipwreck.

John 8:7-9; Ephesians 5:3-4; 1 Timothy 1:5-6;
1 Timothy 4:1-2; Titus 1:15-16
Echoes from Eden, 64, 65.

253. Consistency

The average church is like this: We come on Sunday and we get a little blessing and we lose it until Wednesday. Then we come and get another little blessing and we get back up the peak and then we lose it till Sunday and then we get back on another peak. It's a continual going up to the peak and down into the valley and back to the peak again. Now it's better to do it that way than not to do it at all. But it's a whole lot better to stay on a high level than to come down in the middle of the week and have to come to a prayer meeting to get back up. Prayer meetings are necessary and you should come, but not to heal up your broken wires. We ought to stay one; the mood, the spirituality ought to persist.

Acts 2:42-47; Acts 4:31-33; Philippians 2:1-4;
1 Thessalonians 5:16-17
Success and the Christian, 88, 89.

254. Contempt; Pride: spiritual

It is in the realm of religion that contempt finds its most fruitful soil and flourishes most luxuriantly. It is seen in the cold disdain with which the respectable church woman regards the worldly sister and in the scorn heaped upon the fallen woman by the legally married wife. The sober deacon may find it hard to conceal his contempt for the neighbor who drinks. The evangelical may castigate the liberal in a manner that leaves slight doubt that he feels himself above him in every way. Religion that is not purified by penitence, humility and love will lead to a feeling of contempt for the irreligious and the morally degraded. And since contempt implies a judgment of no worth made against a human brother, the contemptuous man comes under the displeasure of God and lies in danger of hell fire. . . .

To esteem anyone worthless who wears the form of a man is to be guilty of an affront to the Son of Man. We should hate sin in ourselves and in all men, but we should never undervalue the man in whom the sin is found.

Matthew 5:22; Luke 18:9-14; Acts 10:34-35;
Ephesians 2:2-7; James 2:1-5
Of God and Men, 96, 97.

255. Controversy

The nearer we draw to the heart of God the less taste we will have for controversy. The peace we know in God's bosom is so sweet that it is but natural that we want to keep it unbroken to enjoy as fully and as long as possible.

The Spirit-filled Christian is never a good fighter. He is at too many disadvantages. The enemy is always better at invective than he will allow himself to be. The devil has all the picturesque epithets, and his followers have no conscience about using them. The Christian is always more at home blessing than he is opposing. He is, moreover, much thinner-skinned than his adversaries. He shrinks from an angry countenance and draws back from bitter words. They are symbols of a world he has long ago forsaken for the quiet of the kingdom of God where love and good will prevail. All this is in his favor, for it marks him out as a man in whom there is no hate and who earnestly desires to live at peace with all men.

Romans 12:16-18; 2 Corinthians 13:11; Ephesians 4:31-32; 1 Thessalonians 5:13-15
The Next Chapter After the Last, 17.

256. Conversation; Intellectual stimulation

Our intellectual activities in the order of their importance may be graded this way: first, cogitation; second, observation; third, reading.

I wish I could include conversation in this short list. One would naturally suppose that verbal intercourse with congenial friends should be one of the most profitable of all mental activities; and it may have been so once but no more. It is now quite possible to talk for hours with civilized men and women and gain absolutely nothing from it. Conversation today is almost wholly sterile. Should the talk start on a fairly high level, it is sure within a few minutes to degenerate into cheap gossip, shoptalk, banter, weak humor, stale jokes, puns and secondhand quips. So we shall omit conversation from our list of useful intellectual activities, at least until there has been a radical reformation in the art of social discourse.

Romans 14:17-19; Ephesians 4:29; Colossians 3:16-18
Man: The Dwelling Place of God, 144, 145.

257. Conversion; Regeneration; Salvation: transformation

The converted man is both reformed and regenerated. And unless the sinner is willing to reform his way of living he will never know the inward experience of regeneration. This is the vital truth which has gotten lost under the leaves in popular evangelical theology.

The idea that God will pardon a rebel who has not given up his rebellion is contrary both to the Scriptures and to common sense. How horrible to contemplate a church full of persons who have been pardoned but who still love sin and hate the ways of righteousness. And how much more horrible to think of heaven as filled with sinners who had not repented nor changed their way of living.

Matthew 7:15-16; James 2:26; 1 John 1:6-9
The Root of the Righteous, 43.

258. Creation; Science; Atheism; Origins

The human mind requires an answer to the question concerning the origin and nature of things. The world as we find it must be accounted for in some way. Philosophers and scientists have sought to account for it, the one by speculation, the other by observation, and in their labors they have come upon many useful and inspiring facts. But they have not found the final Truth. That comes by revelation and illumination.

They who believe the Christian revelation know that the universe is a creation. It is not eternal, since it had a beginning, and it is not the result of a succession of happy coincidences whereby an all but infinite number of matching parts accidentally found each other, fell into place and began to hum. So to believe would require a degree of credulity few persons possess. "I had rather believe all the fables in the Legend, and the Talmud, and the Alcoram," said Bacon, "than that this universal frame is without a mind. And therefore God never wrought miracles to convince atheism, because His ordinary works convince it."

Genesis 1:1; Psalm 19:1-6; John 1:3; Romans 1:20-23
Man: The Dwelling Place of God, 24.

259. Creation; Wonder

God made the world; it is a beautiful thing and something to venerate. It's a great loss—a tragic loss—that we've suffered in the last generation. We have lost the ability to wonder. We know so everlasting much and we're so sure of ourselves. But David stood and wondered in the presence of God's creation; he raised his eyes and said, "What is man that you are mindful of him?" (Psalm 8:4a). And Isaiah and Jeremiah and Ezekiel and all the rest of them stood and wondered in the presence of God Almighty's creation. . . .

Everything is a bright miracle. It's not only a miracle when Christ turns water into wine; it's also a miracle when the sun rises with its healing rays and drives off the fog and brings out the bud and brings the frog out to croak in the grass and the fish to swim and the bird to whistle and sing in the air. All God's handiwork is a wonderful miracle. If we only knew it, we would find that we are living in a world that is not a broken-off, lost dark no-man's land. It is the back door of heaven, and if we listen we can hear the angels sing.

The footprints of God are everywhere about us. And while we can't see Him, we can see His luminous trail like a bird that sings while hidden in a tree. As Middleton said, "The bird sings darkling." We can't see the bird, but we can hear her sing. God sings among His branches and sings in His universe. You and I cannot gaze upon Him, for no man can see God and live. But we can hear Him sing His song of creation and redemption. And we can feel the pressure of His breath upon us as we move through the world. We'll never see things rightly till we see them as the garments of God.

Psalm 8:3-5; Psalm 19:1-6; Psalm 104; Jeremiah 9:23-24
Success and the Christian, 101, 102, 103.

260. Creeds

I have told you what the great creeds of the church say. If the Bible taught otherwise, I would throw the creeds away. Nobody can come down the years with flowing beard, and with the dust of centuries upon him, and get me to believe a doctrine unless he can give me chapter and verse. I quote the creeds, but I preach them only so far as they summarize the teaching of the Bible on a given subject. If there were divergency from the teachings of the Word of God I would not teach the creed; I would teach the Book, for the Book is the source of all authentic information. However, our fathers did a mighty good job of going into the Bible, finding out what it taught, and then formulating the creeds for us.

How to Be Filled with the Holy Spirit, 14, 15.

261. Creeds

Among certain Christians it has become quite the fashion to cry down creed and cry up experience as the only true test of Christianity. The expression "Not creed, but Christ" (taken, I believe, from a poem by John Oxenham) has been widely accepted as the very voice of truth and given a place alongside of the writings of the prophets and apostles.

When I first heard the words they sounded good. One got from them the idea that the advocates of the no-creed creed had found a precious secret that the rest of us had missed; that they had managed to cut right through the verbiage of historic Christianity and come direct to Christ without bothering about doctrine. And the words appeared to honor our Lord more perfectly by focusing attention upon Him alone and not upon mere words. But is this true? I think not. . . .

Now the truth is that creed is implicit in every thought, word or act of the Christian life. It is altogether impossible to come to Christ without knowing at least something about Him; and what we know about Him is what we believe about Him; and what we believe about Him is our Christian creed. Otherwise stated, since our creed is what we believe, it is impossible to believe on Christ and have no creed. . . .

While we may worship (and thousands of Christians do) without the use of any formal creed, it is impossible to worship acceptably without some knowledge of the One we seek to worship. And that knowledge is our creed whether it is ever formalized or not.

Jude 3
That Incredible Christian, 20, 21.

262. Criticism

"Let not thy peace depend on the tongues of men," said the wise old Christian mystic, Thomas a Kempis; "for whether they judge well or ill, thou art not on that account other than thyself."

The desire to stand well with our fellow men is a natural one, and quite harmless up to a point, but when that desire becomes so all-consuming that we cannot be happy apart from the praises of men, it is no longer harmless, it is sinful in itself and injurious in its effects.

One of the first things a Christian should get used to is abuse. . . .

To do nothing is to get abused for laziness, and to do anything is to get abused for not doing something else.

Was it not Voltaire who said that some people were like insects, they would never be noticed except that they sting? A traveler must make up his mind to go on regardless of the insects that make his trip miserable. . . .

One thing is certain, a Christian's standing before God does not depend upon his standing before men. A high reputation does not make a man dearer to God, nor does the tongue of the slanderer influence God's attitude toward His people in any way. He knows us each one, and we stand or fall in the light of His perfect knowledge.

Galatians 1:9-10; 1 Thessalonians 2:2-4; 1 Timothy 4:12; Hebrews 13:17
The Next Chapter After the Last, 94, 95.

263. Criticism

1. Don't defend your church or organization against criticism. If the criticism is false it can do no harm. If it is true you need to hear it and do something about it. . . .

4. Keep your heart open to the correction of the Lord and be ready to receive His chastisement regardless of who holds the whip. The great saints all learned to take a licking gracefully—and that may be one reason why they were great saints.

Proverbs 10:17; Hebrews 12:3-6; Revelation 3:17-19
The Root of the Righteous, 29, 30.

264. Criticism

Not too long after an editorial appeared in which I quoted the apostle Paul, I heard from a professor who told me I had it all wrong. Paul did not mean what I had said he meant as I applied his statement to present-day life.

I took time to write a reply. "When it comes to saying what he meant," I began, "Paul's batting average has been pretty good up to now. So I will string along with what Paul plainly, clearly said." I did not figure I needed someone to straighten me out—especially someone who had decided the Bible does not mean what it says.

Jesus Is Victor!, 152, 153.

265. Cross: current view of; Church: current condition

But if I see aright, the cross of popular evangelicalism is not the cross of the New Testament. It is, rather, a new bright ornament upon the bosom of a self-assured and carnal Christianity whose hands are indeed the hands of Abel, but whose voice is the voice of Cain. The old cross slew men; the new cross entertains them. The old cross condemned; the new cross amuses. The old cross destroyed confidence in the flesh; the new cross encourages it. The old cross brought tears and blood; the new cross brings laughter. The flesh, smiling and confident, preaches and sings about the cross; before that cross it bows and toward that cross it points with carefully staged histrionics—but upon that cross it will not die, and the reproach of that cross it stubbornly refuses to bear.

I well know how many smooth arguments can be marshalled in support of the new cross. Does not the new cross win converts and make many followers and so carry the advantage of numerical success? Should we not adjust ourselves to the changing times? Have we not heard the slogan, "New days, new ways"? And who but someone very old and very conservative would insist upon death as the appointed way to life? And who today is interested in a gloomy mysticism that would sentence its flesh to a cross and recommend self-effacing humility as a virtue actually to be practiced by modern Christians? These are the arguments, along with many more flippant still, which are brought forward to give an appearance of wisdom to the hollow and meaningless cross of popular Christianity.

Galatians 6:14
The Pursuit of Man, 53, 54.

266. Cross: demands of; Discipleship; Worldliness; Backsliding

In every Christian's heart there is a cross and a throne, and the Christian is on the throne till he puts himself on the cross; if he refuses the cross he remains on the throne. Perhaps this is at the bottom of the backsliding and worldliness among gospel believers today. We want to be saved but we insist that Christ do all the dying. No cross for us, no dethronement, no dying. We remain king within the little kingdom of Mansoul and wear our tinsel crown with all the pride of a Caesar; but we doom ourselves to shadows and weakness and spiritual sterility.

Romans 6:11-14; Romans 12:1-2; Galatians 5:24
The Root of the Righteous, 66.

267. Cross: foolishness of

At the heart of the Christian system lies the cross of Christ with its divine paradox. The power of Christianity appears in its antipathy toward, never in its agreement with, the ways of fallen men. The truth of the cross is revealed in its contradictions. The witness of the church is most effective when she declares rather than explains, for the gospel is addressed not to reason but to faith. What can be proved requires no faith to accept. Faith rests upon the character of God, not upon the demonstrations of laboratory or logic.

The cross stands in bold opposition to the natural man. Its philosophy runs contrary to the processes of the unregenerate mind, so that Paul could say bluntly that the preaching of the cross is to them that perish foolishness. To try to find a common ground between the message of the cross and man's fallen reason is to try the impossible, and if persisted in must result in an impaired reason, a meaningless cross and a powerless Christianity.

1 Corinthians 1:18,20-21,23-25; 2 Corinthians 2:14
That Incredible Christian, 11.

268. Cross: personal

In our modern gospel churches, Christians have decided where to put the cross. They have made the cross objective instead of subjective. They have made the cross external instead of internal. They have made it institutional instead of experiential.

Now, the terrible thing is that they are so wrong because they are half right. They are right in making the cross objective. It was something that once stood on a hill with a man dying on it, the just for the unjust. They are right that it was an external cross—for on that cross God performed a judicial act that will last while the ages burn themselves out.

So, they are half right. But here is where they are wrong: They fail to see that there is a very real cross for you and me. There is a cross for every one of us—a cross that is subjective, internal, experiential.

Our cross is an experience within. It is a cross we voluntarily take, and it is hard, bitter, distasteful. But we take our cross for Christ's sake, and we are willing to suffer the consequences and despise the shame. . . .

But if we are serious about the Christian faith and the demands of our Lord Jesus Christ, we will acknowledge that the cross on the hill must become the cross in our hearts. When that cross on the hill has been transformed by the miraculous grace of the Holy

Spirit into the cross in the heart, then we begin to know something of its true meaning and it will become to us the cross of power.

Matthew 16:24-26; John 12:24-26; Galatians 2:20
Jesus, Author of Our Faith, 82, 83.

269. Cross: personal; Discipleship

The believer's own cross is one he has assumed voluntarily. Therein lies the difference between his cross and the cross on which Roman convicts died. They went to the cross against their will; he, because he chooses to do so. No Roman officer ever pointed to a cross and said, "If any man will, let him." Only Christ said that, and by so saying He placed the whole matter in the hands of the Christian. He can refuse to take his cross, or he can stoop and take it up and start for the dark hill. The difference between great sainthood and spiritual mediocrity depends upon which choice he makes.

Matthew 9:23-25; Matthew 10:37-39; Luke 9:23
Of God and Men, 45.

270. Cross: personal; Jesus Christ: intimacy with; Trials: necessity of

When we are willing to consider the active will of God for our lives, we come immediately to a personal knowledge of the cross, because the will of God is the place of blessed, painful, fruitful trouble!

The Apostle Paul knew about that. He called it "the fellowship of Christ's sufferings." It is my conviction that one of the reasons we exhibit very little spiritual power is because we are unwilling to accept and experience the fellowship of the Savior's sufferings, which means acceptance of His cross.

How can we have and know the blessed intimacy of the Lord Jesus if we are unwilling to take the route which He has demonstrated? We do not have it because we refuse to relate the will of God to the cross. . . .

All Christians living in full obedience will experience the cross and find themselves exercised in spirit very frequently. If they know their own hearts, they will be prepared to wrestle with the cross when it comes.

Matthew 10:24-25; Romans 8:16-17; Philippians 3:10
I Talk Back to the Devil, 91, 92.

271. Cross: personal; Persecution; Trials: difficulty of

The cross would not be a cross to us if it destroyed in us only the unreal and the artificial. It is when it goes on to slay the best in us that its cruel sharpness is felt. If it slew only our sins it might be bearable, even kind, as the knife of the surgeon is kind when it removes the foreign matter that would take our lives if allowed to remain; but when we must suffer the loss of things both precious and good, then we taste the bitterness of the nails and the thorns.

To value the esteem of mankind and for Christ's sake to renounce it is a form of crucifixion suffered by true Christians since the days of the apostles. For it cannot be denied that the way of the cross is unpopular and that it brings a measure of reproach upon those who take it. It is rare that a separated Christian escapes a certain odium in his lifetime.

Luke 9:23-25; John 15:18-21; Philippians 3:6-8
Born After Midnight, 53.

272. Cross: personal; Trials: necessity of

...God will crucify without pity those whom He desires to raise without measure! ...

God wants to crucify us from head to foot—making our own powers ridiculous and useless—in the desire to raise us without measure for His glory and for our eternal good.

Romans 8:10-11; Galatians 2:20; Philippians 2:5-11
I Talk Back to the Devil, 96, 97.

273. Cross: power of; Cross: current view of

The radical message of the cross transformed Saul of Tarsus and changed him from a persecutor of Christians to a tender believer and an apostle of the faith. Its power changed bad men into good ones. It shook off the long bondage of paganism and altered completely the whole moral and mental outlook of the Western world.

All this it did and continued to do as long as it was permitted to remain what it had been originally, a cross. Its power departed when it was changed from a thing of death to a thing of beauty. When men made of it a symbol, hung it around their necks as an ornament or made its outline before their faces as a magic sign to ward off evil, then it became at best a weak emblem, at worst a positive fetish. As such it is revered today by millions who know absolutely nothing about its power.

Galatians 1:13-17; Philippians 3:6-8; 1 Thessalonians 1:9
The Root of the Righteous, 61, 62.

274. Cults; Conscience; Sin: seared conscience

We wonder how it is that a person who has been brought up in the Word of truth suddenly can turn away from it into some false religion. You may say, "He or she became confused." No. False doctrine can have no power upon a good conscience. But when a conscience has been seared, when a person has played with fire and burned his or her conscience, searing it until he or she can handle the hot iron of sin without cringing, then there is no longer any safety for that person. The man or woman can go off into strange cults, into heresy, into any one of the false religions.

Why is it that people reared in Sunday school, who learned the Ten Commandments, knew the Sermon on the Mount and could recite the story of Christ's birth and crucifixion and resurrection will turn to one of the many false cults rampant in our land? The answer is that they fooled with the inner voice and would not listen to the sound of the preacher within them. God turned from them and let them go. With a seared conscience they wandered into the arms of a false religion.

Romans 1:18-32; Galatians 1:6-7; 1 Timothy 4:1-2
Faith Beyond Reason, 79.

275. Cults; Human potential; Holy Spirit: need for

That is the difference between Christianity and all the Oriental cults and religions. All cult religions try to wake up what you already have, and Christianity says, "What you have is not enough—you will need the enduement which is sent from above!" That is the difference. The others say, "Stir up the thing that is in you," and they expect this to be enough.

By way of illustration, if there were four or five lions coming at you, you would never think of saying to a little French poodle, "Wake up the lion in you." That would not work—it would not be enough. They would chew the little fellow up and swallow him, haircut and all, because a French poodle just isn't sufficient for a pack of lions. Some power outside of himself would have to make him bigger and stronger than the lion if he were to conquer.

That is exactly what the Holy Spirit says He does for the Christian believer, but the cult religions still say, "Concentrate and free your mind and release the creative powers that lie within you."...

All of this teaching about hidden potentials and creative impulses and waking up your true self is hard to defend, for we walk around on the earth barely able to keep going. And as we get older, gravitation will pull and slowly drag us down and finally bump over us. We finally give up with a sigh and go back to mother earth. That's the kind of potential that the human race has—the potential to be a corpse.

Luke 24:49; Romans 7:24-25; 2 Corinthians 2:14; Philippians 4:13; 1 John 4:1
The Counselor, 142, 143.

276. Current conditions: apathy; Confession

Suppose there were an elixir of life that could cure any disease anyone could have, and it was sold down at the corner, and you could buy it for a nickel a bottle. It was the magic elixir of life that would make anybody healthy.

Then suppose that I found an old fellow sitting on a bench and I went and sat down beside him. I noticed by looking at him that he had high blood pressure. I could tell it by the veins that stood out on his forehead. I began to try to tell him, "You have lived long enough on this bench. Get up; there's something better for you," and he began to resist me. Then I would have to preach a whole series of sermons to him to get him to know how sick he is, when just down the street a little way was the cure for what was wrong with him.

That is precisely where we are in the church. You have to work on people for weeks to get them to see that they are in a rut. It would be cruel to do if there was not a remedy. But the justice of God is on the side of the confessing sinner. "If we confess our sins, he is faithful and just and will forgive us our sins and purify us from all unrighteousness" (I John 1:9).

2 Corinthians 4:4; 1 John 1:6-9; 1 John 2:1-2
Rut, Rot or Revival: The Condition of the Church, 44.

277. Current conditions: evil days; Prophecy; Eternal perspective

We must meet the present emergency with a spirit of optimism. This is no time for repining, no time for looking backward, no time for self-pity or defeated complaining. We are on the winning side and we cannot lose. "Surely I am with you always" (Matthew 28:20) makes ultimate defeat impossible.

Surely the days are evil and the times are waxing late, but the true Christian is not caught unawares. He has been forewarned of just such times as these and has been expecting them. Present events only confirm the long-range wisdom of Jesus Christ and prove the authenticity of the prophetic Word. So the believer actually turns defeat into victory and draws strength from the knowledge that the Lord in whom he trusts has foretold events and is in full command of the situation. . . .

We must face today as children of tomorrow. We must meet the uncertainties of this world with the certainty of the world to come. To the pure in heart nothing really bad can happen. He may die, but what is death to a Christian? . . .

Surely this is not the time for pale faces and trembling knees among the sons of the new creation. The darker the night the brighter faith shines and the sooner comes the morning. Look up and lift up your heads; our redemption draws near.

Psalm 2; Matthew 28:18-20; Philippians 1:21-24; 2 Timothy 3:1-7
Of God and Men, 161, 163.

278. Current conditions: shallowness

Suppose some angelic being who had since creation known the deep, still rapture of dwelling in the divine Presence would appear on earth and live awhile among us Christians. Don't you imagine he might be astonished at what he saw?

He might, for instance, wonder how we can be contented with our poor, commonplace level of spiritual experience. In our hands, after all, is a message from God not only inviting us into His holy fellowship but also giving us detailed instructions about how to get there. After feasting on the bliss of intimate communion with God how could such a being understand the casual, easily satisfied spirit which characterizes most evangelicals today? And if our hypothetical being knew such blazing souls as Moses, David, Isaiah, Paul, John, Stephen, Augustine, Rolle, Rutherford, Newton, Brainard and Faber, he might logically conclude that 20th century Christians had misunderstood some vital doctrine of the faith somewhere and had stopped short of a true acquaintance with God.

John 17:3; Ephesians 1:18-21; 1 John 1:1-3
Keys to the Deeper Life, 27, 28.

279. Current conditions: shallowness; Church: apathy

. . . I confess a sadness about the shallowness of Christian thinking in our day. Many are interested in religion as a kind of toy. If we could make a judgment, it would appear that numbers of men and women go to church without any genuine desire to gear into deity. They do not come to meet God and delight in His presence. They do not come to hear from that everlasting world above!

Psalm 95:6-7; Psalm 100; Acts 10:33
Christ the Eternal Son, 38.

280. Current conditions: shallowness; Spiritual depth

Why do the majority of present day Christians prefer shallow religious fiction? Or uninspired Bible talks that never get beyond the "first principles"? . . .

First, present day evangelical Christianity is not producing saints. The whole concept of religious experience has shifted from the transcendental to the utilitarian. God is valued as being useful and Christ appreciated because of the predicaments He gets us out of. He can deliver us from the consequences of our past, relax our nerves, give us peace of mind and make our business a success. The all-consuming love that burns in the writings of an Augustine, a Bernard or a Rolle is foreign to the modern religious spirit. . . .

To come to our devotions straight from carnal or worldly interests is to make it impossible to relish the deep, sweet thoughts found in the great books we are discussing here. We must know their heart-language, must vibrate in harmony with them, must share their inward experiences or they will mean nothing to us. Because we are too often strangers to their spiritual mood, we are unable to profit by them and are forced to turn to one or another form of religious entertainment to make our Christianity palatable enough to endure.

Psalm 73:25; 1 Corinthians 2:12-16; Philippians 3:6-8; Hebrews 5:12-14
The Size of the Soul, 48, 49.

281. Current conditions: shallowness; Spiritual growth

He said that we are to leave the first principles, that is, the elementary instructions of the Christian faith. We are to leave them, but not leave them behind. We are not to leave them as one would leave one house and go to another or leave one city and go to another. We are to leave them behind as a builder who is building a house lays the foundation and leaves it behind as he goes upward. If it's a building like some of the buildings downtown, they leave the foundation far behind and go up several stories until they have thirty, forty or fifty stories towering in the air. They have left the foundation, not that they've departed from it, but they have built upon it. Now that is what the man of God means. . . .

The trouble was the Hebrews never went beyond the foundation. And this exclusive preoccupation with elementary truth is also characteristic of evangelicals today. Conversely, the ignoring of Christian truth is characteristic of the liberals. But exclusive preoccupation with the first principles is characteristic of the average church. He says that keeps us babies all our lives.

Ephesians 4:11-16; Philippians 3:13-14; Hebrews 5:11-6:1
Success and the Christian, 2, 3.

282. Current conditions: shallowness; Spiritual growth

But the spiritual climate into which many modern Christians are born does not make for vigorous spiritual growth. Indeed, the whole evangelical world is to a large extent unfavorable to healthy Christianity. And I am not thinking of Modernism either. I mean rather the Bible-believing crowd that bears the name of orthodoxy.

We may as well face it: the whole level of spirituality among us is low. We have measured ourselves by ourselves until the incentive to seek higher plateaus in the things of the Spirit is all but gone. Large and influential sections of the world of fundamental Christianity have gone overboard for practices wholly unscriptural, altogether unjustifiable in the light of historic Christian truth and deeply damaging to the inner life of the individual Christian. They have imitated the world, sought popular favor, manufactured delights to substitute for the joy of the Lord and produced a cheap and synthetic power to substitute for the power of the Holy Spirit. The glowworm has taken the place of the bush that burned, and scintillating personalities now answer to the fire that fell at Pentecost.

Exodus 3:2-3; Acts 2:1-4; Romans 12:1-2
Of God and Men, 8, 9.

D

283. Dead churches; Revival: need for

If you have any spiritual perception at all, I need not state that in our generation and in every community, large or small, there are churches existing merely as monuments of what they used to be. The glory has departed. The witness of God and of salvation and of eternal life is now just an uncertain sound. The monument is there, but the church has failed.

God does not expect us to give up, to give in, to accept the church as it is and to condone what is happening. He expects His believing children to measure the church against the standards and the blessings promised in the Word of God. Then, with love and reverence and prayer and in the leading of the Spirit of God we will quietly and patiently endeavor to align the church with the Word of God.

When this begins to happen and the Word of God is given its place of priority, the presence of the Holy Spirit will again begin to glow in the church. That is what my heart longs to see.

1 Samuel 4:21-22; Psalm 26:8; Ephesians 5:25-29
Whatever Happened to Worship?, 99.

284. Death: baby's

My own mother-in-law had a baby that died and she went through fire and water and blood and tears and toil, but through it she came to a wonderful spiritual experience. She had to sit up in bed, weak and weary as she was, and make the baby's coffin. Her husband made it out of wood and she made a cloth lining of whatever she could get hold of. When the funeral was held, she stood by the grave with the rest and when everybody was expecting her to break down, she said, "Shall we sing together?" And she led off in the Doxology. Some people went away and said, "Mrs. Pfautz is insane." Others went away with moist eyes and said, "There's a faith and love that can give her newborn to the grave and sing 'Praise God from whom all blessings flow' beside that grave."

2 Samuel 12:23
Success and the Christian, 79.

285. Death: certainty of

In history there is the account of a famous political prisoner standing before his judge. Asked if he had anything to say before sentence was pronounced, the man said "No." The judge intoned, "I therefore pronounce that on a certain day you be hanged by the neck until death. I sentence you to die." It was then that the prisoner spoke: "Your honor, nature has sentenced you to die, as well." In dignity, he turned and walked away to his cell.

Genesis 3:14-19; Ecclesiastes 12:1-8; Hebrews 9:27
Who Put Jesus on the Cross?, 107, 108.

286. Death: certainty of; Mortality

I know there are some bright people who argue against the historicity of the fall of humankind in Adam and Eve. But no person, however brilliant, wise and well-schooled, has been able to escape two brief sentences written across all of his prospects by the great God Almighty. Those two sentences are: "You cannot stay—you must go!" and "You cannot live—you must die."

No human being, regardless of talent, possessions and status, has yet won a final victory over the universal sentence of temporality and mortality. Temporality says, "You must go!" Mortality says, "You must die!"

Genesis 3:1-7,19; Romans 5:12; Hebrews 9:27; James 1:13-15
Tragedy in the Church: The Missing Gifts, 131, 132.

287. Death: enemy

Certain poets have found a morbid pleasure in the law of impermanence and have sung in a minor key the song of perpetual change. Omar the tentmaker was one who sang with pathos and humor of mutation and mortality, the twin diseases that afflict mankind. "Don't slap that clay around so roughly," he exhorts the potter, "that may be your grandfather's dust you make so free with." "When you lift the cup to drink red wine," he reminds the reveler, "you may be kissing the lips of some beauty dead long ago."

This note of sweet sorrow expressed with gentle humor gives a radiant beauty to his quatrains but, however beautiful, the whole long poem is sick, sick unto death. Like the bird charmed by the serpent that would devour it, the poet is fascinated by the enemy that is destroying him and all men and every generation of men.

1 Corinthians 15:25-26,51-57; 2 Timothy 1:10; Revelation 21:4
The Knowledge of the Holy, 78.

288. Death: enemy; Death: triumph in; Heaven: certainty of

There is nothing heroic about our passing, leaving families and friends, but then, death is never heroic and it is never kind. Death is never artistic, always much more likely to be crude and messy and humiliating.

The preacher who once stood with strength and keenness to preach the living Word of God to dying men is now in his bed, his cheeks hollow and his eyes staring, for death is slipping its chilly hand over that earthly tabernacle.

The singer whose gifts have been used to glorify God and to remind men and women of the beauty of heaven above is now hoarse, dry-lipped, whispering only a half-spoken word before death comes.

But this is not the end. I thank God that I know that this is not all there is. My whole everlasting being, my entire personality—all that I have and all that I am are cast out on the promises of God that there is another chapter!

At the close of every obituary of His believing children, God adds the word *henceforth*! After every biography, God adds the word *henceforth*! There will be a tomorrow and this is a reason for Christian joy.

1 Corinthians 15:25-26; 2 Timothy 4:6-8; 1 Peter 1:3-5
Who Put Jesus on the Cross?, 110.

289. Death: no fear of

I once heard a Methodist bishop say that when he was a very young minister he was called to the bed-side of an elderly woman who had obviously but a few hours left for this world. The bishop admitted that he was badly frightened, but the old saint was completely relaxed and radiantly happy. He tried to commiserate with her and muttered something about how sorry he was that she had to die, but she wouldn't hear any such talk. "Why, God bless you, young man," she said cheerfully; "there's nothing to be scairt about. I'm just going to cross over Jordan in a few minutes, and my Father owns the land on both sides of the river."

2 Corinthians 5:1-8; Philippians 1:21-24
Born After Midnight, 118.

290. Death: no fear of; Heaven: longing for

With the promises of God so distinct and beautiful, it is unbecoming that a Christian should make such a fearful thing of death. The fact that we Christians do display a neurosis about dying indicates that we are not where we ought to be spiritually. If we had actually reached a place of such spiritual commitment that the wonders of heaven were so close that we longed for the illuminating Presence of our Lord, we would not go into such a fearful and frantic performance every time we find something wrong with our physical frame.

I do not think that a genuine, committed Christian ever ought to be afraid to die. We do not have to be because Jesus promised that He would prepare a proper place for all of those who are born again, raised up out of the agony and stress of this world through the blood of the everlasting covenant into that bright and gracious world above....

I am sure that our Lord is looking for heavenly minded Christians. His Word encourages us to trust Him with such a singleness of purpose that He is able to deliver us from the fear of death and the uncertainties of tomorrow. I believe He is up there preparing me a mansion—"He is fixing up a mansion which shall forever stand; for my stay shall not be transient in that happy, happy land!"

John 14:2; John 17:20-24; Colossians 3:1-4
Who Put Jesus on the Cross?, 151, 152, 153.

291. Death: preparation for

It is in the record of the early Methodists in England, when there was persecution and testing in every direction, that John Wesley was able to say, "Our people die well!"

In more recent years, I have heard a quotation from a denominational bishop who estimated that only about ten percent of the men are prepared and spiritually ready to die when their time comes.

I believe you can only die well when you have lived well, from a spiritual point of view.

2 Corinthians 7:1; Titus 2:12-14; 1 John 3:2-3
Who Put Jesus on the Cross?, 178.

292. Death: preparation for; Funerals

We share with other believers the hope that for many of us the return of Christ may circumvent death and project us into the Immaculate Presence without the necessity of dying. But if not, then let there be no gloomy faces among the few that gather to pay their last regards. We lived with the Resurrection in our heart and died in the Everlasting Arms. Hosanna! There's no room there for lamentation.

"I have observed," said the old historian, "that these Christians die well." A Christian can die well because he is the only one who dares to die at all. The lost man cannot afford to die, and that he must die is his infinite woe. A Christian dares to die because his Savior has died and risen. Let us renounce paganism at our funerals and die as we lived, like Christians.

Acts 7:60; Philippians 1:21-24;
1 Thessalonians 4:13-18
The Price of Neglect, 11.

293. Death: triumph in

I recall that there was a good man of God by the name of Samuel Rutherford, whose witness shone like a star in dark England in days gone by. He was a poet, an author, and a great preacher—a man who loved Jesus probably better than any man of his times. His convictions were unpopular and he was in trouble because he refused to conform his preaching to the dictates of the state church. When he was an old man, the officials decided to try him as a criminal because he would not submit to the rules of the state church. The date of his trial was set, and he was notified by Parliament that he must appear for trial.

Rutherford knew that he was on his deathbed and so he wrote a letter in reply. He said, "Gentlemen, I have received your summons, but before I got yours, I received one from a higher source. Before the day of my trial, I will be over there where very few kings and great men ever come. Farewell!"

That was Samuel Rutherford, witnessing to all of England that an entire new chapter awaits the Christian when our Lord says, "Welcome home!"

John 12:24-26; 2 Corinthians 5:1-8; 2 Timothy 4:6-8
Who Put Jesus on the Cross?, 111, 112.

294. Death: triumph in;
Heaven: longing for;
World: contentment with

Death is not the worst thing that can happen to a person! . . .

For the Christian, death is a journey to the eternal world. It is a victory, a rest, a delight. I am sure my small amount of physical suffering in life has been mild compared with Paul's. But I think I have some understanding of what he meant when he told the Philippians: "To me, to live is Christ and to die is gain. . . . I desire to depart and be with Christ, which is better by far. . . ." (Philippians 1:21, 23). The more a Christian suffers in the body, the more he or she thinks about the triumph of going home to heaven.

But we modern Christians seem to be a strange breed. We are so completely satisfied with the earthly things we have collected, and we so enjoy this age's creature comforts, that we would rather stay here for a long, long time! Probably we do not tell God about that kind of desire when we pray. We know it would not be considered pious or spiritual if people knew we preferred our position here to the prospect of heaven.

Romans 8:18-23; 2 Corinthians 4:16-18; Philippians 1:21-24
Jesus Is Victor!, 140, 141.

295. Death: triumph in; Worship: for eternity

There was Brother Lawrence, the man who practiced the presence of God. He wouldn't pick up a straw from the ground but for the love of God. When he was dying, they said, "What are you doing, Brother Lawrence?" He said, "I'm doing what I plan to do through all eternity—worship God. When I die I won't change my occupation. I have just been worshiping God for 40 years on earth, and when I get to heaven I'll just keep right on doing what I am doing."

Revelation 4:8-11; Revelation 5:8-14
The Counselor, 116.

296. Dedication; Life purpose; Eternal perspective

The "dedicated" matador would likely win some sort of prize for sheer absurdity and may be allowed to stand as the uncrowned champion of all those who seek to waste their lives in the most foolish way. But dedication to vanity is not confined to bullfighters. The truth is, dedication of the life to anything or anyone short of God Himself, is a prostitution of noble powers and must bring a harvest of grief and disappointment at last. Only God is worthy of the soul He has made in His own image. To devote our lives to any cause, however worthy, is to sell ourselves short. Not money, position, fame, can justly claim our devotion. Art, literature, music also fall short. And, if God is forgotten, even the loftiest and most unselfish task is unworthy of the soul's full surrender. Complete dedication unto death in the cause of freedom, for instance, is a touching thing and has given to history many of her greatest heroes, but only the God of freedom should have our "last full measure of devotion."

Matthew 16:24-26; 1 Timothy 4:8-10; James 4:13-14
The Set of the Sail, 56.

297. Dedication; Revival: conditions for; Apathy

Persistence of the spiritual yearning is often ruined by side interests. God wants His people to talk Christ and to think Christ and to dream Christ and to love His Word and His ways and to be so dedicated to it that the conversation normally swings around to it when they're together. And I do not believe that God can continue to bless nor send anything like a life-giving revival to a church until we are absorbed in it. To get anything done, you've go to be absorbed in it.

Nobody ever did anything when he only did it halfway. Men who have done great things have always had to be dedicated men. To make the electric light and the talking machine, Edison slept only four or five hours a night and worked constantly. To compose great musical scores, men have sat up all through the night. Tchaikovsky used to stay awake hours upon hours; when others were sleeping, he would be working. My opinion of Tchaikovsky's music is such that I wonder why he didn't just take a nap. But anyway, what I'm saying is that in order to get it done, he had to stay awake and do it. Byron, one of the great English poets, said, "I shut myself in my room and work as much as 18 hours at a stretch, never even get out to take a drink of tea." And that's something for an Englishman. So you have to be interested in something. . . .

I recently read the words of a great Christian leader who has been around the world several times. He said, "The only religion that I have found in the world that people don't take seriously is Christianity. The Buddhists take themselves seriously. The Mohammedans take themselves seriously." But Christians play at it too much. We have the truth that would save the world and we're the ones who play like children in the marketplace (Luke 7:32). We've got to be absorbed in the Lord's doings.

Deuteronomy 6:4-9; Luke 7:32; Colossians 3:23
Success and the Christian, 95, 96, 97.

298. Deeper life; Current conditions: shallowness

To speak of the "deeper life" is not to speak of anything deeper than simple New Testament religion. Rather it is to insist that believers explore the depth of the Christian evangel for those riches it surely contains but which we are as surely missing. The "deeper life" is deeper only because the average Christian life is tragically shallow.

Romans 11:33-36; Ephesians 1:3,18-21; 2 Peter 3:18
Keys to the Deeper Life, 32.

299. Deeper life; Discipleship

You'd like to have a deeper life that could be given to you with a syringe or a glass of water and a pill. "Take one pill three times a day." You just can't do that. But that is the way some people get their religion. They want it in pill form, so they buy books. Brethren, there is no such thing. There's a cross, there's a gallows, there's a man with stripes on His back, there's an apostle with no property. There's a tradition of loneliness and weariness and rejection and glory. But there are no pills. It is only Himself, Himself, Himself.

Romans 6:4-7; 2 Corinthians 11:23-33; Galatians 2:20; Philippians 3:10
Success and the Christian, 27.

300. Deeper life; Knowledge of God: spiritual depth

I almost shrink from hearing the expression, "the deeper life," because so many people want to talk about it as a topic—but no one seems to want to know and love God for Himself!

God is the deeper life! Jesus Christ Himself is the deeper life, and as I plunge on into the knowledge of the triune God, my heart moves on into the blessedness of His fellowship. This means that there is less of me and more of God—thus my spiritual life deepens, and I am strengthened in the knowledge of His will.

Jeremiah 9:23-24; John 3:30; Philippians 3:10
I Talk Back to the Devil, 17.

301. Denominations

When we gather for worship, we come in the name of our Lord Jesus Christ. If you bring with you a psychology of denomination, I most heartily recommend that you ask God for a cleansing from it, because we ought not to divide the children of God into imaginary divisions. They're imaginary from God's standpoint. Remember that we are a family and meet in His name around the person of Christ.

Ephesians 4:3-6
Success and the Christian, 119.

302. Denominations

It is a grave error for us evangelicals to assume that the children of God are all in our communion and that all who are not associated with us are *ipso facto* enemies of the Lord. The Pharisees made that mistake and crucified Christ as a consequence.

Matthew 12:24; Matthew 15:1-2; John 9:28-29
Man: The Dwelling Place of God, 19.

303. Dependability

The root of dependability is dead in most churches, except for a faithful few, and these few have to take abuse from the unfaithful, undependable ones. The faithful few can always be depended upon and are always in evidence, so they are criticized for wanting to run the show.

Now, I want to ask you a question, and it is not something new and original. Think about your religious life, your holy habits, your church attendance, your giving to the Lord's work, your pattern of dependability during the past 12 months.

Now, be honest with yourselves, and ask an answer of your own heart: "If everyone in this church had been exactly as dependable as I am, where would our church be today?"

That's a question we ought to ask on our knees with tears and with sorrow, praying that God will help us to be dependable. When you are asked to do something, even if it is something simple, do it. It seems that so many of us only want to do the dramatic things—no one wants to be known as being dependable.

Romans 12:9-13; 1 Corinthians 4:2-3; Philippians 2:19-22; 3 John 5-6
Who Put Jesus on the Cross?, 28, 29.

304. Dependence on God; Confidence

It is itself a cliché that the Christian faith is full of apparent self-contradictions commonly called paradoxes. One such paradox is the necessity to repudiate self and depend wholly upon God while at the same time having complete confidence in our own ability to receive and know and understand with the faculties God Himself has given us. That brand of humility which causes a man to distrust his own mentality to the point of moral diffidence and chronic irresolution is but a weak parody on the real thing. It is a serious reflection upon the wisdom and goodness of God to question His handiwork. "Does the clay say to the potter, what are you making?"

Isaiah 45:9; 2 Corinthians 3:5-6; 2 Corinthians 3:12; 2 Corinthians 4:5-7
God Tells the Man Who Cares, 123, 124.

305. Dependence on God; Pastoral ministry: dependence on God

The work of a minister is, in *fine*, altogether too difficult for any man. He is driven to God for wisdom. He must seek the mind of Christ and throw himself on the Holy Spirit for spiritual power and mental acumen equal to the task.

Jeremiah 9:23-24; 1 Corinthians 15:9-10; 2 Corinthians 3:5-6; Philippians 2:12-13
Of God and Men, 24.

306. Depression

Nevertheless, to sharpen our focus somewhat and bring our picture into better perspective, we point out that Mr. Simpson's conflict with Giant Despair was nothing unusual in one of his temperament. On those occasional descents which he admittedly made into the nether regions, those Dantean visits through the dark forest and into the blind world, he was not alone. The company he shared on those painful journeys (if he could but have remembered it) was probably far better than that he left behind him. For the great had traveled that way. David had wandered there sometimes, his voiceless harp under his arm, all its strings hanging broken and mute; Jeremiah had been often there, and the rough stones of the way had been damp with his tears; even the mighty Elijah had spent a little while in the shadowing vale in full retreat—we wince to admit—from an angry woman; Luther had gone at least once down the dark road and—as if to balance accounts—had been led by a woman back into the sunshine again.

It is characteristic of the God-intoxicated, the dreamers and mystics of the Kingdom, that their flight-range is greater than that of other men. Their ability to sweep upward to unbelievable heights of spiritual transport is equaled only by their sad power to descend, to sit in dazed dejection by the River Chebar or to startle the night watches with their lonely grief. A long list of names could be appended here to support this statement; and it would be a noble and saintly list indeed, for Moses' name would be there, and Thomas Upham's and Brother Lawrence's, and St. Francis', and Madam Guyon's and a host of others. It might well read like a little Who's Who in the Kingdom of God, if the whole truth were told of the gloom of the great, which overtakes them sometimes on the journey to the City of God.

1 Kings 19:4-15; Psalm 13:1-2; Jeremiah 9:1; Lamentations 1:16
Wingspread; A. B. Simpson: A Study in Spiritual Altitude, 71, 72.

307. Devotion to God

One of the old Baptist missionary societies had as its symbol an ox quietly standing between a plow and an altar. Underneath was the legend: "Ready for either or for both!" Plow, if that be God's will. Die on the altar, if that be God's will. Plow awhile, and then die on the altar. I can think of no more perfect symbol of devotion to God.

Philippians 1:20-26
Tragedy in the Church: The Missing Gifts, 109.

308. Devotion to God; Death: triumph in

One of the purest souls ever to live on this fallen planet was Nicholas Herman, that simplehearted Christian, known throughout the world as Brother Lawrence. . . .

He spent his long life walking in the presence of His Lord, and when he came to die there was no need for any particular change in his occupation. At the last hour someone asked him what was going on in his thoughts as death approached. He replied simply: "I am doing what I shall do through all eternity—blessing God, praising God, adoring God, giving Him the love of my whole heart. It is our one business, my brethren, to worship Him and love Him without thought of anything else."

Revelation 4:8-11; Revelation 5:8-14
The Price of Neglect, 22, 23.

309. Devotional mood

Maintenance of the devotional mood is indispensable to success in the Christian life.

Holiness and power are not qualities that can be once received and thereafter forgotten as one might wind a clock or take a vitamin pill. The world is too much with us, not to mention the flesh and the devil, and every advance in the spiritual life must be made against the determined resistance of this trinity of evil. Gains made must be consolidated and held with a resolution equal to that of an army in the field.

To establish our hearts in the devotional mood we must abide in Christ, walk in the Spirit, pray without ceasing and meditate on the Word of God day and night. Of course this implies separation from the world, renunciation of the flesh and obedience to the will of God as we are able to understand it.

And what is the devotional mood? It is nothing else than constant awareness of God's enfolding presence, the holding of inward conversations with Christ and private worship of God in spirit and in truth.

Psalm 1:1-3; John 15:1-7; Galatians 5:16; Ephesians 6:10-12; 1 Thessalonians 5:16-17
The Set of the Sail, 129.

310. Dialogue

In our world are dozens of different kinds of Christianities. Certainly many of them do not seem to be busy and joyful in proclaiming the unique glories of Jesus Christ as the eternal Son of God. Some brands of Christianity will tell you very quickly that they are just trying to do a little bit of good on behalf of neglected people and neglected causes. Others will affirm that we can do more good by joining in the "contemporary dialogue" than by continuing to proclaim the "old, old story of the cross."

But we stand with the early Christian apostles. We believe that every Christian proclamation should be to the glory and the praise of the One whom God raised up after He had loosed the pains of death. I am happy to be identified with Peter and his message at Pentecost. . . .

Peter considered it important to affirm that the risen Christ is now exalted at the right hand of God. He said that fact was the reason for the coming of the Holy Spirit. Frankly, I am too busy serving Jesus to spend my time and energy engaging in contemporary dialogue.

Acts 2:14-36; Philippians 1:9-11; Colossians 1:28-29; 1 Timothy 2:1-8; Hebrews 4:14-16
Jesus, Our Man in Glory, 4, 5.

311. Dialogue; Skeptics; Church: current condition

Christians now chatter learnedly about things simple believers have always taken for granted. They are on the defensive, trying to prove things that a previous generation never doubted. We have allowed unbelievers to get us in a corner and have given them the advantage by permitting them to choose the time and place of encounter. We smart under the attack of the quasi-Christian unbeliever, and the nervous, self-conscious defense we make is called "the religious dialogue."

Under the scornful attack of the religious critic real Christians who ought to know better are now "rethinking" their faith. Scarcely anything has escaped the analysts. With a Freudian microscope they examine everything: foreign missions, the Book of Genesis, the inspiration of the Scriptures, morals, all tried and proven methods, polygamy, liquor, sex, prayer—all have come in for inquisition by those who engage in the contemporary dialogue. Adoration has given way to celebration in the holy place, if indeed any holy place remains to this generation of confused Christians.

Ephesians 5:6; Colossians 2:8-9; 1 Timothy 6:20-21
Man: The Dwelling Place of God, 153, 154.

312. Differences; Wars; Church: conflict

Human life has its central core where lie the things men live by. These things are constant. They change not from age to age, but are the same among all races throughout the world always.

Life also has its marginal zones where lie the things that are relatively unimportant. These change from generation to generation and vary from people to people.

It is at the central core that men are one, and it is on the marginal zones that they differ from each other. Yet the marginal things divide the peoples of the world radically and seriously. Most of the enmities of the earth have arisen from differences that did not matter basically; but because the people could not distinguish things men live by from things they live with these enmities arose between them, and often led to persecutions, murders and bloody wars.

Were men everywhere to ignore the things that matter little or not at all and give serious attention to the few really important things, most of the walls that divide men would be thrown down at once and a world of endless sufferings ended.

Matthew 24:6-7; James 4:1-2
Man: The Dwelling Place of God, 115, 116.

313. Direction; Goals; Church: focus

The Lord would seem to be more concerned with *where* we are going rather than *how fast*. A steady pace in the right direction will lead to the right goal at last, but if the life is aimed at the wrong goal, speed will only take us further astray in a shorter time.

Lack of direction is the cause of many tragic failures in religious activities. The churches are overrun with persons of both sexes (though the vast majority are men) who have never known a clear call of God to anything in particular. Such people are often victims of whim and chance, the easy prey of ambitious leaders who seek to gain prominence by using others for their own ends. The directionless Christian is the one who supports the new and spectacular, regardless of whether or not it is in accord with the Scriptures and the revealed will of God.

A great economizing of time and effort can be effected by learning what we should do and then sticking to it, quietly refusing to be turned aside from our task.

Proverbs 3:5-6; Ephesians 4:14-16; 3 John 9
This World: Playground or Battleground?, 55, 56.

314. Discipleship

Everywhere in fundamentalism we have given up the grossly sinful things. We have all agreed on what those grossly sinful things are. We shudder at the thought of a honky-tonk, though there are some churches and tabernacles that you couldn't tell the difference if somebody didn't yell "Jesus" occasionally to give it a holy atmosphere. Honky-tonks and unholy places, we stay out of them.

There are certain things we don't do and for Christ's sake we have surrendered those evil things. But this is the mark of a common Christian and the man who's never gone beyond that is a mediocre Christian. Paul surrendered the good along with the bad. He said, "Not only the things that are bad have I given up; but what things were gain to me those I counted loss.". . .

Any external treasure that touches your heart is a curse. Paul said, "I give that up so that I might know Him. That I might go on to deeply enriched and increasing intimacy and vast expanses of knowledge of the One who is intimate and illimitable in His beauty and I go on to know Him. And that I might know Him, I give all this up." He never allowed anything to touch his heart.

Luke 14:33; Philippians 3:6-8; Colossians 3:5-11
Success and the Christian, 19, 20, 21.

315. Discipleship; Lordship of Christ

Now, think with me about those who are demi-disciples—that is, part disciples, half disciples. These are men and women who bring their lives partially under the control of Christ, but they leave whole other areas outside His control. Long ago I came to the conclusion that if Jesus Christ is not controlling all of me, the chances are very good that He is not controlling any of me.

Joshua 22:5; 1 Samuel 12:24; Matthew 22:37-39; Matthew 26: 40-41; Luke 9:23-25
Faith Beyond Reason, 58.

316. Discipleship; Preaching: watered down; Commitment

I am having a hard time trying to comprehend what has happened to sound Bible teaching. What has happened to preaching on Christian discipleship and on our daily deportment in the spiritual life? We are making an accommodation. We are offering a take-it-easy, Pollyanna type of approach that does not seem ever to have heard of total commitment to One who is our Lord and Savior.

I regret that more and more Christian believers are being drawn into a hazy, fuzzy kind of teaching that assures everyone who has ever "accepted Christ" that he or she has nothing more to be concerned about. He is OK and he will always be OK because Christ will be returning before things get too tough. Then all of us will wear our crowns, and God will see that we have cities to rule over!

If that concept is accurate, why did our Lord take the stern and unpopular position that Christian believers should be engaged in watching and praying?

Matthew 26:41; Romans 12:1-2; 1 Corinthians 9:24-27; Hebrews 12:1-2
Men Who Met God, 31, 32.

317. Discipleship; Revival: personal; Obedience: need for

And how can we improve the church? Simply and only by improving ourselves: and there is where the difficulty lies. The church in any locality is what its individual members are, no better and no worse. We as members must begin by seeking moral amendment that will result in a positive spiritual renaissance. And that is why improvement is hard to achieve. As long as we can keep the whole thing at arm's length and deal with it academically we may preach and write about it at little or no real cost to ourselves and, it must be admitted, with no real advance in godliness.

If we would be followers of Christ indeed we must become personally and vitally involved in His death and resurrection. And this requires repentance, prayer, watchfulness, self-denial, detachment from the world, humility, obedience and cross carrying. That is why it is easier to talk about revival than to experience it.

Matthew 7:24-27; Romans 6:4-7; James 1:22-25
The Set of the Sail, 154, 155.

318. Discipleship; Service: sacrificial

Some riches are reserved for those who apply to serve in the legion of the expendables, who love not their lives unto the death, who volunteer to suffer for Christ's sake and who follow up their application with lives that challenge the devil and invite the fury of hell.

Such as these have said goodbye to the world's toys; they have chosen to suffer affliction with the people of God. They have accepted toil and suffering as their earthly portion.

Philippians 1:29-30; Hebrews 11:24-26; James 1:12; Revelation 12:11
Renewed Day by Day, Volume 1, Jan. 29.

319. Discipleship; Spiritual warfare

Peter was not promoting or predicting a cold and lifeless and formal spirituality in the Christian church when he advised believers to gird up the loins of their minds and be sober.

He was saying to the early Christians as he hopes to say to us now: "Brethren, if ever there was an hour when we needed to be serious about our Christian faith, this is the hour! We need to be sober men—and spiritual men!"

1 Thessalonians 5:1-8; 2 Timothy 2:3-4; 2 Timothy 4:1-5; 1 Peter 1:6-9, 13
I Call It Heresy!, 135.

320. Discipleship; Sunday Christians

It may be well to look at some of the marks of those who are not really disciples. Some of them have a pious look. In fact, on Sunday mornings, they look as pious as stuffed owls. We have some of them in our evangelical circles. People can afford to be pious at 10:45 a.m. on Sundays. It is a most convenient hour. They do not have to be religious to get up in time for 10:45 a.m. church. They do not lose out on their Sunday dinners, either. They get a little fresh air. The service does not last long. The music is good most of the time. It only costs them the dollar they drop in the offering plate.

So, those who go to church only once a week—on Sunday morning—leave themselves wide open to the suspicion that they are only part-time Sunday-morning disciples. They are not in church enough to prove that they are any other kind of disciple.

Acts 2:42-44; Hebrews 10:24-25
Faith Beyond Reason, 61.

321. Discipline: corrective

How good it would be if we could learn that God is easy to live with. He remembers our frame and knows that we are dust. He may sometimes chasten us, it is true, but even this He does with a smile, the proud, tender smile of a Father who is bursting with pleasure over an imperfect but promising son who is coming every day to look more and more like the One whose child he is.

Psalm 103:13-14; Proverbs 3:12;
Hebrews 12:5-11
The Root of the Righteous, 16.

322. Discipline: personal

But I can hear someone protest, saying "I wanted to get into the Christian life, the spiritual faith, in order that I might be freed from necessity and from a law of having to do things regularly."

Well, you have missed it, my brother! You might as well close your Bible and walk out because you are in the wrong church and the wrong pew and the wrong dispensation! God would have His people learn regular holy habits and follow them right along day by day.

He doesn't ask us to become slaves to habits, but He does insist that our holy habits of life should become servants of His grace and glory.

Romans 6:16-18; Galatians 5:13;
1 Timothy 4:7-8; 2 Timothy 2:14-16
Who Put Jesus on the Cross?, 27.

323. Discipline: personal

I have been forced to admit that one of the things hardest for me to understand and try to reconcile is the complete aimlessness of so many Christians' lives. . . .

Probably the worst part of this situation among us is the fact that so many of our Christian brothers and sisters have unusual gifts and talents and capacities—yet they have not exercised this discipline of girding up the mind and spiritual potential in order to make the necessary progress in the Christian life.

Why should a pastor have to confess total failure from year to year? Why should he have to go from one church to another, starting something, trying something—only to admit failure again?

I don't think he has ever really girded himself. He has abilities but they are not disciplined. He has a fine mind but it is not girded up. He is like a man with a treasured Stradivarius violin that has never been put in tune. He has never taken time to sit down and tune that priceless instrument, therefore he gets no melody and harmony from it.

Philippians 3:13-14; 1 Timothy 4:13-16;
1 Peter 1:6-9, 13
I Call It Heresy!, 142.

324. Discipline: personal; Discipleship

It has become popular to preach a painless Christianity and automatic saintliness. It has become a part of our "instant" culture. "Just pour a little water on it, stir mildly, pick up a gospel tract, and you are on your Christian way."

Lo, we are told, this is Bible Christianity. *It is nothing of the sort!* To depend upon that kind of a formula is to experience only the outer fringe, the edge of what Christianity really is. We must be committed to all that it means to believe in the Lord Jesus Christ. There must be a new birth from above; otherwise we are in religious bondage and legalism and delusion—or worse! But when the wonder of regeneration has taken place in our lives, then comes the lifetime of preparation with the guidance of the Holy Spirit.

Ephesians 4:11-13; Hebrews 12:8-14;
2 Peter 3:18
Jesus, Author of Our Faith, 93.

325. Discipline: personal; Trials: necessity of; Spiritual warfare; Suffering

Then there is the matter of constant consolation and peace—the promise of always feeling relaxed and at rest and enjoying ourselves inwardly.

This, I say, has been held up as being quite the proper goal to be sought in the evil hour in which we live. We forget that our Lord was a man of sorrow and acquainted with grief. We forget the arrows of grief and pain which went through the heart of Jesus' mother, Mary. We forget that all of the apostles except John died a martyr's death. We forget that there were 13 million Christians slain during the first two generations of the Christian era. We forget that they languished in prison, that they were starved, were thrown over cliffs, were fed to the lions, were drowned, that they were sewn in sacks and thrown into the ocean.

Yes, we want to forget that most of God's wonderful people in the early days of the church did not have peace of mind. They did not seek it. They knew that a soldier does not go to the battlefield to relax—he goes to fight. They accepted their position on earth as soldiers in the army of God, fighting along with the Lord Jesus Christ in the terrible war against iniquity and sin. It was not a war against people but against sin and iniquity and the devil!

There was much distress, many heartaches, painful bruises, flowing tears, much loss and many deaths.

But there is something better than being comfortable, and the followers of Christ ought to find it out—the poor, soft, overstuffed Christians of our time ought to find it out! There is something better than being comfortable!

We Protestants have forgotten altogether that there is such a thing as discipline and suffering.

Isaiah 53:3; John 19:26-27; 2 Corinthians 11:23-33; 2 Timothy 2:3-4;
Hebrews 11:32-40
Who Put Jesus on the Cross?, 17, 18, 19.

326. Dishonesty; Oaths; Truth: carelessness regarding

Men and women are well aware of their failures and frailty. They know their weaknesses, their duplicity, their tendency to be less than honest. So they add an oath to their covenant—an appeal to Someone greater than themselves: "So help me, God!"

I have always considered it a little humorous that sinful men who cannot trust each other call on God or the Holy Bible to witness that a sinful being is not going to tell a lie. I suspect there is a chuckle in hell whenever a person in one of our courts promises before God that he or she will "tell the truth, the whole truth and nothing but the truth."

Matthew 5:34-37; Ephesians 4:25; Colossians 3:5-11; James 5:12
Jesus, Our Man in Glory, 87.

327. Disobedience; Sin: consequences of

Of course the Christian can hope for no manifestation of God while he lives in a state of disobedience. Let a man refuse to obey God on some clear point, let him set his will stubbornly to resist any commandment of Christ, and the rest of his religious activities will be wasted. He may go to church for fifty years to no profit. He may tithe, teach, preach, sing, write or edit or run a Bible conference till he gets too old to navigate and have nothing but ashes at the last. "To obey is better than sacrifice."

1 Samuel 15:22; Psalm 51:15-17; Isaiah 1:11-20; Jeremiah 7:22-24
Born After Midnight, 102, 103.

328. Distractions; Devotional life; Meditation; Simplicity

Among the enemies to devotion none is so harmful as distractions. Whatever excites the curiosity, scatters the thoughts, disquiets the heart, absorbs the interests or shifts our life focus from the kingdom of God within us to the world around us—that is a distraction; and the world is full of them. Our science-based civilization has given us many benefits but it has multiplied our distractions and so taken away far more than it has given. . . .

The remedy for distractions is the same now as it was in earlier and simpler times, viz., prayer, meditation and the cultivation of the inner life. The psalmist said "Be still, and know," and Christ told us to enter into our closet, shut the door and pray unto the Father. It still works. . . .

Distractions *must* be conquered or they will conquer us. So let us cultivate simplicity; let us want fewer things; let us walk in the Spirit; let us fill our minds with the Word of God and our hearts with praise. In that way we can live in peace even in such a distraught world as this. "Peace I leave with you, my peace I give unto you."

Psalm 46:10; Matthew 6:6; John 14:27
The Set of the Sail, 130, 131, 132.

329. Distractions; Priorities; Busyness

Failing in his frontal attacks upon the child of God, Satan often turns to more subtle means of achieving his evil purpose. He resorts to devious methods in his attempt to divert the Christian from carrying out the task God has committed to him. He often succeeds by involving the saint in some other lesser occupation and so distracting him. . . .

The great task to which God had called Nehemiah was so important that every other consideration must be waived. Would that we might have such an overpowering sense of being about our Father's business and be so impressed with the grandeur of our task that we would reject every suggestion of the evil one that would bid us take up some lesser pursuit. Let us rout him with the words that date back to 445 B.C., and which cannot be improved upon: "I am carrying on a great project and cannot go down."

Satan's distracting words often come from the most unexpected quarters. Martha would call Mary away from sitting at the feet of the Master. Sometimes, if we are not careful, our best friend may distract us. Or it might be some very legitimate activity. This day's bustle and hurly-burly would too often and too soon call us away from Jesus' feet. These distractions must be immediately dismissed, or we shall know only the "barrenness of busyness."

Nehemiah 6:3; Luke 10:38-42; Acts 6:2
We Travel an Appointed Way, 28, 29.

330. Dogmatics; Separation; Christians: in the world

Well, if to escape the charge of being dogmatic I must accept the changing dogmas of the masses, then I am willing to be known as a dogmatist and no holds barred. We who call ourselves Christians are supposed to be a people apart. We claim to have repudiated the wisdom of this world and adopted the wisdom of the cross as the guide of our lives. We have thrown in our lot with that One who while He lived on earth was the most unadjusted of the sons of men. He would not be integrated into society. He stood above it and condemned it by withdrawing from it even while dying for it. Die for it He would, but surrender to it He would not.

1 Corinthians 1:20-21; 1 Timothy 6:20-21; Jude 3
The Price of Neglect, 69.

331. Doubts

I heard about an old Christian man who testified, "I'll admit that I sometimes have doubts. But always I take them to God immediately. I just dive down to the bottom and examine the foundations of my faith. That tactic has not failed yet. Always I have come to the surface singing "How firm a foundation, ye saints of the Lord, / Is laid for your faith in His excellent Word."

Matthew 14:22-33; 2 Timothy 1:11-12; James 1:5-6
Men Who Met God, 48.

332. Dry spells; Faith: foundation of

Probably nothing else bothers the earnest Christian quite so much as the problem of those dry spells that come to him occasionally, no matter how faithfully he tries to obey God and walk in the light. He can never predict them and he cannot explain them. And there lies his difficulty.

It might comfort one who finds himself in the middle of an emotional desert to know that his experience is not unique. The sweetest and holiest saints whose feet have graced this earth have at some time found themselves there. . . . It is good to know during such an internal drought that it has been a common experience with the saints. . . .

Such times demand that we exercise faith. Moments of great spiritual delight do not require much faith; if we never came down from the mount of blessing we might easily come to trust in our own delights rather than in the unshakeable character of God. It is necessary therefore that our watchful Heavenly Father withdraw His inward comforts from us sometimes to teach us that Christ alone is the Rock upon which we must repose our everlasting trust.

2 Samuel 22:2; 1 Kings 19:9-10; Psalm 18:2
The Root of the Righteous, 126, 128.

E

333. Earthly loves; Deeper life

For the Spirit-filled Christian life means that I am delivered from earthly loves to a point where there is no love that I would not allow Jesus Christ to take away. Be it money, reputation, my home, my friends, my family or whatever it may be. The love of Jesus Christ has come in and swallowed up all other loves and sanctified them, purified them, made them holy and put them in their right relationship to that all-consuming love of God so that they're secondary and never primary.

I want to ask you this question: Is there anything or anyone on Earth that you love so much that you'd fight God if He wanted to take them? Then you are not where you should be and you might as well face up to it and not pretend to be something you're not. Complete freedom means that I want the will of God only. And if it is the will of God for me to have these things, then I love them for His sake, but I love them with a tentative and relative love and not an all-poured-out love that makes me a slave. It means that I love nothing outside the will of God and that I love only what and who He wills that I should love....

If you love anything enough that there's any question about whether God can have it or not, you know nothing about the deeper life.

Matthew 10:37-39; Luke 14:26-27; Philippians 3:6-8
Success and the Christian, 77, 79.

334. Earthly things

There are three very distinct marks of the ancient curse resting upon everything in this world. First, everything is recent. Second, everything is temporal. Third, everything is transient....

Temporal and transient things surround us—but their curse is that they belong to us only for a brief day....

I am sure you have watched a small child viewing a colorful circus parade. The great wagons, the clowns, the elephants, the lions and the tigers, the bands, the costumes, the spangles. Each thing excites the child—the eyes pop out and there are screams of delight. But it is passing. It is temporary. It is transient. The parade goes on down to the railroad station into its train and disappears.

And so it is with everything that the world has to offer us. Some kind of a pretty trinket. Some kind of a pleasing rattle to shake. Some kind of a pacifier for the scene in which we live.

1 Corinthians 7:31; James 4:13-14; 2 Peter 3:10-11; 1 John 2:15-17
Christ the Eternal Son, 60, 61, 62.

335. Earthly things

There are those who would trouble you because you can't get all steamed up about material things. A friend of mine was quite irked because I just can't get all excited and steamed up about earthly things. I can't possibly do it. I can't possibly stand off and strike an attitude of awe at a Buick or a Cadillac or something else. I can't. The houses they're building that are supposed to be so magnificent, I can't get excited about them. When you have seen the house or city that has foundations whose builder and maker is God (Hebrews 11:10), you can't get excited about any house any man in this world ever built.

John 14:1-3; Hebrews 11:8-10; Revelation 21:10-27
Success and the Christian, 18.

336. Earthly things; Eternal perspective

A friend of mine has been quite irked because I cannot get excited and steamed up about earthly things. I just cannot stand and strike an attitude of awe when a friend drives up with one of the classy new automobiles. I hear people describing the magnificent new houses that they are building, and they have excitement in their voices. But the Word of God forces me to remember that when you have seen the house or the city that hath foundations and whose builder and maker is God, you cannot really ever get excited again about any house ever built by any man in this world.

Colossians 3:1-4; Hebrews 11:8-10; 1 John 2:15-17
I Talk Back to the Devil, 67.

337. Earthly things; Knowledge of God: supreme value of

The way to deeper knowledge of God is through the lonely valleys of soul poverty and abnegation of all things. The blessed ones who possess the Kingdom are they who have repudiated every external thing and have rooted from their hearts all sense of possessing. These are the "poor in spirit."...

These blessed poor are no longer slaves to the tyranny of things. They have broken the yoke of the oppressor; and this they have done not by fighting but by surrendering. Though free from all sense of possessing, they yet possess all things. "Theirs is the kingdom of heaven."...

There can be no doubt that this possessive clinging to things is one of the most harmful habits in the life. Because it is natural, it is rarely recognized for the evil that it is. But its outworkings are tragic.

Matthew 5:3; Matthew 16:24-26; 1 Corinthians 4:7; 1 Timothy 6:17-19
The Pursuit of God, 23, 27.

338. Earthly things; Prayers; God: His presence

O God and Father, I repent of my sinful preoccupation with visible things. The world has been too much with me. Thou hast been here and I knew it not. I have been blind to Thy presence. Open my eyes that I may behold Thee in and around me. For Christ's sake, Amen.

Matthew 16:23; Philippians 3:18-21; Colossians 3:1-4
The Pursuit of God, 64, 65.

339. Earthly things; Priorities

The roots of our hearts have grown down into things, and we dare not pull up our rootlet lest we die. Things have become necessary to us, a development never originally intended. God's gifts now take the place of God, and the whole course of nature is upset by the monstrous substitution.

Matthew 6:19-21, 23; Matthew 16:24-26; Matthew 19:21-22; 1 Timothy 6:17-19
The Pursuit of God, 22.

340. Egos; Humility

Years ago God gave me an ice pick and said, "Now Son, among your other duties will be to puncture all the inflated egos you see. Go stick an ice pick in them." And there has been more popping and hissing in my ministry as the air goes out of egos. People hate me for that, but I love them for the privilege of whittling them down to size, because if there is anything that we ought to get straight, it is how little we are.

Psalm 49:10-12; Jeremiah 9:23-24; Daniel 4:25
Success and the Christian, 44, 45.

341. Emotionalism; Obedience: need for

When they want to get blessed, some people try getting worked up psychologically....

Some people try group dynamics. . . .

What is needed is some old-fashioned, salty horse sense. I am sure there are 189 mules in the state of Missouri that have more sense than a lot of the preachers who are trying to teach people how to get the blessing of God in some way other than by the constituted means. When you get people all broken up, dabbing at their eyes and shaking, what is the result? It does not bring them any closer to God. It does not make them love God any better, in accordance with the first commandment. Nor does it give any greater love for neighbors, which is the second commandment. It does not prepare them to live fruitfully on earth. It does not prepare them to die victoriously, and it does not guarantee that they will be with the Lord at last.

The Lord has constituted means. Jesus said in the Gospel of John, "Whoever has my commands and obeys them, he is the one who loves me" (John 14:21a).

Matthew 22:37-39; John 14:21-24; 1 John 5:3
Rut, Rot or Revival: The Condition of the Church, 50, 51, 52.

342. Emotions; Emotionalism; Preaching: manipulation

I have to disagree with religious appeal that supposes if someone in the audience can be moved to shed a tear, a saint has been made. Or that if a husky listener can be touched emotionally to the point that he must blow his nose as though it was Gabriel's trumpet, all will be well with his soul.

I warn you that there is no connection whatsoever between the human manipulation of our emotions, on the one hand, and, on the other, the confirmation of God's revealed truth in our beings through the ministry of His Holy Spirit. When in our Christian experience our emotions are raised, it must be the result of what God's truth is doing for us. If that is not so, it is not properly religious stirring at all.

John 8:31-32
Jesus, Our Man in Glory, 83, 84.

343. Emotions; Happiness

Spiritual people are indifferent to their feelings—they live by faith in God with little care about their emotions. They think God's thoughts and see things as God sees them. They rejoice in Christ and have no confidence in themselves. They are more concerned with obedience than with happiness. This is less romantic, perhaps, but it will stand the test of fire.

Isaiah 55:8-9; Galatians 2:20; Philippians 3:3
This World: Playground or Battleground?, 21, 22.

344. Emotions; Holy Spirit: inward witness

One cause of the decline in the quality of religious experience among Christians these days is the neglect of the doctrine of the inward witness. . . .

In spite of the undeniable lukewarmness of most of us we still fear that unless we keep a careful check on ourselves we shall surely lose our dignity and become howling fanatics by this time next week. We set a watch upon our emotions day and night lest we become over-spiritual and bring reproach upon the cause of Christ. Which all, if I may say so, is for most of us about as sensible as throwing a cordon of police around a cemetery to prevent a wild political demonstration by the inhabitants.

John 15:26; Acts 5:32; Romans 8:16-17
Born After Midnight, 11.

345. Encounter with God

I happen to believe that Abraham's encounters with the living God nearly 4,000 years ago leave modern men and women without excuse.

Abraham stands for every believer. His eager and willing faith becomes every Christian's condemnation. On the other hand, his fellowship with God becomes every believer's encouragement.

If there is a desire in your heart for more of God's blessing in your life, turn your attention to the details of Abraham's encounters with God. You will find yourself back at the center, at the beating heart of living religion.

Genesis 12:1-4; Genesis 15:6; Genesis 17:1,2,5; Genesis 22:13-14; Hebrews 11:8-10
Men Who Met God, 19.

346. Encounter with God

These are elements that are always the same among men and women who have had a personal meeting with God.

First, these great souls always have a compelling sense of God Himself, of His person and of His presence. While others would want to spend their time talking about a variety of things, these godly men and women, touched by their knowledge of God, want to talk about Him. They are drawn away from a variety of mundane topics because of the importance of their spiritual discoveries. . . .

The third element is the permanent and life-changing nature of a true encounter with God. The experience may have been brief, but the results will be evident in the life of the person touched as long as he or she lives.

Psalm 139:7-12; Acts 4:20;
2 Corinthians 5:13-17
Men Who Met God, 16, 17.

347. Encounter with God; Knowledge of God: divine encounter

Is it not true that for most of us who call ourselves Christians there is no real experience? We have substituted theological ideas for an arresting encounter; we are full of religious notions, but our great weakness is that for our hearts there is no one there.

Whatever else it embraces, true Christian experience must always include a genuine encounter with God. Without this, religion is but a shadow, a reflection of reality, a cheap copy of an original once enjoyed by someone else of whom we have heard. It cannot but be a major tragedy in the life of any man to live in a church from childhood to old age and know nothing more real than some synthetic god compounded of theology and logic, but having no eyes to see, no ears to hear, and no heart to love.

Deuteronomy 29:4; Ezekiel 12:2; Luke 24:32; Acts 28:25-27
The Pursuit of Man, 10.

348. Enoch; Faith: daily walk; Walk with God

Enoch recognized the failure of men and women trying to live their lives apart from God and His will. By faith he walked with God on this earth at a time when sin and corruption were wildly rampant all around him.

Enoch's daily walk was a walk of faith, a walk of fellowship with God. What the Scriptures are trying to say to us is this: If Enoch could live and walk with God by faith in the midst of his sinful generation, we likewise should be able to follow his example because the human race is the same and God is the same! . . .

There is only one conclusion to be drawn here. Enoch was translated into the presence of God because of his faith, and thus he escaped death. It is very evident that there was no funeral for Enoch. Those who knew him best surely had to answer many questions. "Where is Enoch?" "What happened to Enoch?" "Why don't we see Enoch around anymore?"

Perhaps members of his own family did not fully understand his walk with God, but they could answer with the facts: "He is gone! God has called him home. God has taken him."

Genesis 5:24; Hebrews 11:5
Jesus, Author of Our Faith, 22, 23.

349. Entertainers; Celebrities

In olden days they crowned the king and tied a cap and bell on the court fool; today we crown the fool and tie a tin can on the king....

It is surely an incredible state of affairs when the entertainer rates higher in public esteem than the doctor, the nurse, the teacher and the statesman upon whose shoulders rest the hopes of whole generations of men. Yet it is so today in our ostensibly civilized society. In America the court fool now wears the crown and rules over the minds of millions of chortling subjects who want nothing higher or better in this life than to kick off their shoes and spend an evening of howling mirth over the hoary chestnuts dished out by the current royal jester, whoever he may happen to be....

Yes, we have crowned the fool and spurned the real kings among us: The farmer who toils for us from sunup to sundown, the teacher who gets old and tired trying to make ladies and gentlemen out of the boys and girls we place in their care, the doctor who brought those boys and girls into the world and who stands to watch over their health while they grow up, the corner policeman who brings at least a semblance of safety to our streets, the soldier whose blood has bought our American soil a hundred times during the years of our history, the patriotic statesman who labors to make and keep our country free. These are underpaid, overlooked and generally tolerated while the court fool struts about over the world as if he were a king indeed instead of the cheap jester that he is.

Isaiah 5:11-12; Ephesians 5:3-4
The Warfare of the Spirit, 17, 18, 19.

350. Entertainment

A German philosopher many years ago said something to the effect that the more a man has in his own heart the less he will require from the outside; excessive need for support from without is proof of the bankruptcy of the inner man.

If this is true (and I believe it is) then the present inordinate attachment to every form of entertainment is evidence that the inner life of modern man is in serious decline. The average man has no central core of moral assurance, no spring within his own breast, no inner strength to place him above the need for repeated psychological shots to give him the courage to go on living. He has become a parasite on the world, drawing his life from his environment, unable to live a day apart from the stimulation which society affords him. . . .

For there are millions who cannot live without amusement; life without some form of entertainment for them is simply intolerable; they look forward to the blessed relief afforded by professional entertainers and other forms of psychological narcotics as a dope addict looks to his daily shot of heroin. Without them they could not summon courage to face existence. . . .

Proverbs 14:12-13; Ecclesiastes 2:1-11
The Root of the Righteous, 30, 31.

351. Entertainment; Distractions; World: contentment with

I should say something else here about this world and its selfish and often godless society. Why is there so much attraction to the magazines, the radio, the television, the sports, the concerts, the fun? We may be reluctant to admit it, but we have an enemy, and he has many helpers. All of these things that surely add up to fun and entertainment have an overall design of keeping people from taking God seriously. There is some great master plan that is surely succeeding in keeping men and women relatively happy in this world without ever a serious thought of God and salvation and eternal life!

Millions of men and women seem to be very content with the arrangement as it is. They do not want to be reminded at all that they are going to die and that after death comes the judgment of a holy and righteous God. They would rather remain gullible and deceived than to learn the truth about this world and the next.

2 Corinthians 5:10; Hebrews 9:27; 1 John 2:15-17
Jesus, Author of Our Faith, 84, 85.

352. Entertainment; Religion: popular

Evangelical Christianity is gasping for breath. We happen to have entered a period when it is popular to sing about tears and prayers and believing. You can get a religious phrase kicked around almost anywhere—even right in the middle of a worldly program dedicated to the flesh and the devil. Old Mammon, with two silver dollars for eyes, sits at the top of it, lying about the quality of the products, shamelessly praising actors who ought to be put to work laying bricks. In the middle of it, someone trained in a studio to sound religious will say with an unctuous voice, "Now, our hymn for the week!" So they break in, and the band goes twinkle, twankle, twinkle, twankle, and they sing something that the devil must blush to hear. They call that religion, and I will concede that religion it is. It is not Christianity, and it is not the Holy Spirit. It is not New Testament and it is not redemption. It is simply making capital out of religion.

Faith Beyond Reason, 12.

353. Entertainment; World: contentment with

When I was a boy on the farm, we "butchered" every year in the early fall. It was my job to coax the fattened hogs into the barn. I would throw them some corn, and they were pleased as they came grunting in with that corn still grinding in their mouths.

But in minutes they were dead. My father would then bleed them and dress them out. That is how we got our supply of pork for the winter.

The gullible pigs have never learned. Wherever they are, they are still being led to the slaughter generation after generation. All it takes is a supply of shelled corn!

You may not like the illustration, but there are plenty of gullible people who have never recognized why they are being kept so busy and so well entertained with the things that are amusing and fun. Paul said that he had caught on—and he reckoned himself dead to this world and this world dead to him.

Proverbs 1:10,15-16; Ecclesiastes 2:1-2; Romans 6:2,11-14
Jesus, Author of Our Faith, 85.

354. Eros; Sex

The period in which we now live may well go down in history as the Erotic Age. Sex love has been elevated into a cult. Eros has more worshipers among civilized men today than any other god. For millions the erotic has completely displaced the spiritual. . . .

Now if this god would let us Christians alone I for one would let his cult alone. The whole spongy, fetid mess will sink some day under its own weight and become excellent fuel for the fires of hell, a just recompense which is meet, and it becomes us to feel compassion for those who have been caught in its tragic collapse. Tears and silence might be better than words if things were slightly otherwise than they are. But the cult of Eros is seriously affecting the Church. The pure religion of Christ that flows like a crystal river from the heart of God is being polluted by the unclean waters that trickle from behind the altars of abomination that appear on every high hill and under every green tree from New York to Los Angeles.

Proverbs 5:1-23; 1 Corinthians 5:1-2; 1 Corinthians 6:9-10; Colossians 3:5-11
Born After Midnight, 36, 37.

355. Error; False teaching

Contrary to popular opinion, the cultivation of a psychology of uncritical belief is not an unqualified good, and if carried too far it may be a positive evil. The whole world has been booby-trapped by the devil, and the deadliest trap of all is the religious one. Error never looks so innocent as when it is found in the sanctuary.

Galatians 1:6-7; 1 Timothy 1:3-4; 1 John 4:1
Man: The Dwelling Place of God, 84.

356. Eternal destiny; Salvation: invitation to; Choices

Every man holds his future in his hand. Not the dominant world leader only, but the inarticulate man lost in anonymity is a "man of destiny." He decides which way his soul shall go. He chooses, and destiny waits on the nod of his head. He decides, and hell enlarges herself, or heaven prepares another mansion. So much of Himself has God given to men. . . .

"If any man will . . . , let him follow me," He says, and some will rise and go after Him, but others give no heed to His voice. So the gulf opens between man and man, between those who will and those who will not. Silently, terribly the work goes on, as each one decides whether he will hear or ignore the voice of invitation. Unknown to the world, perhaps unknown even to the individual, the work of separation takes place. Each hearer of the Voice must decide for himself, and he must decide on the basis of the evidence the message affords. There will be no thunder sound, no heavenly sign or light from heaven. The Man is His own proof. The marks in His hands and feet are the insignia of His rank and office. He will not put Himself again on trial; He will not argue, but the morning of the judgment will confirm what men in the twilight have decided. . . .

Christ will be Lord, or He will be Judge. Every man must decide whether he will take Him as Lord now or face Him as Judge then.

Matthew 16:24-26; John 14:1-6; John 20:27-29; Philippians 2:9-11
The Set of the Sail, 40, 41, 42.

357. Eternal life

God's gifts in nature have their limitations. They are finite because they have been created, but the gift of eternal life in Christ Jesus is as limitless as God. The Christian man possesses God's own life and shares His infinitude with Him. In God there is life enough for all and time enough to enjoy it. Whatever is possessed of natural life runs through its cycle from birth to death and ceases to be, but the life of God returns upon itself and ceases never. And this is life eternal: to know the only true God, and Jesus Christ whom He has sent.

John 10:27-29; John 17:3; 1 John 5:11,12
The Knowledge of the Holy, 73.

358. Eternal perspective; Earthly things

Brother, I remind you of that day when one of those wonderful and handsome and modern vehicles will pull up to your front door. Two gray-faced men will get out with a basket and they will lug you out—away from your radio and television and electric stoves and refrigerators and sweepers and massagers—they will lug you out and someone will prepare for your funeral. . . .

I suppose it may be more comfortable to go to hell in a Cadillac, or to pride your animal nature on food cooked in an automatic oven, but it is hell, nevertheless, when you get there.

Psalm 39:4-6; Matthew 16:24-26; James 4:13-14
Christ the Eternal Son, 61.

359. Eternal perspective; Earthly things; Faith: daily walk

It takes real faith to begin to live the life of heaven while still upon the earth, for this requires that we rise above the law of moral gravitation and bring to our everyday living the high wisdom of God. And since this wisdom is contrary to that of the world, conflict is bound to result. This, however, is a small price to pay for the inestimable privilege of following Christ. . . .

A real Christian need not defend his possession nor his position. God will take care of both. Let go of your treasures and the Lord will keep them for you unto life eternal. Hang unto them and they will bring you nothing but trouble and misery to the end of your days.

It is better to throw our little all to the four winds than to get old and sour defending it. It is better to be cheated a few times than to develop a constant suspicion that someone is trying to cheat us. It is better to have the house burglarized than to spend the rest of our days and nights sitting with a rifle across our knees watching over it. Give it up, and keep it. Defend it, and lose it. That is a law of the kingdom and it applies to every regenerated soul. We can afford to trust God; we can't afford not to.

Matthew 16:24-26; Philippians 4:11-12; Colossians 3:1-4; 1 Timothy 6:17-19
Born After Midnight, 98, 99.

360. Eternal perspective; Materialism; Earthly things

God has revealed Himself many times and in many ways to assure men and women made in His image that there is another and a better world than this vale of tears we refer to as home. . . .

When people around us learn that we are involved in a spiritual kingdom not yet visible, they think we are prime candidates for a mental institution. But this we know: Those same people around us are subject to the cruel tyranny of material and temporal things—things that will decay and pass away. No world dictator ever ruled his cowering subjects with any more fierce and compulsive domination than the material, visible things rule the men and women of this world.

Of all the calamities that have been visited upon this world and its inhabitants, the willing surrender of the human spirit to materialistic values is the worst! We who were made for higher worlds are accepting the ways of this world as the ultimate. That is a tragedy of staggering proportions.

We who were meant to commune with the Creator God, with the angels, archangels and seraphim, have decided instead to settle down here. As well might the eagle leave his lofty domain to scratch in the barnyard with the common hens.

Matthew 6:19-21; Hebrews 1:1-2; 1 John 2:15-17
Men Who Met God, 101, 102.

361. Eternal perspective; Priorities; Values

Apart from God nothing matters. We think that health matters, that freedom matters, or knowledge or art or civilization. And but for one insistent word they would matter indeed. That word is *eternity*.

Grant that men possess perpetual being and the preciousness of every earthly treasure is gone instantly. God is to our eternal being what our heart is to our body. The lungs, the liver, the kidneys have value as they relate to the heart. Let the heart stop and the rest of the organs promptly collapse. Apart from God, what is money, fame, education, civilization? Exactly nothing at all, for men must leave all these things behind them and one by one go to eternity. Let God hide His face and nothing thereafter is worth the effort.

Matthew 6:19-21, 24, 33; Philippians 1:21-24; Philippians 3:6-8
Man: The Dwelling Place of God, 117.

362. Eternal perspective; Science; Life purpose

This is my position: let the scientist stay in his field and I will stay in mine. I am as glad and thankful as anyone for the benefits of research, and I hope scientists will soon find the cure of heart disease, for I have lost many good friends from sudden heart attacks.

But listen to me now about the difference in meaning between the short-term matters of our physical beings and the eternal relationships between the believer and his God.

If you save a person from diptheria when he is a baby, or save him in his teens from smallpox, or save him in his fifties from a heart attack, what have you done?

If that man lives to be ninety and still is without God and does not know why he was born, you have simply perpetuated the life of a mud turtle. That man who has never found God and has never been born again is like a turtle, with two legs instead of four and no shell and no tail, because he still does not know what life has been all about.

Psalm 90:12; Matthew 16:24-26; 1 Corinthians 3:16-23; James 4:13-14
Whatever Happened to Worship?, 60.

363. Eternal perspective; Unsung heroes

I would rather be among those who are unknown, unsung and unheralded doing something through the Spirit of God that will count even a tiny little bit in the kingdom of God than to be involved in some highly-recognized expression of religious activity across which God will ultimately write the judgment: "This too shall pass!"

Exodus 4:10-12; Jeremiah 1:5-8; 1 Corinthians 12:22-25; 1 Corinthians 15:58; 2 Corinthians 10:10
Tragedy in the Church: The Missing Gifts, 32.

364. Eternal perspective; Values

We who follow Christ are men and women of eternity. We must put no confidence in the passing scenes of the disappearing world. We must resist every attempt of Satan to palm off upon us the values that belong to mortality. Nothing less than forever is long enough for us. We view with amused sadness the frenetic scramble of the world to gain a brief moment in the sun. "The book of the month," for instance, has a strange sound to one who has dwelt with God and taken his values from the Ancient of Days. "The man of the year" cannot impress those men and women who are making their plans for that long eternity when days and years have passed away and time is no more.

Psalm 90:4-6; Psalm 103:15-17; Ecclesiastes 12:1,8
The Next Chapter After the Last, 9.

365. Eternal security; Calvinism; Jesus Christ: His intercession

Let this truth penetrate. There is a glorified Human Being at the right hand of God—not a spirit but a Man glorified. He is there interceding for us, representing us. This is why I believe in the security of the saints. How can I help but believe that? If Jesus Christ is at the right hand of God, then He has invested Himself—charged Himself—with full authority, authority given Him by God the Father. My name is on His multistone breastpiece (see Exodus 39:8-14), and I am safe!

Someone once asked Dr. Graham Scroggie, "Are you a Calvinist?" I feel Dr. Scroggie was speaking for me when he replied, "When I am on my knees praying, I am a Calvinist. But when I get into the pulpit to preach I am an Arminian!" That my great High Priest will keep me, I have no doubt. Will He do so because of my goodness? No! Will He keep you because of your goodness? Again, no! We are kept because He is at the throne of God interceding for us.

Exodus 39:8-14; John 10:27-29; Romans 8:34
Jesus Is Victor!, 46, 47.

366. Eternity

We who live in this nervous age would be wise to meditate on our lives and our days long and often before the face of God and on the edge of eternity. For we are made for eternity as certainly as we are made for time, and as responsible moral beings we must deal with both.

Psalm 90:12; Hebrews 9:27
The Knowledge of the Holy, 63, 64.

367. Eternity; Heaven: glory of

So the elder tells John: "These are they who have come out of the great tribulation; they have washed their robes and made them white in the blood of the Lamb. Therefore, "they are before the throne of God and serve him day and night in his temple; and he who sits on the throne will spread his tent over them. Never again will they hunger; never again will they thirst. The sun will not beat upon them, nor any scorching heat. For the Lamb at the center of the throne will be their shepherd; he will lead them to springs of living water. And God will wipe away every tear from their eyes."

Where in all this world could we turn to find anything as beautiful, as powerful, as overwhelming as this description of the overcoming saints of God in heaven? I recommend that we stop reading the shallow, worldly stuff of our day—material that is not doing our souls any good. We should concentrate more of our time and attention on where we are going for eternity.

John 14:1-6; Colossians 3:1-4; Revelation 7:14-17
Jesus Is Victor!, 113, 114.

368. Eternity; Pilgrims

"O Lord, I know that the way of man is not in himself: it is not in man that walketh to direct his steps."

The prophet here turns to a figure of speech, one which appears in the Scriptures so frequently that it is not easy to remember that it is but a figure. Man is seen as a traveler making his difficult way from a past he can but imperfectly recollect into a future about which he knows nothing. And he cannot stay, but must each morning strike his moving tent and journey on toward—and there is the heavy problem—toward what?

It is a simple axiom of the traveler that if he would arrive at the desired destination he must take the right road. How far a man may have traveled is not important; what matters is whether or not he is going the right way, whether the path he is following will bring him out at the right place at last. Sometimes there will be an end to the road, and maybe sooner than he knows; but when he has gone the last step of the way will he find himself in a tomorrow of light and peace, or will the day toward which he journeys be "a day of trouble and distress, a day of wasteness and desolation, a day of darkness and gloominess, a day of clouds and thick darkness"?

Proverbs 20:24; Jeremiah 10:23; Zephaniah 1:15; Matthew 13:3-9, 20-22
The Set of the Sail, 105, 106.

369. Eternity; Salvation: preparation for eternity

... we have such a short time to prepare for such a long time. By that I mean we have now to prepare for then. We have an hour to prepare for eternity. To fail to prepare is an act of moral folly. For anyone to have a day given to prepare, it is an act of inexcusable folly to let anything hinder that preparation. If we find ourselves in a spiritual rut, nothing in the world should hinder us. Nothing in this world is worth it. If we believe in eternity, if we believe in God, if we believe in the eternal existence of the soul, then there is nothing important enough to cause us to commit such an act of moral folly.

Failing to get ready in time for eternity, and failing to get ready now for the great then that lies out yonder, is a trap in plain sight. There is an odd saying in the Old Testament, "How useless to spread a net in full view of all the birds" (Proverbs 1:17). When the man of God wrote that, he gave the birds a little credit. It would be silly for a bird watching me set the trap to conveniently fly down and get into it. Yet there are people doing that all the time. People who have to live for eternity fall into that trap set for them in plain sight.

Proverbs 1:17; Acts 4:12; 2 Corinthians 6:1-2
Rut, Rot or Revival: The Condition of the Church, 87, 88.

370. Evangelicalism; Fundamentalism; Holy Spirit: need for

I have to tell the truth, and the truth is not very well received, even by the saints. The simple truth is that unless we have a lighting down upon evangelicalism, upon fundamentalism, upon our gospel churches, unless the Dove of God can come down with His wings outspread and make Himself known and felt among us, that which is fundamentalism will be liberalism in years to come. And liberalism will be unitarianism.

The Counselor, 165.

371. Evangelism: concern for lost

Then there's the poor sick world out there. I, for my part, do not want to be happy while the world perishes. Nobody loves the world quite enough. The Man who loved the world enough to die for it died for it, and Paul, the man who loved Israel enough to want to perish for Israel, cried out he wanted to be accursed for Israel's sake. We don't seem to have it much these days. Much of our Christianity is social instead of spiritual. We should be a spiritual body with social overtones, but most of our churches are social bodies with spiritual overtones. The heart of the Church ought always to be Christ and the Holy Spirit. The heart of the Church ought always to be heaven and God and righteousness. Those who loved the Lord spoke often one to another, and what they spoke about were spiritual things.

Psalm 126:5-6; John 3:16; Acts 2:46-47; Romans 9:1-3
The Counselor, 168.

372. Evangelism: concern for lost

The testimony of the true follower of Christ might well be something like this: The world's pleasures and the world's treasures henceforth have no appeal for me. I reckon myself crucified to the world and the world crucified to me. But the multitudes that were so dear to Christ shall not be less dear to me. If I cannot prevent their moral suicide, I shall at least baptize them with my human tears. I want no blessing that I cannot share. I seek no spirituality that I must win at the cost of forgetting that men and women are lost and without hope. If in spite of all I can do they will sin against light and bring upon themselves the displeasure of a holy God, then I must not let them go their sad way unwept. I scorn a happiness that I must purchase with ignorance. I reject a heaven that I must enter by shutting my eyes to the sufferings of my fellow men. I choose a broken heart rather than any happiness that ignores the tragedy of human life and human death. Though I, through the grace of God in Christ, no longer lie under Adam's sin, I would still feel a bond of compassion for all of Adam's tragic race, and I am determined that I shall go down to the grave or up into God's heaven mourning for the lost and the perishing.

And thus and thus will I do as God enables me. Amen.

Psalm 126:5-6; Romans 9:1-3; 2 Corinthians 5:12-15
The Next Chapter After the Last, 36.

373. Evangelism: divine power in

Every notable advance in the saving work of God among men will, if examined, be found to have two factors present: several converging lines of providential circumstances and a person.

Exodus 3:7-10; Ezekiel 22:30; John 1:6-7
Let My People Go: The Life of Robert A. Jaffray, 50.

374. Evangelism: divine power in

. . . by *power* I mean that divine afflatus which moves the heart and persuades the hearer to repent and believe in Christ. It is not eloquence; it is not logic; it is not argument. It is not any of these things, though it may accompany any or all of them. It is more penetrating than thought, more disconcerting than conscience, more convincing than reason. It is the subtle *wonder* that follows anointed preaching, a mysterious operation of spirit on spirit. Such power must be present in some degree before anyone can be saved. It is the ultimate enabling without which the most earnest seeker must fall short of true saving faith.

Acts 1:8; Ephesians 2:8-10; Colossians 2:13
Paths to Power, 13.

375. Evangelism: divine power in; Communism

A friend of mine went to see a man who was the head of a local communist cell in a local communist headquarters where they send out literature. The communist said, "Come in, Reverend, and sit down." He went in and sat. "Now, we're communists," he said, "you know that, and you're a minister. Of course, we're miles apart. But," he said, "I want to tell you something. We learned our technique from your book of Acts." He said, "We learned how to win and conquer from your book of Acts." And he said, "You who believe the Bible have thrown overboard the methods of the early church and we who don't believe it have adopted them and they're working."

Acts 2:46-47; Acts 4:32-33; Acts 17:6
Success and the Christian, 10, 11.

376. Evangelism: divine power in; Evangelism: lack of involvement in; Cults; Church: apathy

If we evangelicals had one-third of the enthusiasm of some of the cults we could take a continent. We have the power and they do not—that is, we have power available to us and they do not. We have a lazy bunch of evangelicals on our hands.

Rut, Rot or Revival: The Condition of the Church, 97.

377. Evangelism: divine power in; Truth: necessity of response; Salvation: Holy Spirit's work

The uncomprehending mind is unaffected by truth. The intellect of the hearer may grasp saving knowledge while yet the heart makes no moral response to it. A classic example of this is seen in the story of Benjamin Franklin and George Whitefield. In his autobiography Franklin recounts in some detail how he listened to the mighty preaching of the great evangelist. He even walked around the square where Whitefield stood to learn for himself how far that golden voice carried. Whitefield talked with Franklin personally about his need of Christ and promised to pray for him. Years later Franklin wrote rather sadly that the evangelist's prayers must not have done any good, for he was still unconverted. . . .

The inward operation of the Holy Spirit is necessary to saving faith. The gospel is light but only the Spirit can give sight. When seeking to bring the lost to Christ we must pray continually that they may receive the gift of seeing. And we must pit our prayer against that dark spirit who blinds the hearts of men.

2 Corinthians 4:4; Ephesians 2:8-10
Born After Midnight, 62, 63.

378. Evangelism: humanistic approach to; Church: current condition

... any evangelism which by appeal to common interests and chatter about current events seeks to establish a common ground where the sinner can feel at home is as false as the altars of Baal ever were. Every effort to smooth out the road for men and to take away the guilt and the embarrassment is worse than wasted; it is evil and dangerous to the souls of men.

One of the most popular current errors, and the one out of which springs most of the noisy, blustering religious activity being carried on in evangelical circles these days, is the notion that as times change the church must change with them. Christians must adapt their methods by the demands of the people. If they want 10-minute sermons, give them 10-minute sermons. If they want truth in capsule form, give it to them. If they want pictures, give them plenty of pictures. If they like stories, tell them stories. If they prefer to absorb their religious instruction through the drama, go along with them—give them what they want. "The message is the same, only the method changes," say the advocates of compromise.

Isaiah 6:9-10
God Tells the Man Who Cares, 14, 15.

379. Evangelism: humanistic approach to; Shallow belief; Discipleship

The flaw in current evangelism lies in its humanistic approach. It struggles to be supernaturalistic but never quite makes it. It is frankly fascinated by the great, noisy, aggressive world with its big names, its hero worship, its wealth and its garish pageantry. To the millions of disappointed persons who have always yearned for worldly glory but never attained to it, the modern evangel offers a quick and easy short cut to their heart's desire. Peace of mind, happiness, prosperity, social acceptance, publicity, success in sports, business, the entertainment field, and perchance to sit occasionally at the same banquet table with a celebrity—all this on earth and heaven at last. Certainly no insurance company can offer half as much.

In this quasi-Christian scheme of things God becomes the Aladdin lamp who does the bidding of everyone that will accept His Son and sign a card. The total obligation of the sinner is discharged when he accepts Christ. After that he has but to come with his basket and receive the religious equivalent of everything the world offers and enjoy it to the limit. Those who have not accepted Christ must be content with this world, but the Christian gets this one with the one to come thrown in as a bonus.

Matthew 5:14-16; Matthew 10:34-39; John 12:24-26
Born After Midnight, 22.

380. Evangelism: lack of involvement in; Cults

We are 20th century Christians. Some of us are Christians only because it is convenient and pleasant and because it is not costing us anything. But here is the truth, whether we like it or not: the average evangelical Christian who claims to be born again and have eternal life is not doing as much to propagate his or her faith as the busy adherents of the cults handing out their papers on the street corners and visiting from house to house.

We are not willing to take the spit and the contempt and the abuses those cultists take as they knock on doors and try to persuade everyone to follow them in their mistaken beliefs. The cultists can teach us much about zeal and effort and sacrifice, but most of us do not want to get that serious about our faith—or our Savior.

Luke 16:27-28; Acts 20:24; Romans 10:1-3
Jesus Is Victor!, 114, 115.

381. Evangelism: lack of involvement in; Evangelism: urgency of

Let a flood or a fire hit a populous countryside and no able-bodied citizen feels that he has any right to rest till he has done all he can to save as many as he can. While death stalks farmhouse and village no one dares relax; this is the accepted code by which we live. The critical emergency for some becomes an emergency for all, from the highest government official to the local Boy Scout troop. As long as the flood rages or the fire roars on, no one talks of "normal times." No times are normal while helpless people cower in the path of destruction.

In times of extraordinary crisis ordinary measures will not suffice. The world lives in such a time of crisis. Christians alone are in a position to rescue the perishing. We dare not settle down to try to live as if things were "normal." Nothing is normal while sin and lust and death roam the world, pouncing upon one and another till the whole population has been destroyed.

To me it has always been difficult to understand those evangelical Christians who insist upon living in the crisis as if no crisis existed. They say they serve the Lord, but they divide their days so as to leave plenty of time to play and loaf and enjoy the pleasures of the world as well. They are at ease while the world burns; and they can furnish many convincing reasons for their conduct, even quoting Scripture if you press them a bit.

I wonder whether such Christians actually believe in the fall of man.

Isaiah 6:8; Ezekiel 33:8-9; Romans 9:1-3
Born After Midnight, 30, 31.

382. Evangelism: true conversion

First, we must consider the person who becomes a disciple of Christ on impulse. This is likely to be the person who came in on a wave of enthusiasm, and I am a little bit suspicious of anyone who is too easily converted. I have a feeling that if he or she can be easily converted to Christ, he or she may be very easily flipped back the other way. I am concerned about the person who just yields, who has no sales resistance at all. . . .

Actually, I go along with the man or woman who is thoughtful enough about this decision to say truthfully: "I want a day to think this over," or "I want a week to read the Bible and to meditate on what this decision means."

I have never considered it a very great compliment to the Christian church that we can generate enthusiasm on such short notice. The less there is in the kettle, the quicker it begins to boil. There are some who get converted on enthusiasm and backslide on principle!

John 8:31-32
Faith Beyond Reason, 55, 56, 57.

383. Evangelism: urgency of; Fall of man

The fall of man has created a perpetual crisis. It will last until sin has been put down and Christ reigns over a redeemed and restored world.

Until that time the earth remains a disaster area and its inhabitants live in a state of extraordinary emergency. . . .

To me, it has always been difficult to understand those evangelical Christians who insist upon living in the crisis as if no crisis existed. They say they serve the Lord, but they divide their days so as to leave plenty of time to play and loaf and enjoy the pleasures of the world as well. They are at ease while the world burns. . . .

I wonder whether such Christians actually believe in the Fall of man!

Romans 5:19; 2 Corinthians 5:19-21
Renewed Day by Day, Volume 1, Jan. 17.

384. Evangelism: urgency of; Priorities; Eternity

I remind you that it is characteristic of the natural man to keep himself so busy with unimportant trifles that he is able to avoid the settling of the most important matters relating to life and existence.

Men and women will gather anywhere and everywhere to talk about and discuss every subject from the latest fashions on up to Plato and philosophy—up and down the scale. They talk about the necessity for peace. They may talk about the church and how it can be a bulwark against communism. None of these things are embarrassing subjects.

But the conversation all stops and the taboo of silence becomes effective when anyone dares to suggest that there are spiritual subjects of vital importance to our souls that ought to be discussed and considered. There seems to be an unwritten rule in polite society that if any religious subjects are to be discussed, it must be within the framework of theory—"Never let it get personal!"

All the while, there is really only one thing that is of vital importance—the fact that our Lord Jesus Christ "was wounded for our transgressions; he was bruised for our iniquities; the chastisement of our peace was upon him; and with his stripes we are healed."

Isaiah 53:5
Who Put Jesus on the Cross?, 3, 4.

385. Evangelism: wrong emphasis

Evangelical Christians commonly offer Christ to mankind as a nostrum to cure their ills, a way out of their troubles, a quick and easy means to the achievement of personal ends. They use the right words, but their emphasis is awry. The message is so presented as to leave the hearer with the impression that he is being asked to give up much to gain more. And that is not good, however well intentioned it may be.

What we do is precisely what a good salesman does when he presents the excellence of his product as compared with that of his closest competitor. The customer chooses the better of the two, as who would not? But the weakness of the whole salesmanship technique is apparent: the idea of selfish gain is present in the whole transaction.

Ephesians 1:4-6,12-14
Man: The Dwelling Place of God, 12.

386. Evangelism: wrong emphasis

In our eagerness to make converts I am afraid we have lately been guilty of using the technique of modern salesmanship, which is of course to present only the desirable qualities in a product and ignore the rest. We go to men and offer them a cozy home on the sunny side of the brae. If they will but accept Christ He will give them peace of mind, solve their problems, prosper their business, protect their families and keep them happy all day long. They believe us and come, and the first cold wind sends them shivering to some counselor to find out what has gone wrong; and that is the last we hear of many of them. . . .

By offering our hearers a sweetness-and-light gospel and promising every taker a place on the sunny side of the brae, we not only cruelly deceive them, we guarantee also a high casualty rate among the converts won on such terms. On certain foreign fields the expression "rice Christians" has been coined to describe those who adopt Christianity for profit. The experienced missionary knows that the convert that must pay a heavy price for his faith in Christ is the one that will persevere to the end. He begins with the wind in his face, and should the storm grow in strength he will not turn back for he has been conditioned to endure it.

By playing down the cost of discipleship we are producing rice Christians by the tens of thousands right here on the North American continent.

Matthew 13:3-9,20-22; 1 John 2:19
That Incredible Christian, 116, 117.

387. Evangelism: wrong emphasis; Cross: current view of

All unannounced and mostly undetected there has come in modern times a new cross into popular evangelical circles. It is like the old cross, but different: the likenesses are superficial; the differences, fundamental. . . .

The old cross would have no truck with the world. For Adam's proud flesh it meant the end of the journey. It carried into effect the sentence imposed by the law of Sinai. The new cross is not opposed to the human race; rather, it is a friendly pal and, if understood aright, it is the source of oceans of good clean fun and innocent enjoyment. It lets Adam live without interference. His life motivation is unchanged; he still lives for his own pleasure, only now he takes delight in singing choruses and watching religious movies instead of singing bawdy songs and drinking hard liquor. The accent is still on enjoyment, though the fun is now on a higher plane morally if not intellectually.

The new cross encourages a new and entirely different evangelistic approach. The evangelist does not demand abnegation of the old life before a new life can be received. He preaches not contrasts but similarities. He seeks to key into public interest by showing that Christianity makes no unpleasant demands; rather, it offers the same thing the world does, only on a higher level. Whatever the sin-mad world happens to be clamoring after at the moment is cleverly shown to be the very thing the gospel offers, only the religious product is better.

The new cross does not slay the sinner, it redirects him. It gears him into a cleaner and jollier way of living and saves his self-respect. To the self-assertive it says, "Come and assert yourself for Christ." To the egotist it says, "Come and do your boasting in the Lord." To the thrill seeker it says, "Come and enjoy the thrill of Christian fellowship." The Christian message is slanted in the direction of the current vogue in order to make it acceptable to the public.

1 Corinthians 1:18; 2 Corinthians 5:17; Galatians 2:20
Man: The Dwelling Place of God, 42, 43.

388. Evangelism: wrong emphasis; Discipleship

Any appeal to the public in the name of Christ that rises no higher than an invitation to tranquillity must be recognized as mere humanism with a few words of Jesus thrown in to make it appear Christian. . . .

Christ calls men to carry a cross; we call them to have fun in His name. He calls them to forsake the world; we assure them that if they but accept Jesus the world is their oyster. He calls them to suffer; we call them to enjoy all the bourgeois comforts modern civilization affords. He calls them to self-abnegation and death; we call them to spread themselves like green bay trees or perchance even to become stars in a pitiful fifth-rate religious zodiac. He calls them to holiness; we call them to a cheap and tawdry happiness that would have been rejected with scorn by the least of the Stoic philosophers.

Matthew 10:37-39; Luke 9:23-25; Philippians 1:29-30
Born After Midnight, 141.

389. Evangelism: wrong emphasis; Testimonials; Shallow belief

To make converts here we are forced to play down the difficulties and play up the peace of mind and worldly success enjoyed by those who accept Christ. We must assure our hearers that Christianity is now a proper and respectable thing and that Christ has become quite popular with political bigwigs, well-to-do business tycoons and the Hollywood swimming pool set. Thus assured, hell-deserving sinners are coming in droves to "accept" Christ for what they can get out of Him; and though one now and again may drop a tear as proof of his sincerity, it is hard to escape the conclusion that most of them are stooping to patronize the Lord of glory much as a young couple might fawn on a boresome but rich old uncle in order to be mentioned in his will later on.

Born After Midnight, 17.

390. Excess; America: excess

Were I to select a word which I felt best described the modern American temper that word would be excess.

Almost everything we do, we overdo. We are forever creating monstrosities. If it moves, it moves too fast; if it is high, it is too high; if it makes noise, the noise is ridiculously loud; if we make a car, it is sure to be grotesquely large and gaudy with vastly more power than is required for the transportation we desire. We have too many telephones, too many filling stations, too many stores. Our national debt is astronomical, our waste incredible; our highways are too many, too complex and too expensive. Vacations are too long and too strenuous. Our swapping of Christmas gifts has become an irksome rat race not remotely related to the blessed Advent. Music we hear everywhere till our ears are suffocated in a welter of inappropriate melody. . . .

Without doubt we are out of control and it may be that we have reached the point of no return. We may never recover from our mighty binge. It should be said, however, that if we alone are destroying ourselves by excess, it is because we are the only nation rich enough to do it successfully and to get such a whale of a lot of pleasure out of the job.

Proverbs 23:4; Luke 12:19-21; 1 Timothy 6:9-10
The Warfare of the Spirit, 86, 87.

391. Excess; Sin: good perverted

It has been obvious to me that almost every sin is but a natural good perverted or carried to excess. Self-respect is turned into pride; natural appetite becomes gluttony; sleep goes on to become sloth; sex goes awry and turns to sodomy; love degenerates into lechery; praise sinks to flattery; determination hardens into obstinacy; a natural childish love of play grows up with the man and becomes a multi- billion dollar business wherein tens of thousands of able-bodied persons waste their lives playing for the amusement of the millions of bored adults who are more than willing to work hard to obtain money to watch them play.

Proverbs 23:20-21; Proverbs 24:30-31; Romans 1:26-27
The Warfare of the Spirit, 88.

392. Existentialism; Accountability; Atheism; Sartre, Jean-Paul

It has always seemed to me completely inconsistent that existentialism should deny the existence of God and then proceed to use the language of theism to persuade men to live right. The French writer, Jean-Paul Sartre, for instance, states frankly that he represents atheistic existentialism. "If God does not exist," he says, "we find no values or commands to turn to which legitimize our conduct. So in the bright realm of values, we have no excuse behind us, nor justification before us. We are all alone, with no excuses." Yet in the next paragraph he states bluntly, "Man is responsible for his passion," and further on, "A coward is responsible for his cowardice." And such considerations as these, he says, fill the existentialist with "anguish, forlornness and despair."

It seems to me that such reasoning must assume the truth of everything it seeks to deny. If there were no God there could be no such word as "responsible." No criminal need fear a judge who does not exist; nor would he need to worry about breaking a law that had not been passed. It is the knowledge that the law and the judge do in fact exist that strikes fear to the lawbreaker's heart. There is someone to whom he is accountable; otherwise the concept of responsibility could have no meaning.

That Incredible Christian, 80, 81.

393. Eyes of God

When we lift our inward eyes to gaze upon God we are sure to meet friendly eyes gazing back at us, for it is written that the eyes of the Lord run to and fro throughout all the earth. The sweet language of experience is "Thou God seest me" (Genesis 16:13). When the eyes of the soul looking out meet the eyes of God looking in, heaven has begun right here on this earth.

Genesis 16:13; 2 Chronicles 16:9; Zechariah 4:10; Titus 2:11-14
The Pursuit of God, 83.

F

394. Failure

If it were true that the Lord would put the Christian on the shelf every time he failed and blundered and did something wrong, I would have been a piece of statuary by this time! I know God and He isn't that kind of God.

Psalm 32:1-2; Titus 2:14; 1 John 1:6-9
I Talk Back to the Devil, 126.

395. Faith: and feelings; Promises of God

You may not be feeling well physically today. Have you learned to be thankful anyhow and to rejoice in the promises of God? God's eternal blessings do not depend on how you feel today. If my eternal hope rested on how I felt physically, I might as well begin packing for a move to some other region! Even if I do not feel heavenly, my feelings in no way change my heavenly hope and prospect.

I dare not relate even a fraction of my faith and hope to my emotions of the moment and to how I feel today. My eternal hope depends on God's well-being—on whether God Himself is able to make good on His promises. And about that there is no doubt.

Daniel 3:17; 2 Corinthians 4:16-18;
Philippians 4:4,11-12
Jesus, Our Man in Glory, 82, 83.

396. Faith: and works

The supreme purpose of the Christian religion is to make men like God in order that they may act like God. In Christ the verbs *to be* and *to do* follow each other in that order. . . .

Rightly understood, faith is not a substitute for moral conduct but a means toward it. The tree does not serve in lieu of fruit but as an agent by which fruit is secured. Fruit, not trees, is the end God has in mind in yonder orchard; so Christ-like conduct is the end of Christian faith. To oppose faith to works is to make the fruit the enemy to the tree; yet that is exactly what we have managed to do. And the consequences have been disastrous. . . .

A proper understanding of this whole thing will destroy the false and artificial either/or. Then we will have not less faith but more godly works; not less praying but more serving; not fewer words but more holy deeds; not weaker profession but more courageous possession; not a religion as a substitute for action but religion in faith-filled action.

Matthew 7:20; John 15:8; James 2:17,26
Of God and Men, 63, 65, 66.

397. Faith: and works; Discipleship

I don't think you can be a Christian without being a disciple. The idea that I can come to the Lord and by grace have all of my sins forgiven and have my name written in heaven, and have the Carpenter go to work on a mansion in my Father's house, and at the same time raise hell on my way to heaven is impossible and unscriptural. It cannot be found in the Bible.

We are never saved by our good works, but we are not saved apart from good works. Out of our saving faith in Jesus Christ, there springs immediately goodness and righteousness. Spring is not brought by flowers, but you cannot have spring without flowers. It isn't my righteousness that saves, but the salvation I have received brings righteousness.

Amos 3:3; Titus 2:11-14
The Counselor, 133.

398. Faith: and works; Gospel: moral implications

That many of our hotly defended beliefs are no more than reactions to what we consider false doctrines would not be difficult to prove. The doctrine of justification by works (itself a serious error), for instance, has driven some teachers to espouse the equally damaging error of salvation without works. To many people the thought of "works" is repugnant because of its association with the effete Judaism of the New Testament era. The upshot of the matter is that we have salvation without righteousness and right doctrine without right deeds. Grace is twisted out of its moral context and made the cause of lowered standards of conduct in the church.

Galatians 5:13; Ephesians 2:8-10; James 2:14-26
This World: Playground or Battleground?, 49, 50.

399. Faith: and works; Obedience: need for

The truth is that faith and obedience are two sides of the same coin and are always found together in the Scriptures. As well try to pry apart the two sides of a half-dollar as to separate obedience from faith. The two sides, while they remain together and are taken as one, represent good sound currency and constitute legal tender everywhere in the United States. Separate them and they are valueless. Insistence upon honoring but one side of the faith-obedience coin has wrought frightful harm in religious circles. Faith has been made everything and obedience nothing. The result among religious persons is moral weakness, spiritual blindness and a slow but constant drift away from New Testament Christianity.

James 2:18-26
The Size of the Soul, 160.

400. Faith: and works; Salvation: by faith alone

The effort to be forgiven by works is one that can never be completed because no one knows or can know how much is enough to cancel out the offense; so the seeker must go on year after year paying on his moral debt, here a little, there a little, knowing that he sometimes adds to his bill much more than he pays. The task of keeping books on such a transaction can never end, and the seeker can only hope that when the last entry is made he may be ahead and the account fully paid. This is quite the popular belief, this forgiveness by self-effort, but it is natural heresy and can at last only betray those who depend upon it.

Romans 3:28; Ephesians 2:8-10; Titus 3:4-7
That Incredible Christian, 99.

401. Faith: confirmation of

The difference between faith as it is found in the New Testament and faith as it is found now is that faith in the New Testament actually produced something—there was a confirmation of it.

Faith now is a beginning and an end. We have faith in faith—but nothing happens. They had faith in a risen Christ and something did happen. That's the difference.

Matthew 7:15-16; Galatians 5:22-23; James 2:18-26
The Counselor, 4.

402. Faith: confirmation of; Discipleship

There is, however, one serious flaw in all this: it is that many—would I overstate the case if I said the majority?—of those who confess their faith in Christ and enter into association with the community of believers have little joy in their hearts, no peace in their minds, and from all external appearances are no better morally than the ordinary educated citizen who takes no interest whatever in religion and, of course, makes no profession of Christianity. Why is this?

I believe it is the result of an inadequate concept of Christianity and an imperfect understanding of the revolutionary character of Christian discipleship. . . .

True faith brings a spiritual and moral transformation and an inward witness that cannot be mistaken. These come when we stop believing in belief and start believing in the Lord Jesus Christ indeed.

Romans 8:16-17; 2 Corinthians 5:17; Philippians 4:6-7
Man: The Dwelling Place of God, 60, 61.

403. Faith: confirmation of; Lordship of Christ; Obedience: need for

The difficulty we modern Christians face is not misunderstanding the Bible, but persuading our untamed hearts to accept its plain instructions. Our problem is to get the consent of our world-loving minds to make Jesus Lord in fact as well as in word. For it is one thing to say, "Lord, Lord," and quite another thing to obey the Lord's commandments. We may sing, "Crown Him Lord of all," and rejoice in the tones of the loud-sounding organ and the deep melody of harmonious voices, but still we have done nothing until we have left the world and set our faces toward the city of God in hard practical reality. When faith becomes obedience then it is true faith indeed.

Matthew 7:21-23; Luke 6:46; James 2:22
The Pursuit of Man, 120, 121.

404. Faith: daily walk

Faith is the least self-regarding of the virtues. It is by its very nature scarcely conscious of its own existence. Like the eye which sees everything in front of it and never sees itself, faith is occupied with the Object upon which it rests and pays no attention to itself at all. While we are looking at God we do not see ourselves—blessed riddance. The man who has struggled to purify himself and has had nothing but repeated failures will experience real relief when he stops tinkering with his soul and looks away to the perfect One. While he looks at Christ, the very things he has so long been trying to do will be getting done within him. It will be God working in him to will and to do.

2 Chronicles 20:12; Psalm 123:1-2; Philippians 2:12-13
The Pursuit of God, 82, 83.

405. Faith: daily walk; Christian life

The book of Acts lays strong emphasis upon steadfastness in the faith, as do the Pauline epistles and the Book of Hebrews. Obviously the apostles conceived the Christian life to be a long tough journey, requiring a lot of faith and determination but ending in glory at last. . . .

True faith is not an end; it is a means to an end. It is not a destination; it is a journey, and the initial act of believing in Christ is a gate leading into the long lane we are to travel with Christ for the rest of our earthly days. That journey is hard and tired, but it is wonderful also, and no one ever regretted the weariness when he came to the end of the road.

Romans 8:18-19; 1 Corinthians 15:58; Hebrews 12:1-2
The Next Chapter After the Last, 84, 85.

406. Faith: daily walk; Faith: defective

To many Christians Christ is little more than an idea, or at best an ideal; He is not a fact. Millions of professed believers talk as if He were real and act as if He were not. And always our actual position is to be discovered by the way we act, not by the way we talk. . . .

Many of us Christians have become extremely skillful in arranging our lives so as to admit the truth of Christianity without being embarrassed by its implications. We fix things so that we can get on well enough without divine aid, while at the same time ostensibly seeking it. We boast in the Lord but watch carefully that we never get caught depending on Him. . . .

Pseudo-faith always arranges a way out to serve in case God fails it. Real faith knows only one way and gladly allows itself to be stripped of any second ways or makeshift substitutes. For true faith, it is either God or total collapse. And not since Adam first stood up on the earth has God failed a single man or woman who trusted Him.

Joshua 23:14; 2 Chronicles 20:12; Luke 6:44-45
The Price of Neglect, 12, 13.

407. Faith: defective

Do you remember a rather comic character by the name of Sancho Panza in that well-known book, *Don Quixote*? There is an incident in the book in which Señor Panza clung to a window sill all night, afraid that if he let go he would plunge and die on the ground below. But when the morning light came, red-faced and near exhaustion, he found that his feet were only two inches above the grass. Fear kept him from letting go, but he could have been safe on the ground throughout the long night.

I use that illustration to remind us that there are many professing Christians whose knuckles are white from blindly hanging on to their own window sill. The Lord has been saying, "Look on me and let go!" But they have refused.

Matthew 6:25-34; Philippians 4:6-7;
1 Peter 5:7
I Talk Back to the Devil, 88.

408. Faith: defective

As we examine the nature of believing faith in our day, we find ourselves asking, "Where is the mystery? Where is the reverence, the awe, the true fear of God among us?"

Genesis 17:1, 2-5; Isaiah 6:5,8
Men Who Met God, 22.

409. Faith: definition of; Salvation: by faith alone

In a dramatic story in the Book of Numbers (21:4-9) faith is seen in action. Israel became discouraged and spoke against God, and the Lord sent fiery serpents among them. "And they bit the people; and much people of Israel died" (v. 6). Then Moses sought the Lord for them and He heard and gave them a remedy against the bite of the serpents. He commanded Moses to make a serpent of brass and put it upon a pole in sight of all the people, "and it shall come to pass, that every one that is bitten, when he looketh upon it, shall live" (v. 8). Moses obeyed, "and it came to pass, that if a serpent had bitten any man, when he beheld the serpent of brass, he lived" (v. 9). . . .

Our plain man, in reading this, would make an important discovery. He would notice that *look* and *believe* are synonymous terms. "Looking" on the Old Testament serpent is identical with "believing" on the New Testament Christ. That is, the *looking* and the *believing* are the same thing. And he would understand that, while Israel looked with their external eyes, believing is done with the heart. I think he would conclude that *faith is the gaze of a soul upon a saving God.*

Numbers 21:4-9; Psalm 123:1-2;
John 3:14-15; Hebrews 12:1-2
The Pursuit of God, 88, 89.

410. Faith: expectation

True faith is never found alone; it is always accompanied by expectation. The man who believes the promises of God expects to see them fulfilled. Where there is no expectation, there is no faith.

Psalm 27:13; Romans 8:22-25; Hebrews 11:1-2
God Tells the Man Who Cares, 166.

411. Faith: expectation; Patience: God's timing; Prayer: unanswered

Faith in one of its aspects moves mountains; in another it gives patience to see the promises afar off and to wait quietly for their fulfillment. Insistence upon an immediate answer to every request of the soul is an evidence of religious infantilism. It takes God longer to grow an oak than to grow an ear of popcorn.

Matthew 11:23; Romans 12:9-13; Hebrews 11:13-16
The Next Chapter After the Last, 9, 10.

412. Faith: expectation; Unbelief

Unbelief says: Some other time, but not now; some other place, but not here; some other people, but not us. Faith says: Anything He did anywhere else He will do here; anything He did any other time He is willing to do now; anything He ever did for other people He is willing to do for us! With our feet on the ground, and our head cool, but with our heart ablaze with the love of God, we walk out in this fullness of the Spirit, if we will yield and obey. God wants to work through you!

The Counselor has come, and He doesn't care about the limits of locality, geography, time or nationality. The Body of Christ is bigger than all of these. The question is: Will you open your heart?

Matthew 13:58; 1 Thessalonians 2:13; Hebrews 4:2
The Counselor, 121.

413. Faith: foundation of

. . . faith is good only when it engages truth; when it is made to rest upon falsehood it can and often does lead to eternal tragedy.

For it is not enough that we believe; we must believe in the right thing about the right One!

Acts 4:12; Romans 15:13; 2 Timothy 1:11-12
Renewed Day by Day, Volume 1, Jan. 9.

414. Faith: foundation of; Bible: authority of; Church: authority

Faith in Jesus is not commitment to your church or denomination. I believe in the local church; I am not a tabernacle man. I believe in the divine assembly. We ought to realize that we are, as a group of Christians, a divine assembly, a cell in the body of Christ, alive with His life. But not for one second would I try to create in you a faith that would lead you to commit yourself irrevocably to a local church or to your church leaders.

You are not asked to follow your church leaders. You are not asked like a little robin on the nest to open your innocent little mouth and just take anything I put in. If what I put in is not biblical food, regurgitate and do not be afraid to do it. Call me or come see me or write me an anonymous letter. But do something about it. Do not, by any means, swallow what your leaders give you. Here is the book, the Bible: go to it.

Faith is faith in Jesus Christ, God's Son. It is total faith in Christ and not in a denomination or church, though you may love the church and respect and love your leaders and your denomination. But your commitment is to Christ.

John 5:36-40; John 17:11; 1 John 4:1
Rut, Rot or Revival: The Condition of the Church, 53, 54.

415. Faith: foundation of; Depression; Emotions

Faith is at the foundation of all Christian living, and because faith has to do with the character of God, it is safe from all vacillations of mood. A man may be believing soundly and effectively even when his mood is low, so low that he is hardly aware that he is alive emotionally at all.

Psalm 43:5; Psalm 71:12-14; Lamentations 3:19-23
The Next Chapter After the Last, 51.

416. Faith: foundation of; Faith: expectation

A father and his nine-year-old son have a close and trusting relationship. The father reminds his boy that in a month he will be observing his 10th birthday.

"Son," he begins, "I know that you want a bicycle. I am going to order a brand new red and white bicycle, and it will be here in time for you to begin riding it on the morning of your birthday. It will be your very own bicycle—you will be the owner!"

Is that excited boy going to wait a month before he tells his friends that he is the owner of a shining new bicycle? Oh, no! He runs out immediately to give the great news to his friends. He is full of faith. He is full of expectancy. He already knows within himself the pride of ownership. His faith has given substance to his boyish hope. His faith has given a reality to the bicycle he has not yet seen!

He is not reporting to his friends an imaginary projection of his mind. He has his father's word. He is able to speak with assurance: "Believe it or not, I own one of the most beautiful bicycles in the whole world!"

That boy knows he can trust the character of his father. His faith is not in the factory that makes the bicycle. It rests in the character and the ability of his father to keep the promise he has made.

But, of course, there is one little friend in the neighborhood who remains cynical and unbelieving.

"Don't give me that dreamy line about having a bicycle," the friend insists with some belligerence. "Who is going to believe your story? I don't see any shiny new bicycle in your front yard."

For an answer, the boy with the faith, the boy who already knows the delight of anticipation, simply smiles a knowing smile. "Just give me till my birthday, and when you see me riding my bike past your house, you will wish my father was your father, too!"

Romans 8:22-25; 2 Corinthians 4:16-18; Hebrews 11:1-2
Jesus, Author of Our Faith, 14, 15.

417. Faith: foundation of; Faith: gift of God

True faith rests upon the character of God and asks no further proof than the moral perfections of the One who cannot lie. It is enough that God said it, and if the statement should contradict every one of the five senses and all the conclusions of logic as well, still the believer continues to believe. "Let God be true, but every man a liar" is the language of true faith. Heaven approves such faith because it rises above mere proofs and rests in the bosom of God. . . .

Faith as the Bible knows it is confidence in God and His Son Jesus Christ; it is the response of the soul to the divine character as revealed in the Scriptures; and even this response is impossible apart from the prior inworking of the Holy Spirit. Faith is a gift of God to a penitent soul and has nothing whatsoever to do with the senses or the data they afford. Faith is a miracle; it is the ability God gives to trust His Son, and anything that does not result in action in accord with the will of God is not faith but something else short of it.

Romans 3:4; Ephesians 2:8-10; Titus 1:2
Man: The Dwelling Place of God, 32, 33.

418. Faith: foundation of;
Heaven: certainty of

True faith is not the intellectual ability to visualize unseen things to the satisfaction of our imperfect minds; it is rather the moral power to trust Christ. To be contented and unafraid when going on a journey with his father the child need not be able to imagine events; he need but know the father. Our earthly lives are one shining web of golden mystery which we experience without understanding, how much more our life in the Spirit. Jesus Christ is our all in all. We need but trust Him and He will take care of the rest. . . .

God has not failed me in this world; I can trust Him for the world to come.

Joshua 23:14; 1 Kings 8:56; Isaiah 42:16; 2 Corinthians 4:16-18; 2 Corinthians 5:1-8
That Incredible Christian, 70.

419. Faith: foundation of;
Knowledge of God: basis for faith

If our faith is to have a firm foundation we must be convinced beyond any possible doubt that God is altogether worthy of our trust. . . .

As long as we question the wisdom of any of God's ways our faith is still tentative and uncertain. While we are able to understand, we are not quite believing. Faith enters when there is no supporting evidence to corroborate God's word of promise and we must put our confidence blindly in the character of the One who made the promise. . . .

A promise is only as good as the one who made it, but it is as good, and from this knowledge springs our assurance. By cultivating the knowledge of God we at the same time cultivate our faith.

Psalm 22:3-5; Psalm 107:6-9; Romans 4:19-21
That Incredible Christian, 26, 28.

420. Faith: foundation of;
Knowledge of God: basis for faith; Church: concept of God

All things else being equal, the destiny of a man or nation may safely be predicted from the idea of God which that man or that nation holds. No nation can rise higher than its conception of God. . . .

A church is strong or weak just as it holds to a high or low idea of God. For faith rests not primarily upon promises, but upon character. A believer's faith can never rise higher than his conception of God. A promise is never better or worse than the character of the one who makes it. An inadequate conception of God must result in a weak faith, for faith depends upon the character of God just as a building rests upon its foundation. . . .

Job told us, "Acquaint thyself with him and be at peace"; and Paul said, "So then faith cometh by hearing, and hearing by the word of God." These two verses show the way to a strong and lasting faith: *Get acquainted with God through reading the Scriptures, and faith will come naturally.*

Job 22:21; Romans 10:17; Hebrews 10:19-23; 1 John 5:3-10
The Set of the Sail, 38, 39.

421. Faith: foundation of; Promises of God

Study the Scriptures and you will find that we are not going to have more faith by counting the promises of God. Faith does not rest upon promises. Faith rests upon character. Faith must rest in confidence upon the One who makes the promises.

Jesus, Author of Our Faith, 6.

422. Faith: foundation of; Promises of God

So, what is the promise for? A promise is given to me so that I may know intelligently what God has planned for me, what God will give me, and so what to claim. Those are the promises and they are intelligent directions. They rest upon the character and ability of the One who made them.

Let me illustrate. My estate consists principally of my books. I have a little household furniture, but not too much and none of it too expensive. That and my books are about all I have. But suppose when my heirs gather to listen to the reading of my will, they hear, "I leave to my son Lowell a yacht in the Gulf of Mexico; I leave to my son Stanley an estate of one hundred acres in Florida; I leave to my son Wendell all the mineral rights that I hold in Nevada." You know what would happen, do you not? Those boys of mine, gathered for the reading of the will, would say in sympathy, "Poor Dad! He must have been mentally deranged to write a will like that! It is a meaningless will because he owned none of those things. He cannot make good on that will!"

But when the richest man in the country dies, and they call in the heirs, everyone listens closely for his or her own name because this is a will with resources behind it. The man has made the will in order that his heirs may know what they can claim. Just so, faith does not rest merely on promises. It goes back to the character of the One who makes the promises.

Romans 4:19-21; Ephesians 3:20,21;
1 Thessalonians 5:23-24; 1 Peter 1:3-5
Faith Beyond Reason, 42, 43.

423. Faith: gift of God; Apologetics; Holy Spirit: conviction

Now, with all my heart I believe in the historicity of the Christian gospel, but that does not mean that the eternal fate of the individual man depends upon historic evidence. The Holy Spirit is here now to convince the world, and however we treat the warnings of the Holy Spirit is exactly how we treat Jesus Christ Himself.

If faith must depend upon a man knowing enough of the historical evidences to arrive at a scholarly belief in the deity of Jesus, then there could only be a relatively few people saved. But I do not have to be a scholar, a logician, or a lawyer to arrive at belief in the deity of the Lord Jesus Christ, for the Holy Spirit has taken the deity of Christ out of the hands of the scholars and put it in the consciences of men. The Spirit of God came to lift it out of the history books and write it on the fleshy tablets of the human heart. . . .

I find myself wondering about the great majority of preachers and teachers in Christian circles who seem so intent upon making the deity of Christ rest upon historical evidence. I think they must not discern that the Holy Spirit has taken that matter completely out of the realm of evidence and has put it as a burning point in the human conscience. It is no longer an intellectual problem—it is a moral problem!

Matthew 16:17; John 16:8; Ephesians 2:8-10
Echoes from Eden, 30, 31, 32.

424. Faith: gift of God; Man: sinfulness of; Conscience

In spite of our effort to make sinners think they are unhappy the fact is that wherever social and health conditions permit the masses of mankind enjoy themselves very much. Sin has its pleasures (Hebrews 11:25) and the vast majority of human beings have a whale of a time living. The conscience is a bit of a pest but most persons manage to strike a truce with it quite early in life and are not troubled much by it thereafter.

It takes a work of God in a man to sour him on the world and to turn him against himself; yet until this has happened to him he is psychologically unable to repent and believe. Any degree of contentment with the world's moral standards or his own lack of holiness successfully blocks off the flow of faith into the man's heart. Esau's fatal flaw was moral complacency; Jacob's only virtue was his bitter discontent.

John 6:37,44; Ephesians 2:8-10; Hebrews 11:24-26
The Set of the Sail, 143, 144.

425. Faith: intellectual only

Much of our trust in God depends on the fact that things have never gone wrong for us. The crisis time has never come. We figure that God is out there somewhere in case we come to that place of "last resort."

Men Who Met God, 73.

426. Faith: power of God

Your faith can stand in the text and you can be as dead as the proverbial doornail, but when the power of God moves in on the text and sets the sacrifice on fire, then you have Christianity. We try to call that revival, but it is not revival at all. It is simply New Testament Christianity. It is what it ought to have been in the first place, and was not. . . .

A church can go on holding the creed and the truth for generations and grow old. New people can follow and receive that same code and also grow old. Then some revivalist comes in and fires his guns and gets everybody stirred, and prayer moves God down on the scene and revival comes to that church. People who thought they were saved get saved. People who had only believed in a code now believe in Christ. And what has really happened? It is simply New Testament Christianity having its place. It is not any deluxe edition of Christianity; it is what Christianity should have been from the beginning.

Romans 13:11-14; Hebrews 6:11-12; Revelation 3:1-3
Faith Beyond Reason, 26, 27.

427. Faith: power of God; A.B. Simpson

At 36, [A.B.] Simpson was a Presbyterian preacher so sick that he said, "I feel I could fall into the grave when I have a funeral." He could not preach for months at a time because of his sickness. He went to a little camp meeting in the woods and heard a quartet sing, "No man can work like Jesus/ No man can work like Him." Simpson went off among the pine trees with that ringing in his heart: "Nobody can work like Jesus; nothing is too hard for Jesus. No man can work like Him." The learned, stiff-necked Presbyterian threw himself down upon the pine needles and said, "If Jesus Christ is what they said He was in the song, heal me." The Lord healed him, and he lived to be 76 years old. Simpson founded a society that is now one of the largest evangelical denominations in the world, The Christian and Missionary Alliance.

We are his descendants and we sing his songs. But are we going to allow ourselves to listen to that which will modify our faith, practices and beliefs, water down our gospel and dilute the power of the Holy Spirit? I, for one, am not!

Genesis 18:14; Jeremiah 32:17,27; James 5:15
Rut, Rot or Revival: The Condition of the Church,
108, 109.

428. Faith: shield of

The apostle Paul calls faith a shield. The man of faith can walk at ease, protected by his simple confidence in God. God loves to be trusted, and He puts all heaven at the disposal of the trusting soul.

Ephesians 6:16; 1 Thessalonians 5:1-8
That Incredible Christian, 51.

429. Faithfulness

I know that faithfulness is not a very dramatic subject and there are many among us in the Christian faith who would like to do something with more dash and more flair than just being faithful. Even in our Christian circles, publicity is considered a great and necessary thing, so we are prone to want to do something that will be recognized and perhaps get our picture in the paper. Thank God for the loyal and faithful Christians who have only one recognition in mind, and that is to hear their Lord say in that Great Day: "Well done, . . . enter into the joy of thy Lord."

Matthew 25:21,23; 1 Corinthians 4:2-3;
1 Corinthians 15:58
Who Put Jesus on the Cross?, 21, 22.

430. Faithfulness; Unsung heroes

The learned historians tell of councils and persecutions and religious wars, but in the midst of all the mummery were a few who saw the Eternal City in full view and managed almost to walk on earth as if they had already gone to heaven. These were the joyous ones who got little recognition from the world of institutionalized religion, and might have gone altogether unnoticed except for their singing.

Unsung but singing: this is the short and simple story of many today whose names are not known beyond the small circle of their own company. Their gifts are not many nor great, but their song is sweet and clear!

Psalm 95:1-2; Acts 16:25; Ephesians 5:18-19; James 5:13
Renewed Day by Day, Volume 1, Jan. 21.

431. Faithful service; Comparison

It is good to come to the understanding that while God wants us to be holy and Spirit-filled, He does not expect us to look like Abraham or to play the harp like David or to have the same spiritual insight given to Paul.

All of those former heroes of the faith are dead. You are alive in your generation. A Bible proverb says that it is better to be a living dog than a dead lion. You may wish to be Abraham or Isaac or Jacob, but remember that they have been asleep for long centuries, and you are still around! You can witness for your Lord today. You can still pray. You can still give of your substance to help those in need. You can still encourage the depressed.

I hope you have not missed something good from God's hand because you felt you did not measure up to Gideon or Isaiah. In this your generation, give God all of your attention! Give Him all of your love! Give Him all of your devotion and faithful service! You do not know what holy, happy secret God may want to whisper to your responsive heart.

Ecclesiastes 9:4; Acts 13:36; 1 Corinthians 12:18-27
Jesus, Author of Our Faith, 72.

432. Faithful service; True greatness

Judged by our tentative human standards mankind may be divided into four distinct classes: Those who are great but not good; those who are good but not great; those who are both great and good, and those who are neither good nor great. . . .

Then there are the men who are *good but not great*, and we may thank God that there are so many of them, being grateful not that they failed to achieve greatness but that by the grace of God they managed to acquire plain goodness. . . .

Every pastor knows this kind—the plain people who have nothing to recommend them but their deep devotion to their Lord and the fruit of the Spirit which they all unconsciously display. Without these the churches as we know them in city, town and country could not carry on. These are the first to come forward when there is work to be done and the last to go home when there is prayer to be made. They are not known beyond the borders of their own parish because there is nothing dramatic in faithfulness or newsworthy in goodness, but their presence is a benediction wherever they go. They have no greatness to draw to them the admiring eyes of carnal men but are content to be good men and full of the Holy Spirit, waiting in faith for the day that their true worth shall be known. When they die they leave behind them a fragrance of Christ that lingers long after the cheap celebrities of the day are forgotten.

Romans 12:3-8,11; 1 Corinthians 4:2-3; Galatians 5:22-23
God Tells the Man Who Cares, 98, 99, 100.

433. Fall of man; Man: alienation from God

When man fell through sin, he began to think of himself as having a soul instead of being one. It makes a lot of difference whether a man believes that he is a body having a soul or a soul having a body!

For the moral "unlikeness" between man and God the Bible has a word—alienation. The Holy Spirit presents a frightful picture of this alienation as it works itself out in human character. Fallen human nature is precisely opposite to the nature of God as revealed in Jesus Christ. Because there is no moral likeness there is no communion, hence the feeling that God is far away in space.

Isaiah 29:13; Matthew 15:8; Ephesians 2:1-3,19-20
Echoes from Eden, 5, 6.

434. Fall of man; Man: sinfulness of

The fall of man has created a perpetual crisis. It will last until sin has been put down and Christ reigns over a redeemed and restored world.

Until that time the earth remains a disaster area and its inhabitants live in a state of extraordinary emergency. . . .

It is not enough to say that we live in a state of moral crisis; that is true, but it is not all. . . .

So the Fall was a moral crisis but it has affected every part of man's nature, moral, intellectual, psychological, spiritual and physical. His whole being has been deeply injured; the sin in his heart has overflowed into his total life, affecting his relation to God, to his fellow men and to everyone and everything that touches him.

Genesis 3:14-19; Romans 5:12; 1 Corinthians 15:25-26
Born After Midnight, 28, 29.

435. Fall of Man; Sin: prevalence of

By that moral disaster known in theology as the fall of man an entire order of beings was wrenched violently loose from its proper place in the creational scheme and quite literally turned upside down. Human beings who had been specifically created to admire and adore the Deity turned away from Him and began to pour out their love first upon themselves and then upon whatever cheap and tawdry objects their lusts and passions found. The first chapter of Romans describes the journey of the human heart downward from the knowledge of God to the basest idolatry and fleshly sins. History is little more than the story of man's sin, and the daily newspaper a running commentary on it.

Genesis 3; Romans 1; Ephesians 2:1-3
Born After Midnight, 124, 125.

436. False hope

I recall a recent poll in which it was reported that 82 per cent of the American people expressed a belief in God and the expectation of going to heaven. Personally, I do not like to deal in percentages, but from what I know personally of American men and women I should like boldly and bluntly to say that I will guess that about three-fourths of that 82 percent are indulging an invalid hope.

It is sad, but it must be said that the earthly hope of men and women without God and without Christ and without faith is a vain hope.

Matthew 7:21-23; Ephesians 2:12-13
I Call It Heresy!, 40.

437. False teachers

Beware of any man who claims to be wiser than the apostles or holier than the martyrs of the Early Church. The best way to deal with him is to rise and leave his presence. You cannot help him and he surely cannot help you.

Matthew 7:15-16; Romans 16:17-18; 2 John 10-11
Man: The Dwelling Place of God, 126.

438. False teachers

The temptation to forget the few spiritual essentials and to go wandering off after unimportant things is very strong, especially to Christians of a certain curious type of mind. Such persons find the great majors of the faith of our fathers altogether too tame for them. Their souls loathe that light bread; their appetites crave the gamy tang of fresh-killed meat. They take great pride in their reputation as being mighty hunters before the Lord, and any time we look out we may see them returning from the chase with some new mystery hanging limply over their shoulder.

Usually the game they bring down is something on which there is a biblical closed season. Some vague hint in the Scriptures, some obscure verse about which the translators disagree, some marginal note for which there is not much scholarly authority: these are their favorite meat. They are especially skillful at propounding notions which have never been a part of the Christian heritage of truth. Their enthusiasm mounts with the uncertainty of their position, and their dogmatism grows firmer in proportion to the mystery which surrounds their subject.

Acts 17:21; Colossians 1:27
The Next Chapter After the Last, 12, 13.

439. False teaching

It is astonishing what some people will believe when they get going. They properly hold it a sin to doubt the Bible, so they refuse to doubt anything that is served up along with the Bible, however ridiculous and unscriptural it may be. If the story has a flavor of wonder about it, these uncritical friends will accept it without question and repeat it in an awed voice with much solemn shaking of the bowed head. Multiply such people in any given church, and you have a perfect soil for the growth of every kind of false teaching and fanatical excess.

We need to cultivate a healthy skepticism toward everything that cannot be supported by the plain teaching of the Bible. Belief is faith only when it has God's revealed truth for its object; beyond that it may be fully as injurious as unbelief itself.

Acts 17:11; Acts 20:28-31; 1 John 4:1
We Travel an Appointed Way, 5, 6.

440. False teaching

This new doctrine, this new religious habit, this new view of truth, this new spiritual experience—*how has it affected my attitude toward and my relation to God, Christ, the Holy Scrip-*

tures, self, other Christians, the world and sin. By this sevenfold test we may prove everything religious and know beyond a doubt whether it is of God or not. By the fruit of the tree we know the kind of tree it is. So we have but to ask about any doctrine or experience, What is this doing to me? and we know immediately whether it is from above or from below.

Matthew 7:15-16; 1 Thessalonians 5:20-21; 1 John 4:1
Man: The Dwelling Place of God, 121.

441. False teaching

In our constant struggle to believe we are likely to overlook the simple fact that a bit of healthy disbelief is sometimes as needful as faith to the welfare of our souls.

I would go further and say that we would do well to cultivate a reverent skepticism. It will keep us out of a thousand bogs and quagmires where others who lack it sometimes find themselves. It is no sin to doubt some things, but it may be fatal to believe everything. . . .

Faith never means gullibility. The man who believes everything is as far from God as the man who refuses to believe anything.

Acts 17:11; 1 John 4:1
The Root of the Righteous, 119, 120.

442. Fame; Celebrities

The social royalty of a few generations ago has passed away. Though their names were in the Who's Who they didn't happen to know what's what!

Matthew 6:19-21; 1 Timothy 6:17-19; 1 John 2:15-17
I Call It Heresy!, 103.

443. Fanatics

People use the word *fanatic* whenever you get a little bit joyful about the Lord. They say you are a fanatic. Webster says that a fanatic is somebody who is too enthusiastic about religion, as if you could be too enthusiastic about religion.

Rut, Rot or Revival: The Condition of the Church, 48.

444. Fanatics; Extremists; Amen

I think it is ironic that the devil gives the world all of its extremists in every realm—entertainment, politics, society, education, anarchy, intrigue—you name it! Yet it is the same devil that frightens believers about the great danger of becoming "extreme."

I passed an auditorium recently where one of the young crowd of singing stars was appearing. Police were having great trouble with the crowds and in the erotic fury of that concert, girls began to tear off their clothes; many were weeping and screaming. Those who had fainted were being carried out.

It is the same devil, but he uses different tactics in dealing with Christians. Should a Christian get blessed and say, "Amen," the devil quickly intervenes and whispers, "Don't be a fanatic—you ought to stay quiet and stable in the faith!"

Psalm 98:1-6; Psalm 150; Isaiah 44:23
I Talk Back to the Devil, 11, 12.

445. Fear

No matter what the circumstances, we Christians should keep our heads. God has not given us the spirit of fear, but of power, of love and of a sound mind. It is a dismal thing to see a son of heaven cringe in terror before the sons of earth. We are taught by the Holy Spirit in Scriptures of truth that fear is a kind of prison for the mind and that by it we may spend a lifetime in bondage....

I could quote hundreds of passages from the Holy Scriptures to show that God keeps His people and that there is nothing in earth or in hell that can harm a trusting soul. The past is forgiven, the present is in God's keeping and a thousand bright promises give assurance for the future. Yet we are sometimes terrified by the adversary. This is not uncommon but it is unnecessary. We should not try to excuse it, but rather acknowledge it as evidence of our spiritual immaturity.

Joshua 1:7-8; John 14:27; Ephesians 6:10-12; 2 Timothy 1:6-7
The Warfare of the Spirit, 55, 56.

446. Fear; God: His love; God: His sovereignty

The world is full of enemies, and as long as we are subject to the possibility of harm from these enemies, fear is inevitable. The effort to conquer fear without removing the causes is altogether futile. The heart is wiser than the apostles of tranquillity. As long as we are in the hands of chance, as long as we look for hope to the law of averages, as long as we must trust for survival to our ability to out think or outmaneuver the enemy, we have every good reason to be afraid. And fear hath torment.

To know that love is of God and to enter into the secret place leaning upon the arm of the Beloved—this and only this can cast out fear. Let a man become convinced that nothing can harm him and instantly for him all fear goes out of the universe. The nervous reflex, the natural revulsion to physical pain may be felt sometimes, but the deep torment of fear is gone forever. God is love and God is sovereign. His love disposes Him to desire our everlasting welfare and His sovereignty enables Him to secure it. Nothing can hurt a good man.

Romans 8:35-39; 2 Timothy 1:6-7; 1 John 4:7-8,18
The Knowledge of the Holy, 154, 155.

447. Fear; God: His sovereignty

Living in this generation, we are fully aware that the competitive world and our selfish society have brought many new fears to the human race. I can empathize with those troubled beings who lie awake at night worrying about the possible destruction of the race through some evil, misguided use of the world's store of nuclear weapons. The tragedy is that they have lost all sense of the sovereignty of God! I, too, would not sleep well if I could not trust moment by moment in God's sovereignty and omnipotence and in His grace, mercy and faithfulness.

The prevailing attitudes of fear, distrust and unrest permeating our world are known to all of us. But in God's plan some of us also know a beautiful opposite: the faith and assurance found in the church of Jesus Christ. God still has a restful "family" in His church.

Psalm 3:3-6; Psalm 4:8; Proverbs 3:24
Jesus Is Victor!, 14, 15.

448. Fear; Will of God

The only fear I have is to fear to get out of the will of God. Outside of the will of God, there's nothing I want, and in the will of God there's nothing I fear, for God has sworn to keep me in His will. If I'm out of His will, that is another matter. But if I'm in His will, He's sworn to keep me.

And He's able to do it, He's wise enough to know how to do it and He's kind enough to want to do it. So really there's nothing to fear.

I get kidded by my family and friends about this, but I don't really think I'm afraid of anything. Someone may ask, "What about cancer? Do you ever fear that you'll die of cancer?" Maybe so, but it will have to hurry up, or I'll die of old age first. But I'm not too badly worried because a man who dies of cancer in the will of God, is not injured; he's just dead. You can't harm a man in the will of God.

Psalm 119:165; Proverbs 3:1-2; Isaiah 26:3
Success and the Christian, 80, 81.

449. Fear of God

A truth fully taught in the Scriptures and verified in personal experience by countless numbers of holy men and women through the centuries might be condensed thus into a religious axiom: *No one can know the true grace of God who has not first known the fear of God.* . . .

I do not believe that any lasting good can come from religious activities that do not root in this quality of creature-fear. The animal in us is very strong and altogether self-confident. Until it has been defeated God will not show Himself to the eyes of our faith. Until we have been gripped by that nameless terror which results when an unholy creature is suddenly confronted by that One who is the holiest of all, we are not likely to be much affected by the doctrine of love and grace as it is declared by the New Testament evangel. The love of God affects a carnal heart not at all; or if at all, then adversely, for the knowledge that God loves us may simply confirm us in our self-righteousness.

Exodus 3:5-6; Psalm 111:10; Proverbs 9:10; Revelation 1:17
The Root of the Righteous, 38, 39.

450. Fear of God

Whence then does the true fear of God arise? From the knowledge of our own sinfulness and a sense of the presence of God. . . .

A congregation will feel this mysterious terror of God when the minister and the leaders of the church are filled with the Spirit. When Moses came down from the mount with his face shining the children of Israel were afraid with a fear born out of that supernatural sight. Moses did not need to threaten them. He had only to appear before them with that light on his face.

Exodus 34:29; Isaiah 6:5, 8; Luke 5:8
The Root of the Righteous, 41.

451. Fear of God; God: His transcendence; God: His awesomeness

In olden days men of faith were said to "walk in the fear of God" and to "serve the Lord with fear." However intimate their communion with God, however bold their prayers, at the base of their religious life was the conception of God as awesome and dreadful. This idea of God transcendent runs through the whole Bible and gives color and tone to the character of the saints. This fear of God was more than a natural apprehension of danger; it was a nonrational dread, an acute feeling of personal insufficiency in the presence of God the Almighty.

Wherever God appeared to men in Bible times the results were the same—an overwhelming sense of terror and dismay, a wrenching sensation of sinfulness and guilt. When God spoke, Abram stretched himself upon the ground to listen. When Moses saw the Lord in the burning bush, he hid his face in fear to look upon God. Isaiah's vision of God wrung from him the cry, "Woe is me!" and the confession, "I am undone; because I am a man of unclean lips."

Exodus 3:1-6; Nehemiah 5:9; Psalm 2:10-11; Isaiah 6:5, 8
The Knowledge of the Holy, 110, 111.

452. Fear of God; Submission; God: His awesomeness

These experiences show that a vision of the divine transcendence soon ends all controversy between the man and his God. The fight goes out of the man and he is ready with the conquered Saul to ask meekly, "Lord, what wilt thou have me to do?" Conversely, the self-assurance of modern Christians, the basic levity present in so many of our religious gatherings, the shocking disrespect shown for the Person of God, are evidence enough of deep blindness of heart. Many call themselves by the name of Christ, talk much about God, and pray to Him sometimes, but evidently do not know who He is. "The fear of the Lord is a fountain of life," but this healing fear is today hardly found among Christian men.

Proverbs 14:27; Isaiah 6:5, 8; Daniel 10:5-9; Acts 9:6
The Knowledge of the Holy, 112.

453. Fear of God; Worship: reverential fear

When we come into this sweet relationship, we are beginning to learn astonished reverence, breathless adoration, awesome fascination, lofty admiration of the attributes of God and something of the breathless silence that we know when God is near.

You may never have realized it before, but all of those elements in our perception and consciousness of the divine Presence add up to what the Bible calls "the fear of God.". . .

There are very few unqualified things in our lives, but I believe that the reverential fear of God mixed with love and fascination and astonishment and admiration and devotion is the most enjoyable state and the most purifying emotion the human soul can know.

Psalm 4:4; Psalm 33:6-9; 2 Corinthians 7:1
Whatever Happened to Worship?, 30, 31.

454. Following Christ; Christians: other-worldly

If we truly want to follow God, we must seek to be other-worldly. This I say knowing well that word has been used with scorn by the sons of this world and applied to the Christian as a badge of reproach. So be it. Every man must choose his world. If we who follow Christ, with all the facts before us and knowing what we are about, deliberately choose the Kingdom of God as our sphere of interest, I see no reason why anyone should object. If we lose by it, the loss is our own; if we gain, we rob no one by so doing. The "other world," which is the object of this world's disdain and the subject of the drunkard's mocking song, is our carefully chosen goal and the object of our holiest longing.

Matthew 16:24-26; Philippians 3:10; Colossians 3:1-4
The Pursuit of God, 52, 53.

455. Forgiveness; Grace

One of the old German devotional philosophers took the position that God loves to forgive big sins more than He does little sins because the bigger the sin, the more glory accrues to Him for his forgiveness. I remember the writer went on to say that not only does God forgive sins and enjoy doing it, but as soon as He has forgiven them, He forgets them and trusts the person just as if he or she had never sinned. I share his view that God not only forgives great sins as readily as little ones, but once He has forgiven them He starts anew right there and never brings up the old sins again. . . .

When a person makes a mistake and has to be forgiven, the shadow may hang over him or her because it is hard for other people to forget. But when God forgives, He begins the new page right there, and then the devil runs up and says, "What about this person's past?" God replies: "What past? There is no past. We started out fresh when he came to Me and I forgave him!"

Psalm 103:10-12; Luke 7:36-50; Romans 8:1
Faith Beyond Reason, 112.

456. Forgiveness; Grace; Failure

If you think that there is anyone in the world so good that God could do something for that person's sake, you don't know sin; and if you think there is anything that God will not do for you for His sake and for His name, you don't know God!

If you have failed, remember that you are not responsible to men in this regard. You stand responsible before your heavenly Father and Jesus Christ at the right hand of God. Let us be encouraged by this good news!

Psalm 23:3; Psalm 106:8; Romans 9:14-16; Ephesians 2:4-10; 1 John 2:12
I Talk Back to the Devil, 9.

457. Forgiveness; Mercy

I recall a true story told us by Rev. D.C. Kopp, missionary to Africa, on one of his furloughs from the Congo. He described the office of deacon in the national church and told of a fine stalwart Christian brother who had the job of disciplining the converts.

One young convert was proving to be a source of real trouble in the church because he was inclined to break the rules and do the things that a Christian brother should not do.

After he had been disciplined many times, this concerned deacon called in the erring brother once more and told him frankly, "Now, brother, you have been failing us and disappointing us and disgracing your Christian calling and it is about enough! When we started dealing with you we had a bottle of forgiveness, but I am here to tell you that that bottle is just about empty! We are just about through with you!"

The missionary got a chuckle out of that incident for he thought it was a quaint and picturesque way to let the brother know that he was no longer passing inspection. But, on the other hand, it is far from being a demonstration of God's dealing with us for the bottle of God's forgiveness has neither top nor bottom!

God has never yet said to a man, "The bottle of my mercy is just about empty!"

Psalm 51:1; Psalm 100:5; Lamentations 3:19-23
I Call It Heresy!, 52, 53.

458. Freedom; Body of Christ

The spirit of complete inward freedom is a precious heritage from the cross and should be treasured as one of life's most wonderful possessions. It is our privilege to be wholly free from evil habits, from superstition, from the fear of men, from the slavery of popular customs, from the necessity of pleasing the self-elected dictators of society. Such freedom is wondrously delightful, near to the joy of heaven itself.

Our Lord said, "And ye shall know the truth, and the truth shall make you free. . . . If the Son therefore shall make you free, ye shall be free indeed."

Yet such a happy soul has no feeling of independence; he is deeply conscious that he is a member of a larger body of which Christ is the head, and he willingly acknowledges his indebtedness to all other Christians. . . .

It is most important that this truth be grasped firmly and taught faithfully, for as long as we are in this mortal body, there will always be danger from one or the other of these two extremes, slavish dependence or arrogant independence.

John 8:31-32,36; Romans 14:7-9; Galatians 5:1,13
The Next Chapter After the Last, 60, 61.

459. Freedom; Christians: true freedom

That is one of the great fallacies held by unbelievers—thinking that the Christian must surrender his or her freedom in order to be a Christian. The notion is one of Satan's inventions, but it is still effective in our day. The devil is able to make sinners imagine they are free!

But it is the Christian who is really free. The Christian has liberty from his or her burden of guilt. The Christian is free from the nasty temper and human jealousies. The Christian is free from slavery to alcohol, tobacco and other substances. Best of all, the Christian is finally free from a thousand fears, including the fear of death and hell.

The unsaved person is hanging on to his or her freedom to sin, to pile up judgment, to get old and to die without God.

John 8:31-32; Romans 6:16-18; Romans 8:15; Galatians 5:1,13
Men Who Met God, 66.

460. Freedom; Conviction

A free Christian should act from within with a total disregard for the opinions of others. If a course is right he should take it because it is right, not because he is afraid not to take it. And if it is wrong he should avoid it though he lose every earthly treasure and even his very life as a consequence.

Fear of the opinion of the group tends to regiment the members of denominations and churches and force them into a cookie-cutter uniformity. The desire to stand well within our own circle of religious friends destroys originality and makes imitators of us. Various churches have their approved experiences, their religious accents, even their accepted religious tones; these become standard for the group and are to the local fellowship what circumcision was to Israel, a ceremonial token of acceptance into the clan.

The great fault in all this is that it shifts the life motivation from within to without, from God to our fellowman. Any act done because we are afraid not to do it is of the same moral quality as the act that is not done because we are afraid to do it. Fear, not love and faith, dictates the conduct, and whatsoever is not of faith is sin.

Romans 14:5,23
Of God and Men, 118.

461. Freedom; Conviction; Expectations

There is a foolish consistency which brings us into bondage to the consciences of other people. Our Christian testimony has created a certain expectation in the minds of our friends, and rather than jeopardize our standing with them we dutifully act in accordance with their expectation even though we have no inward conviction on the matter. We are simply afraid not to do what people expect of us. We cannot face our public after we have failed to do what we know they expected us to do.

This morality by public pressure is not pure morality at all. At best it is a timid righteousness of doubtful parentage; at worst it is the child of weakness and fear. A free Christian should act from within with a total disregard for the opinions of others. If a course is right he should take it because it is right, not because he is afraid not to take it. And if it is wrong he should avoid it, though he lose every friend, his property, his freedom and even his very life as a consequence....

Make a complete surrender to God; love Him with all your heart and love every man for His sake. Determine to obey your own convictions as they crystallize within you as a result of prayer and constant study of the Scriptures. After that you may safely ignore the expectations of your friends as well as the criticisms of your enemies. You will experience first the shocked surprise of the regimented army of lock-step believers, then their grudging admiration, and if you continue to walk the way of love and courage they will take heart from your example, throw off the bondage of fear and go forth as ransomed men and women to walk in the sweet liberty wherewith Christ has made them free.

Matthew 7:1; Romans 14:5; Galatians 5:1
The Price of Neglect, 62, 63, 64.

462. Freedom; Liberty; Servanthood

Freedom is liberty within bounds: liberty to obey holy laws, liberty to keep the commandments of Christ, to serve mankind, to develop to the full all the latent possibilities within our redeemed natures. True Christian liberty never sets us free to indulge our lusts or to follow our fallen impulses. . . .

Unqualified freedom in any area of human life is deadly. In government it is anarchy, in domestic life free love, and in religion antinomianism. The freest cells in the body are cancer cells, but they kill the organism where they grow. A healthy society requires that its members accept a limited freedom. Each must curtail his own liberty that all may be free, and this law runs throughout all the created universe, including the kingdom of God. . . .

The ideal Christian is one who knows he is free to do as he will and wills to be a servant. This is the path Christ took; blessed is the man who follows Him.

1 Corinthians 8:9; 1 Corinthians 9:19; Galatians 5:1,13; 1 Peter 2:16
God Tells the Man Who Cares, 185, 186, 187, 189.

463. Free will; Repentance

It is inherent in the nature of man that his will must be free. Made in the image of God who is completely free, man must enjoy a measure of freedom. This enables him to select his companions for this world and the next; it enables him to yield his soul to whom he will, to give allegiance to God or the devil, to remain a sinner or become a saint. . . .

God will take nine steps toward us, but He will not take the tenth. He will *incline* us to repent, but He cannot do our repenting for us. It is of the essence of repentance that it can only be done by the one who committed the act to be repented of. God can wait on the sinning man; He can withhold judgment; He can exercise long-suffering to the point where He appears "lax" in His judicial administration; but He cannot force a man to repent. To do this would be to violate the man's freedom and void the gift God originally bestowed upon him. . . .

The true saint is one who acknowledges that he possesses from God the gift of freedom. He knows that he will never be cudgeled into obedience nor wheedled like a petulant child into doing the will of God; he knows that these methods are unworthy both of God of his own soul. He knows he is free to make any choice he will, and with that knowledge he chooses forever the blessed will of God.

Deuteronomy 30:19; Joshua 24:14-15; 2 Peter 3:9
That Incredible Christian, 29, 30, 31.

464. Friends: fair-weather

The woods are strangely silent now, where a few short weeks ago a thousand bird voices chorused the rising and setting of the sun.

Where are they, those rustic Carusos of the tree and bush, those Asaphs of the field and the hedgerow? Shame to tell, but they have gone from us just when we needed them most. They have fled to the south to escape the first breath of winter. They nested in our trees and fed in our grainfields while the summer was with us, but they forgot so soon, and they left us without so much as a friendly dip of a departing wing. And we are hurt a little, for we loved them well, and in spite of past experiences we trusted them, too. Nothing with so much melody in its throat could be faithless, so we thought, but we were wrong again—they have betrayed our confidence. They are gone, and while we are shivering beneath our turned-up coat collars they will be soaring over meadows alive with warmth and flowers and bright-hued insects.

Well, we can forgive them, for apparently nature made them to inhabit the sunshine; the frost kills their enthusiasm and destroys their song. They are summer friends, and we may as well accept them for what they are. But the flight of the summer birds can point up a moral for us if we are wise enough to see it, and the consideration of the birds might well make some of us uncomfortable. For there are Christians that seem built for the sunshine only. They require a favorable temperature before they can act like Christians—they have never learned to carry their own climate with them. Those who manage to generate an unbelievable amount of enthusiasm while things are going well disappear at the first sign of trouble. They cannot serve God in the snow—they are strictly summer birds. They desert us at the approach of winter....

Far too many religious persons are summer friends.

Matthew 26:56; 2 Timothy 4:16; Revelation 2:4-5
This World: Playground or Battleground?, 46, 47, 48.

465. Friends: right kind

Who are your friends? It is important to make and cherish the right kind of friends.

I value friendship very highly. We can appreciate and honor one another in friendship, whether or not the other person is a believer. Because it is possible that friendships can be beautiful and helpful, I have always felt something like a churlish heel to insist that certain friendships must be broken off if you want to truly serve God. But our Lord Jesus said it more bluntly than I ever could say it. He told us that in being His disciples we must take up our cross and follow Him. He said there would be instances when we must forsake those who would hold us back—even if they were our own relatives and close friends. Jesus Christ must be first in your heart and mind. It is He who reminds you that the salvation of your soul is of prime importance.

Better to have no friends and be an Elijah, alone, than to be like Lot in Sodom, surrounded by friends who all but damned him. If you give your cherished friendship to the ungodly counselor and the mocker, you have given the enemy the key to your heart. You have opened the gate, and the city of your soul will be overwhelmed and taken!

Genesis 13:12-13; 1 Kings 19:10; Psalm 1:1-3; Matthew 10:34-39
Tragedy in the Church: The Missing Gifts, 127, 128.

466. Friendship with God

The idea of the divine-human friendship originated with God. Had not God said first "Ye are my friends" it would be inexcusably brash for any man to say "I am a friend of God." But since He claims us for His friends it is an act of unbelief to ignore or deny the relationship....

The infinite God and the finite man can merge their personalities in the tenderest, most satisfying friendship. In such relationship there is no idea of equality; only of likeness where the heart of man meets the heart of God....

The more perfect our friendship with God becomes the simpler will our lives be. Those formalities that are so necessary to keep a casual friendship alive may be dispensed with when true friends sit in each other's presence. True friends trust each other.

There is a great difference between having "company" and having a friend in the house. The friend we can treat as a member of the family, but company must be entertained.

God is not satisfied until there exists between Him and His people a relaxed informality that requires no artificial stimulation. The true friend of God may sit in His presence for long periods in silence. Complete trust needs no words of assurance. Such words have long ago been spoken and the adoring heart can safely be still before God.

Unquestionably the highest privilege granted to man on earth is to be admitted into the circle of the friends of God.

Psalm 62:1,5-8; Psalm 63; John 15:14-16; 1 John 1:1-3
That Incredible Christian, 119, 120, 121.

467. Friendship with God

The whole outlook of mankind might be changed if we could all believe that we dwell under a friendly sky and that the God of heaven, though exalted in power and majesty, is eager to be friends with us.

Proverbs 18:24; John 15:14-16
The Knowledge of the Holy, 129.

468. Friendship with God

God's love tells us that He is friendly and His Word assures us that He is our friend and wants us to be His friends. No man with a trace of humility would first think that he is a friend of God; but the idea did not originate with men. Abraham would never have said, "I am God's friend," but God Himself said that Abraham was His friend. The disciples might well have hesitated to claim friendship with Christ, but Christ said to them, "Ye are my friends." Modesty may demur at so rash a thought, but audacious faith dares to believe the Word and claim friendship with God. We do God more honor by believing what He has said about Himself and having the courage to come boldly to the throne of grace than by hiding in self-conscious humility among the trees of the garden.

Proverbs 18:24; John 15:14-16; Hebrews 4:16; James 2:23
The Knowledge of the Holy, 155.

469. Friendship with God; God: His presence

After all, what higher privilege and experience is granted to mankind on earth than to be admitted into the circle of the friends of God? . . .

It is well for us to remember that Divine-human friendship originated with God. Had God not first said "You are My friends," it would be inexcusably brash for any man to say, "I am a friend of God." But since God claims us for His friends, it is an act of unbelief to deny the offer of such a relationship. . . .

The spiritual giants of old were those who at some time became acutely conscious of the presence of God. They maintained that consciousness for the rest of their lives. . . .

The essential point is this: These were men who met and experienced God! How otherwise can the saints and prophets be explained? How otherwise can we account for the amazing power for good they have exercised over countless generations?

Is it not that indeed they had become friends of God? Is it not that they walked in conscious communion with the real Presence and addressed their prayers to God with the artless conviction that they were truly addressing Someone actually there?

John 15:14-16; Hebrews 11
Men Who Met God, 13, 14.

470. Fundamentals; Simplicity; Priorities

In life there will be found certain great fundamentals, like pillars bearing up the weight of some mighty building. . . .

The wise man will simplify his life by going to the center of it. He will look well to the foundations and, having done that, he will not worry about the rest.

Life as we know it in our painfully intricate civilization can be deadly unless we learn to distinguish the things that matter from those that do not. It is never the major things that destroy us, but invariably the multitude of trifling things which are mistakenly thought to be of major importance. These are so many that, unless we get out from under them, they will crush us body and soul. . . .

Every believer as well as every minister of Christ must decide whether he will put his emphasis upon the majors or the minors. He must decide whether he will stay by the sober truths which constitute the beating heart of the Scriptures or turn his attention to those marginal doctrines which always bring division and which, at their best, could not help us much on our way to the Celestial City.

Acts 15:24-29; Romans 2:18; Philippians 1:9-11
The Next Chapter After the Last, 11, 14.

471. Fund-raising; Church: finances

Now, let's get something straight at the outset. When Jesus said that His disciples could lay up treasures in heaven, He did not mean to imply or infer that if you give $10 to foreign missions this year, you will have $10 waiting for you in heaven!

You actually would not believe some of the gross misinterpretations which have been placed upon this teaching in order to get people to part with money for religious purposes.

I have seen a printed certificate issued by a certain tabernacle and which purports to be a bond issued against the Bank of Heaven. They printed it with all those fancy little curlicues, with gold and gilt edges, and stamped with an official-looking seal that really made it appear bona fide.

While I didn't memorize the wording of the text on the printed bond, it was something to this effect: "You pay into this church the sum of $100, and then, when the Lord comes, you take this bond with you, and you will get your $100 back, plus 100 percent interest."

Yes, I tell you, I saw that certificate as it had been issued. People often say to me, "Now, Brother Tozer, be charitable!" But I can't be charitable with a skunk! That kind of thing needs to be exposed before the whole wide world.

That is religious racketeering, pure and simple!

Matthew 6:19-21; Acts 20:33; 1 Thessalonians 2:4-6
The Tozer Pulpit, Volume 1, Book 1, 45, 46.

472. Funerals; Death: triumph in

We have long been of the opinion that for the blood-washed Christian the worst thing about dying is the funeral. Even among gospel Christians the funeral obsequies have degenerated into a gloomy ordeal that leaves everybody miserable for days. The only one not affected by the general heaviness that hangs over everything is the servant of God who has died and in whose honor the service is held. He has gone where the wicked cease from troubling and the weary be at rest. The minister and the undertaker, however, see to it that those who remain are neither untroubled nor at rest.

An odd contradiction exists here, for dolefulness is just what everybody is trying to avoid. Every effort is made to create the impression that the deceased is not really dead, and that the cemetery is not a graveyard at all but a pleasant park where everything is bright and full of cheer. Strangely enough, in spite of this obvious effort, the average funeral (even the Christian funeral) succeeds only in accenting the presence of death all the more. The dimmed lights, the low music, the smell of cut flowers, the unnatural tones of the minister and his slow march ahead of the coffin all contribute to the feeling of utter futility with which the service is charged. . . .

The note of joyous triumph is gone. The whole mood reflects the plaintive hopelessness of paganism. By our conduct at the funeral of those who sleep in Jesus we cancel out the testimony they gave while they lived. It is time for a change.

John 14:1-3; 2 Corinthians 5:1-8; Philippians 1:21-24; 1 Thessalonians 4:13-18
The Price of Neglect, 8, 9, 11.

473. Futility: feelings of; Individual importance

Many people are having their greatest battles over their deepening sense of futility and uselessness. It is important that we grasp God's revelation that every one of us is essential to His great plan for the ages. You will seek answers in vain from fellow men and women. Seek your answers rather from God and His Word. He is sovereign; He is still running His world.

God wants us to know that He must have all the parts in order to compose His great eternal symphony. He would have us assured that each one of us is indispensable to His grand theme!

Psalm 23; Psalm 100:3; Isaiah 12:2; 1 Corinthians 12:18-27
Jesus, Our Man in Glory, 33, 34.

474. Futility: of the world; Peace: false

It is time that we Christians awake to the fact that the world cannot help us in anything that matters. Not the educators nor the legislators nor the scientists can bring us tranquillity of heart, and without tranquillity whatever else they give us is useless at last. For more than half a lifetime I have listened to their promises, and they have so far failed to make good on one of them. To turn to God is now the only reasonable thing to do; we have no second choice. "Lord, to whom shall we go? thou hast the words of eternal life." . . .

All they have given us is the control of a few diseases and the debilitating comforts of push-button living. These have extended our lives a little longer so we are now able to stay around to see our generation die one by one; and when the riper years come upon us they retire us by compulsion and turn us out to clutter up a world that has no place for us, a world that does not understand us and that we do not understand.

Ecclesiastes 12:1-8; Isaiah 55:1-2; John 6:68
Born After Midnight, 110, 111.

475. Future; Faith: confidence in God

It is wholly impossible for us to know what lies before us, but it is possible to know something vastly more important. A quaint but godly American preacher of a generation past said it for us. "Abraham went out not knowing whither he went," said he, "but he knew Who was going with him." We cannot know for certain the what and the whither of our earthly pilgrimage, but we can be sure of the Who. And nothing else really matters.

Genesis 12:1-4; John 10:4; 2 Timothy 1:11-12; Hebrews 11:8-10
The Warfare of the Spirit, 104.

476. Future; Faith: expectation

Now, in conclusion, the Christian's future is still before him. I will give you time to smile at that, because it sounds like a self-evident bromide if ever one was uttered. But I assure you that it is not a self-evident banality; it is rather a proof that we ought to ponder soberly the fact than many Christians already have their future behind them. Their glory is behind them. The only future they have is their past. They are always lingering around the cold ashes of yesterday's burned-out campfire. Their testimonies indicate it, their outlook and their uplook reveal it and their downcast look betrays it! Above all, their backward look indicates it. I always get an uneasy feeling when I find myself with people who have nothing to discuss but the glories of the days that are past.

Yes, the Christian's future is before him. The whole direction of the Christian's look should be forward. . . .

Prospect is the word for you and me. Look forward! Look ahead! Live with faith and expectation because the Christian's future is more glorious than his past!

Luke 9:57-62; Philippians 3:13-14; Hebrews 12:1-2
I Call It Heresy!, 86, 87, 88.

477. Future; God: His sovereignty

First, the Holy Scriptures tell us what we could never learn any other way: They tell us what we are, who we are, how we got here, why we are here and what we are required to do while we remain here. They trace our history from the beginning down to the present time and on into the centuries and millenniums ahead. They track us into the atomic age, through the space age and on into the golden age. They reveal that at an appropriate time the direction of the world will be taken away from men and placed in the hands of the Man who alone has the wisdom and power to rule it....

All this being true, still we Christians can sing at the foot of the threatening volcano. Things have not gotten out of hand. However bad they look, the Lord sits king forever and reigns over the affairs of men. He makes the wrath of man to praise Him and the remainder of wrath He will restrain (see Psalm 29:10, 76:10).

Psalm 2; Psalm 76:10; Daniel 4:17,34-35
Of God and Men, 30, 31, 32.

478. Future; Hope; Eternal perspective; Prophecy

As we move into deeper personal acquaintance with the Triune God I think our life emphasis will shift from the past and the present to the future. Slowly we will become children of a living hope and sons of a sure tomorrow. Our hearts will be tender with memories of yesterday and our lives sweet with gratitude to God for the sure way we have come; but our eyes will be focused more and more upon the blessed hope of tomorrow.

Much of the Bible is devoted to prediction. Nothing God has yet done for us can compare with all that is written in the sure word of prophecy. And nothing He has done or may yet do for us can compare with *what He is and will be to us.*

1 Corinthians 2:9-10; Titus 2:11-14; 1 Peter 1:3-5
Of God and Men, 155.

479. Future; Hope; Eternity

Amid all the world religions, only Christianity is able to proclaim the Bible's good news that God, the Creator and Redeemer, will bring a new order into being! Indeed, that is the only good news available to a fallen race today. God has promised a new order that will be of eternal duration and infused with eternal life.

How amazing!

It is a promise from God of a new order to be based upon the qualities the exact opposite of mankind's universal blight—temporality and mortality. God promises the qualities of perfection and eternity—qualities that cannot now be found anywhere on this earth.

What a prospect!

Acts 1:9-11; 1 Corinthians 15:51,57; Revelation 21-22
Tragedy in the Church: The Missing Gifts, 130, 131.

G

480. Giving

Some people have the brass to think they are bailing out the living God when they drop a ten dollar bill in the church offering plate on Sunday.

I do not think I exaggerate when I say that some of us put our offering in the plate with a kind of triumphant bounce as much as to say: "There—now God will feel better!"

This may hurt some of you but I am obliged to tell you that God does not need anything you have. He does not need a dime of your money. It is your own spiritual welfare at stake in such matters as these. There is a beautiful and enriching principle involved in our offering to God what we are and what we have, but none of us are giving because there is a depression in heaven.

The Bible teaching is plain: you have the right to keep what you have all to yourself—but it will rust and decay, and ultimately ruin you.

Matthew 6:19-21; 2 Corinthians 8:2-5; 1 Timothy 6:17-19
Christ the Eternal Son, 39, 40.

481. Giving; Church: finances

Remember, *my giving will be rewarded not by how much I gave but by how much I had left.* Ministers are sometimes tempted to shy away from such doctrine as this lest they offend the important givers in their congregation. But it is better to offend men than to grieve the blessed Spirit of God which dwells in the church. No man ever yet killed a true church by withdrawing his gifts from it because of a personal pique. The Church of the First-born is not dependent upon the patronage of men. No man has ever been able really to harm a church by boycotting it financially. The moment we admit that we fear the displeasure of the carnal givers in our congregations we admit also that our congregations are not of heaven but of the earth. A heavenly church will enjoy a heavenly and supernatural prosperity. She cannot be starved out. The Lord will supply her needs.

2 Corinthians 9:7-8; Philippians 4:18-19; 1 Timothy 6:17-19
God Tells the Man Who Cares, 183.

482. Giving; Fund-raising

It is to the everlasting credit of God's children that they can be moved to sacrificial giving by a touching story or the sight of human suffering. It is only necessary to fly around the world and return with pictures of human misery, and God's dear sheep will promptly go down on their hunkers and permit themselves to be sheared down to the skin by persons morally unworthy to clean out the sheep pen. The tender-hearted saints think with their feelings and pour out consecrated wealth indiscriminately on projects wholly unworthy of their support. Most Christians are hesitant to question the honesty of anyone who says complimentary things about the Lord and perspires when he preaches. To such they give vast amounts of money and never ask for nor expect an accounting. This speaks well for their hearts but does not say too much in favor of their spiritual discernment....

Furthermore, we must all make an accounting to God for our disposal of the wealth we enjoy. Giving to further dishonest projects is wasting God's money, and in the great day we will tell God why we did it. It will pay us to use prayerful caution before we make our gifts. Let us not give less, but let us give more wisely. Some day we'll be glad we did.

2 Corinthians 5:10; 1 Timothy 6:17-19; 2 John 10-11
This World: Playground or Battleground?, 76, 77.

483. Giving; Prosperity

I hear people testify that they give their tithe because God makes their nine-tenths go farther than the ten-tenths. That is not spirituality; that is just plain business. I insist that it is a dangerous thing to associate the working of God with our prosperity and success down here. I cannot promise that if you will follow the Lord you will soon experience financial prosperity, because that is not what He promised His disciples. Down through the years, following the Lord has meant that we count all things but loss for the excellency of the knowledge of Christ.

Luke 14:33; Philippians 3:6-8; Hebrews 11:24-26
I Talk Back to the Devil, 73.

484. Glamor

The mania after glamor and the contempt of the ordinary are signs and portents in American society. Even religion has gone glamorous. And in case you do not know what glamor is, I might explain that it is a compound of sex, paint, padding and artificial lights. It came to America by way of the honky-tonk and the movie lot, got accepted by the world first and then strutted into the church—vain, self-admiring and contemptuous. Instead of the Spirit of God in our midst, we now have the spirit of glamor, as artificial as painted death and as hollow as the skull, which is its symbol.

Isaiah 3:16-26; 1 Timothy 2:9-10; 1 Peter 3:1-7
This World: Playground or Battleground?, 94.

485. Glorified body; Heaven: glory of; Trials: attitude toward

But in this service I attended, they had asked a young girl to sing, and she was a hunchback, terribly deformed and twisted.

There she stood, about as high as the desk, and with her face set almost down on her breast.

Sweetly she began to sing and you knew she was singing her testimony of faith and love.

> "My soul is so happy in Jesus—for He is
> so precious to me,
> Tis heaven below, my Redeemer to know,
> For He is so precious to me."

Then when she came into the last verse she sounded the personal word of her experience and hope in the faith:

> "Where, some day, through faith in His wonderful grace,
> I know I'll be like Him, and look on His face."

A little hunchback girl—not much to look at, sickly and pale, deformed in physical body, but radiant in soul and spirit because she had grasped the promise that one day she will be like Him, laying her cross and her burden down!

I dare you to show me anything better than that. . . .

It makes no difference who we are or where we live or the status we may have in life—if we have placed our faith and trust in our glorified Savior we shall receive an eternal tabernacle worthy of our soul for it will be a body like unto His glorified body.

What have you ever heard in this life that can compare with that promise?

2 Corinthians 5:1-8; Philippians 3:18-21; 1 John 3:2-3
Echoes from Eden, 94, 95.

486. God: His awesomeness; Flippancy

A person who has sensed what Isaiah sensed will never be able to joke about "the Man upstairs" or the "Someone up there who likes me."

One of the movie actresses who still prowled around the nightclubs after her supposed conversion to Christ was quoted as telling someone, "You ought to know God. You know, God is just a livin' doll!" I read where another man said, "God is a good fellow."

I confess that when I hear or read these things I feel a great pain within. My brother or sister, there is something about our God that is *different*, that is beyond us, that is above us—transcendent. We must be humbly willing to throw our hearts open and to plead, "God, shine Thyself into my understanding for I will never find Thee otherwise."

Psalm 33:6-9; Psalm 96:7-9; Isaiah 6:1-8; Hebrews 4:14-16
Whatever Happened to Worship?, 74, 75.

487. God: His awesomeness; Worship: awe

I have said it before and I will say it again: This low concept of God is our spiritual problem today. Mankind has succeeded quite well in reducing God to a pitiful nothing!

The God of the modern context is no God at all. He is simply a glorified chairman of the board, a kind of big businessman dealing in souls. The God portrayed in much of our church life today commands very little respect.

We must get back to the Bible and to the ministration of God's Spirit to regain a high and holy concept of God. Oh, this awesome, terrible God, the dread of Isaac! This God who made Isaiah cry out, "I am undone!" This God who drove Daniel to his knees in honor and respect.

To know the Creator and the God of all the universe is to revere Him. It is to bow down before Him in wonder and awesome fear.

Psalm 95:6-7; Isaiah 6:5-8; Daniel 6:10
Men Who Met God, 79, 80.

488. God: His gifts; Blessings: unlimited

"God's gifts," said Meister Eckhart, "are meted out according to the taker, not according to the giver." Did we enjoy God's gifts according to the giver there would be no spiritual poverty among us, for surely there is no lack in God. . . .

I cannot want a benefit as eagerly as God wants to give it to me. My asking is likely to be limited by many human factors, and my boldest request is sure to be small. God's willingness to give is unlimited and His ability to perform what He wills is boundless.

Psalm 50:10-12; 2 Corinthians 9:7-8; Ephesians 3:20-21
That Incredible Christian, 77.

489. God: His glory

If all this sounds strange to modern ears, it is only because we have for a full half century taken God for granted. The glory of God has not been revealed to this generation of men. The God of contemporary Christianity is only slightly superior to the gods of Greece and Rome, if indeed He is not actually inferior to them in that He is weak and helpless while they at least had power.

The Knowledge of the Holy, 13.

490. God: His glory

Only engrossment with God can maintain perpetual spiritual enthusiasm because only God can supply everlasting novelty. In God every moment is new and nothing ever gets old. Of things religious we may become tired; even prayer may weary us; but God never. He can show a new aspect of His glory to us each day for all the days of eternity and still we shall have but begun to explore the depths of the riches of His infinite being.

Psalm 89:5-9; Isaiah 40:25,26; Romans 11:33-36; Revelation 4:8-11
God Tells the Man Who Cares, 127, 128.

491. God: His glory; Evangelism: God first

Always and always God must be first. The gospel in its scriptural context puts the glory of God first and the salvation of man second. The angels, approaching from above, chanted "Glory to God in the highest, and on earth peace, good will toward men." This puts the glory of God and the blessing of mankind in their proper order, as do also the opening words of the prayer, "Our Father which art in heaven, hallowed by thy name." Before any petitions are allowed, the name of God must be hallowed. God's glory is and must forever remain the Christian's true point of departure. Anything that begins anywhere else, whatever it is, is certainly not New Testament Christianity.

Matthew 6:9; Luke 2:14; Ephesians 1:4-6
Born After Midnight, 23.

492. God: His goodness

Always God's goodness is the ground of our expectation. Repentance, though necessary, is not meritorious but a condition for receiving the gracious gift of pardon which God gives of His goodness. Prayer is not in itself meritorious. It lays God under no obligation nor puts Him in debt to any. He hears prayer because He is good, and for no other reason. Nor is faith meritorious; it is simply confidence in the goodness of God, and the lack of it is not a reflection upon God's holy character.

Romans 2:4; Romans 11:22; Ephesians 2:8-10; 2 Peter 3:9
The Knowledge of the Holy, 129.

493. God: His grace

Grace is the good pleasure of God that inclines Him to bestow benefits upon the undeserving. It is a self-existent principle inherent in the divine nature and appears to us as a self-caused propensity to pity the wretched, spare the guilty, welcome the outcast, and bring into favor those who were before under just disapprobation. Its use to us sinful men is to save us and make us sit together in heavenly places to demonstrate to the ages the exceeding riches of God's kindness to us in Christ Jesus.

We benefit eternally by God's being just what He is. Because He is what He is, He lifts up our heads out of the prison house, changes our prison garments for royal robes, and makes us to eat bread continually before Him all the days of our lives.

2 Samuel 9:13; Ephesians 2:4-10; Titus 3:4-7
The Knowledge of the Holy, 145, 146.

494. God: His grace; Forgiveness

We who feel ourselves alienated from the fellowship of God can now raise our discouraged heads and look up. Through the virtues of Christ's atoning death the cause of our banishment has been removed. We may return as the Prodigal returned, and be welcome. As we approach the Garden, our home before the Fall, the flaming sword is withdrawn. The keepers of the tree of life stand aside when they see a son of grace approaching.

Genesis 3:24; Luke 15:20-24; Ephesians 2:12-13
The Knowledge of the Holy, 149, 150.

495. God: His grace; Forgiveness

By our own attitudes we may determine our reception by Him. Though the kindness of God is an infinite, overflowing fountain of cordiality, God will not force His attention upon us. If we would be welcomed as the Prodigal was, we must come as the Prodigal came; and when we so come, even though the Pharisees and the legalists sulk without, there will be a feast of welcome within, and the music and dancing as the Father takes His child again to His heart.

The greatness of God rouses fear within us, but His goodness encourages us not to be afraid of Him. To fear and not be afraid—that is the paradox of faith.

Luke 7:47-48; Luke 15:20-24; Hebrews 4:14-16
The Knowledge of the Holy, 131.

496. God: His holiness

Neither the writer nor the reader of these words is qualified to appreciate the holiness of God. Quite literally a new channel must be cut through the desert of our minds to allow the sweet waters of truth that will heal our great sickness to flow in. We cannot grasp the true meaning of the divine holiness by thinking of someone or something very pure and then raising the concept to the highest degree we are capable of. God's holiness is not simply the best we know infinitely bettered. We know nothing like the divine holiness. It stands apart, unique, unapproachable, incomprehensible and unattainable. The natural man is blind to it. He may fear God's power and admire His wisdom, but His holiness he cannot even imagine.

Only the Spirit of the Holy One can impart to the human spirit the knowledge of the holy....

1 Samuel 2:2; Isaiah 6:3; Ephesians 1:17; Revelation 4:8
The Knowledge of the Holy, 162, 163.

497. God: His immutability

For a moral being to change it would be necessary that the change be in one of three directions. He must go from better to worse or from worse to better; or, granted that the moral quality remain stable, he must change within himself, as from immature to mature or from one order of being to another. It should be clear that God can move in none of these directions. His perfections forever rule out any such possibility.

Malachi 3:6; James 1:17
The Knowledge of the Holy, 75, 76.

498. God: His immutability; God: His mercy

What peace it brings to the Christian's heart to realize that our Heavenly Father never differs from Himself. In coming to Him at any time we need not wonder whether we shall find Him in a receptive mood. He is always receptive to misery and need, as well as to love and faith. He does not keep office hours nor set aside periods when He will see no one. Neither does He change His mind about anything. Today, this moment, He feels toward His creatures, toward babies, toward the sick, the fallen, the sinful, exactly as He did when He sent His only-begotten Son into the world to die for mankind.

God never changes moods or cools off in His affections or loses enthusiasm. His attitude toward sin is now the same as it was when He drove out the sinful man from the eastward garden, and His attitude toward the sinner the same as when He stretched forth His hands and cried, "Come unto me, all ye that labour and are heavy laden, and I will give you rest."

Genesis 2:24; Malachi 3:6;
Matthew 11:28-30; James 1:17
The Knowledge of the Holy, 82.

499. God: His leading; Distractions

Imagine! Moses hired a guide to lead Israel through the wilderness! The circumstances being what they were, this seems almost incredible, but Moses was a man capable of making mistakes like the rest of us. And hiring Hobab was a serious mistake....

What need do we have of Hobab's eyes? Surely none at all. Yet the Church has a whole army of Hobabs to which it looks eagerly for guidance and leadership. That Hobab has no place in the divine plan never seems to matter at all. That Hobab is an intruder, that his eyes are not sharp enough to search out the path, that he is altogether superfluous and actually in the way is passed over by almost everyone. God seems so far away, the Bible is such an old book, faith makes such heavy demands upon our flesh, and Hobab is so near at hand and so real and easy to lean on—so we act like men of earth instead of like men of heaven, and Hobab gets the job.

Now, who is Hobab? and how can we identify him? The answer is easy. Hobab is anything gratuitously introduced into the holy work of God which does not have biblical authority for its existence....

Hobab is not an individual. He is whatever takes our attention from the cloud and fire; he is whatever causes us to lean less heavily upon God and look less trustfully to the guiding Spirit. Each one of us must look out for him in our own life and in our church. And when we discover him we must get rid of him right away.

Numbers 10:29-32; Proverbs 3:5-6;
Jeremiah 9:23-24
The Price of Neglect, 18, 19, 20, 21.

500. God: His love; God: His goodness

There is a sweet wisdom in love that is above reason—it rises above it and goes far beyond it. Who could ever imagine the God of all the universe condensing Himself into human form and, out of His love, dying for His alienated people? It seems an unreasonable thing to do, but it was reasonable in that it was the supreme wisdom of the mighty God!

The saintly Lady Julian, centuries ago, cherished this love that is ours in Christ. She wrote: "Out of His goodness, God made us. Out of His goodness, He keeps us. When man had sinned, He redeemed us again out of His goodness. Then do you not suppose that God will give His children the best of everything out of His goodness?"

Matthew 7:7-11; John 3:16; Romans 5:8
Jesus Is Victor!, 45.

501. God: His love; God: His kindness

In our desire after God let us keep always in mind that God also has desire, and His desire is toward the sons of men, and more particularly toward those sons of men who will make the once-for-all decision to exalt Him over all. Such as these are precious to God above all treasures of earth or sea. In them God finds a theater where He can display His exceeding kindness toward us in Christ Jesus. With them God can walk unhindered; toward them He can act like the God He is.

Psalm 139:17-18; Ephesians 2:2-7; Titus 3:4-7
The Pursuit of God, 98.

502. God: His love; Individual importance

We will eternally thank God for the Christian message and the Christian hope and the miracle of transformed human lives that assures us that God cares and that He loves us individually.

We will eternally thank God also that His care and concern are not tailored for the nice people and the respectable people and those who have some means of helping themselves. . . .

He knows very well that he does not matter to the mayor of the city. He knows that he does not matter to the chief of police. He knows that he is not in the heart of the governor or the president or the members of the president's cabinet.

But the shining beauty and the radiance of the message finally get through to him:

"You matter to the living and loving God of all creation. Above everyone else in the whole universe, He cares for you and calls to you and has gracious plans for you!"

That is the high compression. That is the dazzling facet of the diamond of truth which God has thrown almost with a happy carelessness out to the world, saying "Take it!"

What a message for the sinner! What a message for the failure. What a message for the loneliest of the lonely.

John 3:16; Romans 5:8; 1 John 4:10
Christ the Eternal Son, 92, 93, 94, 95.

503. God: His majesty

Old Novatian said, "That in the contemplation of God's majesty, all eloquence is done," which is to say that God is always greater than anything that can be said about Him. No language is worthy of Him. He is more sublime than all sublimity, loftier than all loftiness, more profound than all profundity, more splendid than all splendor, more powerful than all power, more truthful than all truth. Greater than all majesty, more merciful than all mercy, more just than all justice, more pitiful than all pity. Nothing anybody can say about Him is enough.

Psalm 89:5-9; Psalm 96:1-6; Psalm 104:1; Isaiah 40:25-26
Success and the Christian, 39.

504. God: His majesty; Concept of God; Church: services

I am positively sure after many years of observation and prayer that the basis of all of our trouble today, in religious circles, is that our God is too small.

When he says magnify the Lord, he doesn't mean that you are to make God big, but you are to see Him big. When we take a telescope and look at a star, we don't make the star bigger, we only see it big. Likewise you cannot make God bigger, but you are only to see Him bigger. . . .

My brethren, God calls us to magnify Him, to see Him big. A meeting is not big because a lot of people are present. A meeting is big because a number of people see a big God in the meeting. And the bigger God is seen, the greater the meeting. A friend of mine has a little saying, "I would rather have a big, little meeting than a little, big meeting." There are a lot of big meetings that are little because the God in them is a small God. And there are a lot of little meetings that are big because God is big in the midst of them.

Psalm 34:3; Psalm 40:16; Luke 1:46
Success and the Christian, 36, 37, 40.

505. God: His majesty; Concept of God; Spiritual victory

The decline of the knowledge of the holy has brought on our troubles. A rediscovery of the majesty of God will go a long way toward curing them. It is impossible to keep our moral practices sound and our inward attitudes right while our idea of God is erroneous or inadequate. If we would bring back spiritual power to our lives, we must begin to think of God more nearly as He is.

1 Chronicles 29:11-13; 2 Chronicles 5:13-14; Psalm 93:1-2
The Knowledge of the Holy, viii.

506. God: His majesty; God: His sovereignty

The gradual disappearance of the idea and feeling of majesty from the Church is a sign and a portent. The revolt of the modern mind has had a heavy price, how heavy is becoming more apparent as the years go by. Our God has now become our servant to wait on our will. "The Lord is my *shepherd,*" we say, instead of "*The Lord* is my shepherd," and the difference is as wide as the world.

We need to have restored again the lost idea of sovereignty, not as a doctrine only but as the source of a solemn religious emotion. We need to have taken from our dying hand the shadow scepter with which we fancy we rule the world. We need to feel and know that we are but dust and ashes, and that God is the disposer of the destinies of men.

Genesis 18:27; 1 Samuel 3:18; Psalm 23:1; Psalm 115:3; Daniel 4:34-35
The Pursuit of Man, 41, 42.

507. God: His majesty; Humanism; Meditation

. . . we must practice the art of long and loving meditation upon the majesty of God. This will take some effort, for the concept of majesty has all but disappeared from the human race. The focal point of man's interest is now himself. Humanism in its various forms has displaced theology as the key to the understanding of life.

Psalm 63:6-8; Psalm 77:11-15
The Knowledge of the Holy, 182.

508. God: His mercy

There is an old story that fits perfectly here about the Jewish rabbi centuries ago who consented to take a weary traveler into his house for a night's rest.

After they had eaten together, the rabbi said, "You are a very old man, are you not?"

"Yes," the traveler replied, "I am almost a century old."

As they talked, the rabbi brought up the matter of religion and asked the visitor about his faith and about his relation to God.

"Oh, I do not believe in God," the aged man replied. "I am an atheist."

The rabbi was infuriated. He arose and opened the door and ordered the man from his house.

"I cannot keep an atheist in my house overnight," he reasoned.

The weary old man said nothing but hobbled to the door and stepped out into the darkness. The rabbi again sat down by his candle and Old Testament, when it seemed he heard a voice saying, "Son, why did you turn that old man out?"

"I turned him out because he is an atheist and I cannot endure him overnight!"

But then the voice of God said, "Son, I have endured him almost 100 years—don't you think you could endure him for one night?"

The rabbi leaped from his chair, rushed into the darkens and, over- taking the older man, brought him back into the house and then treated him like a long lost brother.

It was the mercy of God that had endured the atheist for nearly 100 years. . . .

Exodus 34:6-7; Romans 2:4; Ephesians 2:2-7
I Call It Heresy!, 54, 55.

509. God: His mercy

What an example we have set for us by the life and faith of the old Puritan saint, Thomas Hooker, as his death approached.

Those around his bedside said, "Brother Hooker, you are going to receive your reward."

"No, no!" he breathed. "I go to receive mercy!"

Psalm 130:7; Lamentations 3:23-24
I Call It Heresy!, 58.

510. God: His mercy

When through the blood of the everlasting covenant we children of the shadows reach at last our home in the light, we shall have a thousand strings to our harps, but the sweetest may well be the one tuned to sound forth most perfectly the mercy of God.

For what right will we have to be there? Did we not by our sins take part in that unholy rebellion which rashly sought to dethrone the glorious King of creation? And did we not in times past walk according to the course of this world, according to the evil prince of the power of the air, the spirit that now works in the sons of disobedience? And did we not all at once live in the lusts of our flesh? And were we not by nature the children of wrath, even as others? But we who were one time enemies and alienated in our minds through wicked works shall then see God face to face and His name shall be in our foreheads. We who earned banishment shall enjoy communion; we who deserve the pains of hell shall know the bliss of heaven. And all through the tender mercy of our God, whereby the Dayspring from on high hath visited us.

Luke 1:78; Ephesians 2:2-7; 1 John 3:2-3
The Knowledge of the Holy, 139, 140.

511. God: His omnipresence; Peace: in trials; Trials: God's presence in

The certainty that God is always near us, present in all parts of His world, closer to us than our thoughts, should maintain us in a state of high moral happiness most of the time. But not all the time. It would be less than honest to promise every believer continual jubilee and less than realistic to expect it. As a child may cry out in pain even when sheltered in its mother's arms, so a Christian may sometimes know what it is to suffer even in the conscious presence of God. Though "alway rejoicing," Paul admitted that he was sometimes sorrowful, and for our sakes Christ experienced strong crying and tears though He never left the bosom of the Father (John 1:18).

But all will be well. In a world like this tears have their therapeutic effects. The healing balm distilled from the garments of the enfolding Presence cures our ills before they become fatal. The knowledge that we are never alone calms the troubled sea of our lives and speaks peace to our souls.

Psalm 139:7-12; John 1:18; 2 Corinthians 6:10
The Knowledge of the Holy, 118, 119.

512. God: His omniscience; God: His compassion

And to us who have fled for refuge to lay hold upon the hope that is set before us in the gospel, how unutterably sweet is the knowledge that our Heavenly Father knows us completely. No talebearer can inform on us, no enemy can make an accusation stick; no forgotten skeleton can come tumbling out of some hidden closet to abash us and expose our past; no unsuspected weakness in our characters can come to light to turn God away from us, since He knew us utterly before we knew Him and called us to Himself in the full knowledge of everything that was against us. "For the mountains shall depart, and the hills be removed; but my kindness shall not depart from thee, neither shall the covenant of my peace be removed, saith the Lord that hath mercy on thee."

Our Father in heaven knows our frame and remembers that we are dust. He knew our inborn treachery, and for His own sake engaged to save us (Isa. 48:8-11). His only begotten Son, when He walked among us, felt our pains in their naked intensity of anguish. His knowledge of our afflictions and adversities is more than theoretic; it is personal, warm, and compassionate. Whatever may befall us, God knows and cares as no one else can.

Psalm 103:13-14; Psalm 139:1-6; Isaiah 48:8-11; Isaiah 54:10; Hebrews 4:14-16
The Knowledge of the Holy, 88, 89.

513. God: His perfection; Christlikeness; Discipline: corrective

Know that our living Lord is unspeakably pure. He is sinless, spotless, immaculate, stainless. In His person is an absolute fullness of purity that our words can never express. This fact alone changes our entire human and moral situation and outlook. We can always be sure of the most important of all positives: God is God and God is right. He is in control. Because He is God He will never change!

I repeat: God is right—always. That statement is the basis of all we are thinking about God.

When the eternal God Himself invites us to prepare ourselves to be with Him throughout the future ages, we can only bow in delight and gratitude, murmuring, "Oh, Lord, may Your will be done in this poor, unworthy life!"

I can only hope that you are wise enough, desirous enough and spiritual enough to face up to the truth that every day is another day of spiritual preparation, another day of testing and discipline with our heavenly destination in mind.

Malachi 3:6; Titus 2:11-14; Hebrews 12:8-14; 1 John 3:2-3
Jesus, Author of Our Faith, 92, 93.

514. God: His presence; Burning bush

If the bush had been burning in that way in our day, do you know what we would do? We would advertise a great Bible conference. We would spend tens of thousands of dollars promoting an international "retreat." We would eat up all the ham and sweet potatoes in the area while we talked and gossiped. Then we would pass a resolution to build a fence around the area containing that miraculous desert bush.

Friend, our preservation and our security do not depend on bylaws and regulations. Our security lies in the presence of God in the midst of His people.

Exodus 3:2-3
Men Who Met God, 75.

515. God: His presence; Communion with God

The greatest fact of the tabernacle was that *Jehovah was there*; a Presence was waiting within the veil.

Similarly, the presence of God is the central fact of Christianity. At the heart of the Christian message is God Himself waiting for His redeemed children to push in to conscious awareness of His presence.

Exodus 29:44-46; Exodus 40:34-35; 2 Corinthians 6:16
The Pursuit of God, 34, 35.

516. God: His presence; Faith: daily walk; Encounter with God

Wherever faith has been original, wherever it has proved itself to be real, it has invariably had upon it a sense of the *present God*. The holy Scriptures possess in marked degree this feeling of actual encounter with a real Person. The men and women of the Bible talked with God. They spoke to Him and heard Him speak in words they could understand. With Him they held person to person converse, and a sense of shining reality is upon their words and deeds. . . .

It was this that filled with abiding wonder the first members of the Church of Christ. The solemn delight which those early disciples knew sprang straight from the conviction that there was One in the midst of them. They knew that the Majesty in the heavens was confronting them on earth: they were in the very Presence of God. And the power of that conviction to arrest attention and hold it for a lifetime, to elevate, to transform, to fill with uncontrollable moral happiness, to send men singing to prison and to death, has been one of the wonders of history and a marvel of the world.

Genesis 32:30; Exodus 33:11; Acts 16:25; 1 John 1:1-3
The Pursuit of Man, 7, 8.

517. God: His presence; Faith: daily walk; Loneliness

We habitually stand in our *now* and look back by faith to see the past filled with God. We look forward and see Him inhabiting our future; but our *now* is uninhabited except for ourselves. Thus we are guilty of a kind of pro tem atheism which leaves us alone in the universe while, for the time, God is not. We talk of Him much and loudly, but we secretly think of Him as being absent, and we think of ourselves as inhabiting a parenthetic interval between the God who was and the God who will be. And we are lonely with an ancient and cosmic loneliness. We are each like a little child lost in a crowded market, who has strayed but a few feet from its mother, yet because she cannot be seen the child is inconsolable. So we try by every method devised by religion to relieve our fears and heal our hidden sadness; but with all our efforts we remain unhappy still, with the settled despair of men alone in a vast and deserted universe.

But for all our fears we are not alone. Our trouble is that we *think* of ourselves as being alone. Let us correct the error by thinking of ourselves as standing by the bank of a full flowing river; then let us think of that river as being none else but God Himself. We glance to our left and see the river coming full out of our past; we look to the right and see it flowing on into our future. *But we see also that it is flowing through our present.* And in our today it is the same as it was in our yesterday, not less than, nor different from, but the very same river, one unbroken continuum, undiminished, active and strong as it moves sovereignly on into our tomorrow.

Deuteronomy 4:7; Psalm 145:18; Isaiah 55:6-8; Hebrews 13:8
The Pursuit of Man, 5, 6, 7.

518. God: His sovereignty

Now, I think that God first makes things orderly for utility. Whenever He made something in this universe it was because He had a purpose for it. I do not believe there is anything in the universe that just got here by accident. Everything in the universe has a meaning.

My father was philosophical about many things and I remember that he used to sit during the summertime and ponder why God made the mosquitoes. I still do not have the answer, but I am just a human being, and just because I do not have the answer, I am not going to accuse the Creator of making a cosmic blunder. I know the mosquito is not a blunder—he is just a pest. But God made him.

The same principle is true of a great many other things. I do not know why God does some things, but I am convinced that nothing is accidental in His universe. The fact that we do not know the reason behind some things is not basis enough for us to call them divine accidents.

Psalm 37:3-6; Isaiah 55:8-9; Romans 9:19-21; Romans 11:33-36
Who Put Jesus on the Cross?, 120, 121.

519. God: His sovereignty; Accidents

To the child of God, there is no such thing as accident. He travels an appointed way. The path he treads was chosen for him when as yet he was not, when as yet he had existence only in the mind of God.

Accidents may indeed appear to befall him and misfortune stalk his way; but these evils will be so in appearance only and will seem evils only because we cannot read the secret script of God's hidden providence and so cannot discover the ends at which He aims. . . .

The man of true faith may live in the absolute assurance that his steps are ordered by the Lord. For him, misfortune is outside the bounds of possibility. He cannot be torn from this earth one hour ahead of the time which God has appointed, and he cannot be detained on earth one moment after God is done with him here. He is not a waif of the wide world, a foundling of time and space, but a saint of the Lord and the darling of His particular care.

Psalm 37:13-16, 23-24; Psalm 139:16; Jeremiah 1:5
We Travel an Appointed Way, 3, 4.

520. God: His sovereignty; Communism

In the dark days of World War 2, when the outcome of that conflagration was still in the balance, this was my Christian counsel to my congregation:

"No matter how things look to us now, sin and murder and violence cannot win at last. Righteousness and godliness cannot fail at last. Prophecy must be fulfilled. We will see the day when Germany's mouthing maniac will go down like a rotten tree felled on the hillside. Let us stay by our faith. It is still right to be good, and it is still wrong to follow evil. God must still rule His world, and Christ must still be the acclaimed King throughout the universe." I believed it then. I believe it yet.

Since those days, communism has reared its head. Millions have feared that it was only a matter of time until the world would be under Communist ideology and control. Silly, frightened people declared they would "rather be Red than dead." But communism cannot prevail, and I will tell you why. It has nothing to do with politics or economics or public ownership of property.

Communism cannot prevail because it begins with materialism. It teaches that there is no God and no Christ, no heaven and no hell. It declares that mankind has no soul and that prayer to God is nonsense. Communism is a negation of everything good and pure, everything divine and holy. It cannot prevail because our God in heaven has His plan and program for creation. There is no human being and no human philosophy or force able to wrest dominion from our living God.

Psalm 2; Philippians 2:9-11; Revelation 5:1-8,13
Jesus Is Victor!, 83, 84.

521. God: His sovereignty; God: His care; Trials: God's presence in

I wrote a little editorial squib some time ago under the title, "We Travel an Appointed Way." I pointed out that we are not orphans in the world and that we do not live and breathe by accident and that we are God's children by faith. I said that it is true that our heavenly Father goes before us and that the Shepherd goes before and leads the way.

Some dear man who was among the readers wrote to me and said: "I was brought up a Methodist. In your comments, do you mean this to be foreordination? That is what the Presbyterians believe. Just what do you mean?"

I wrote him a letter, saying "Dear Brother: When I said we travel an appointed way I was not thinking about foreordination, predestination, eternal security, or the eternal decrees.

"I was just thinking," I told him, "about how nice it is for the steps of a good man to be ordered by the

Lord; and that if a consecrated Christian will put himself in the hands of God, even the accidents will be turned into blessings. Not only that, but our God will make the devil himself work for the glorification of His saints."

It has always been the experience of the children of God that when we walk daily in the will of God, even that which looks like tragedy and loss in the end will turn out to be blessing and gain.

I did not mean to go down that deep—I was just saying that our heavenly Father leads our way and that the steps of a good man are ordered by the Lord, I am sure the Methodist brother can go to sleep tonight knowing that he does not have to turn Presbyterian to be certain that God is looking after him.

Psalm 37:23-24; Proverbs 20:24; Romans 8:28-30; 1 Peter 1:2
Christ the Eternal Son, 42, 43.

522. God: His sovereignty; Jesus Christ: His sustaining power

Christian believers, of all people, should have a sensible view of the "nuclear threat." What is it that attracts neutrons so irrevocably to the nucleus of an atom? My answer: the living breath of God speaking in His world. It is Jesus, the eternal Son, the express image of God's person, sustaining all things by His powerful Word (Hebrews 1:3). "In him all things hold together" (Colossians 1:17).

Few liberals or modernists will agree with me in that view. They dispute God's sovereignty and His power. *But they are scared.* Given the world we live in, the most assuring viewpoint a person can hold is the one I hold. The voice of God fills His world, and Jesus Christ, the living Word, holds everything together.

Colossians 1:15-17; Hebrews 1:3; Hebrews 4:12
Jesus, Our Man in Glory, 73.

523. God: His sovereignty; Trials: attitude toward; Spiritual victory

Revelation describes the age-ending heavenly and earthly events when our Lord and Savior is universally acknowledged to be King of kings and Lord of lords. All will acclaim Him victor. God's Revelation leaves us with no doubt about that.

In our present period of time, however, there is little recognition of God's sovereignty or of His plan for His redeemed people. Go into the marketplace, into our educational institutions and—yes—even into our popular religious circles, and you will find a growing tendency to make mankind large and to make God small. Human society is now taking it for granted that if God indeed exists, He has become our servant, meekly waiting upon us for our will.

In the face of this kind of human thinking, I want to make a case for the committed Christians in this world. We are the true realists. We confess that we do not hold the powers of life and death in our own hands. We have sensed the importance of John's vision in the Revelation. We are assured that God is alive and well and that He has never abdicated His throne. While others may wonder and speculate concerning God's place in the universe, we are assured that He has never yielded to any of His creatures His divine rights as Lord of man and nature.

It is for this reason that the Christian believer, related to God by faith, is assured of final victory. Even in the midst of earthly trials, he or she is joyful.

Romans 8:18-19; 1 Peter 1:6-7; Revelation 1:1-3; Revelation 11:15
Jesus Is Victor!, 15, 16.

524. God: His voice

The voice of God today is a quiet voice. The voice of God's love and grace is constant—never strident, never compulsive. God has sent His messengers to every generation. He has spoken through the urgent voice of the prophet. He has spoken through the concerned voice of the preacher and the evangelist. He has spoken through the sweet voice of the gospel singer. He has spoken through the voices of plain, sincere, loving men and women who have given faithful witness to the transforming new birth from above and the joys that God's children will know throughout the eternity to come. . . .

These voices repeat the offer of our Lord: "Take my yoke upon you and learn from me, for I am gentle and humble in heart, and you will find rest for your souls" (Matthew 11:29).

Matthew 11:28-30; Hebrews 1:1-2
Jesus Is Victor!, 128, 129.

525. God: His wisdom; God: His work

Wisdom, among other things, is the ability to devise perfect ends and to achieve those ends by the most perfect means. It sees the end from the beginning, so there can be no need to guess or conjecture. Wisdom sees everything in focus, each in proper relation to all, and is thus able to work toward predestined goals with flawless precision.

All God's acts are done in perfect wisdom, first for His own glory, and then for the highest good of the greatest number for the longest time. And all His acts are as pure as they are wise, and as good as they are wise and pure. Not only could His acts not be better done: a better way to do them could not be imagined. An infinitely wise God must work in a manner not to be improved upon by finite creatures. O Lord, how manifold are Thy works! In wisdom hast Thou made them all. The earth is full of Thy riches!

Psalm 33:11; Psalm 104:24; Psalm 139; Isaiah 46:10; Jeremiah 10:12-15
The Knowledge of the Holy, 93, 94.

526. God: His work; Faith: expectation

We would all be better Christians and wiser students if we would remember this—God rarely uses periods. There is rarely a full stop in His dealings with us—it is more likely to be with the effect of a colon or a semi-colon. In most instances, what God does becomes a means toward something else that He is planning to do....

Can any man who is begotten of the Spirit and has become a Christian believer presume to say, "I have arrived! Put a period there and write finis across my experience"?

No, of course not. God begets us into His provision and that which is still before us is always bigger than that which is behind us.

1 Corinthians 9:24-27; Philippians 3:12; 1 Thessalonians 5:23-24
I Call It Heresy!, 77.

527. Godliness; Celebrities; Humble service; Eternal perspective

After more than thirty years of observing the religious scene I have been forced to conclude that saintliness and church leadership are not often synonymous....

Were the church a pure and Spirit-filled body, wholly led and directed by spiritual considerations, certainly the purest and the saintliest men and women would be the ones most appreciated and most honored; but the opposite is true. Godliness is no longer valued, except for the very old or the very dead. The saintly souls are forgotten in the whirl of religious activity. The noisy, the self-assertive, the entertaining are sought after and rewarded in every way, with gifts, crowds, offerings and publicity. The Christlike, the self-forgetting, the other-worldly are jostled aside to make room for the latest converted playboy who is usually not too well converted and still very much of a playboy....

The wise Christian will be content to wait for that day. In the meantime, he will serve his generation in the will of God. If he should be overlooked in the religious popularity contests he will give it but small attention. He knows whom he is trying to please and he is willing to let the world think what it will of him. He will not be around much longer anyway, and where he is going men will be known not by their Hooper rating but by the holiness of their character.

Acts 13:36; Philippians 2:25-30;
1 Thessalonians 5:12-13; 2 Timothy 4:6-8
Man: The Dwelling Place of God, 97, 98, 99.

528. Godliness; Fellowship: need for; Denominations

After my conversion at age 17, I traveled in fundamental Christian circles. I yearned earnestly for godliness for my own life and for those around me. I had a great desire to be in fellowship with those who were saintly.

I confess that I found much theology but little saintliness! I confess also, at this later date, that I do not care what denomination or group my brothers and sisters in Christ come from if the saintliness of God by the presence of His Holy Spirit is upon them. If Jesus is being glorified in their spiritual lives and service, my heart that still yearns for godly fellowship is attracted to them.

Exodus 3:2-3; Colossians 1:18; 1 Timothy 4:7-8
Men Who Met God, 76.

529. Godliness; Holiness: meaning of; Christlikeness

If anyone should wonder what I mean by godliness, saintliness, holiness, I'll explain. I mean a life and a heart marked by *meekness* and *humility*. The godly soul will not boast nor show off. I mean *reverence*. The godly man will never take part in any religious exercise that shows disrespect for the Deity. The cozy, cute terms now applied to God and Christ will never pass his lips. He will never join in singing religious songs that are light, humorous or irreverent. He will cultivate a spirit of complete sincerity and discuss God and religion only in grave and reverent tones.

Further, I mean *separation* from the world unto God in an all-out, irrevocable committal. The holy man will not envy the world, nor will he imitate it or seek its approval. His testimony will be, "I am crucified unto the world and the world unto me." He will not depend upon it for his enjoyments, but will look above and within for the joy that is unspeakable and full of glory.

In short, any true work of God in the churches will result in an intensified spirit of worship and an elevated appreciation of the basic Christian virtues as they are set forth in the New Testament. It will result in self-denial and cross carrying among the people. It will make men Christlike, will free them from a thousand carnal sins they did not even know were sins before. It will free them from earthly entanglements and focus their whole attention upon things above.

Romans 6:4-7; Galatians 6:14; Colossians 3:1-4; Titus 1:7-9
The Price of Neglect, 92, 93.

530. God's ways/Man's ways

In the Kingdom of God the surest way to lose something is to try to protect it, and the best way to keep it is to let it go....

Here is seen the glaring disparity between the ways of God and the ways of men. When the world takes its hands off a prized possession someone grabs it and disappears. Therefore the world must conserve by defending. So men hoard their heart's treasures, lock up their possessions, protect their good name with libel laws, hedge themselves about with protective devices of every sort and guard their shores with powerful armed forces. This is all according to Adam's philosophy which springs from his fallen nature and is confirmed by thousands of years of practical experience. To challenge it is to invite the scorn of mankind; and yet our Lord did challenge it. . . .

Between spiritual laws and the laws of human society there is a great gulf. In His wisdom God moves on the high road according to His eternal purposes; man on the low road moves along as best he can, improvising and muddling through according to no certain plan, hoping that things will come out all right and almost always seeing his hopes disappointed.

Isaiah 55:8-9; Matthew 16:24-26; Romans 11:33-36
Born After Midnight, 96, 97.

531. Gospel: accept Christ; Gospel: need for accuracy

Being spiritually lazy we naturally tend to gravitate toward the easiest way of settling our religious questions for ourselves and others; hence the formula "Accept Christ" has become a panacea of universal application, and I believe it has been fatal to many. . . .

The trouble is that the whole "Accept Christ" attitude is likely to be wrong. It shows Christ applying to us rather than us to Him. It makes Him stand hat-in-hand awaiting our verdict on Him, instead of our kneeling with troubled hearts awaiting His verdict on us. It may even permit us to accept Christ by an impulse of mind or emotions, painlessly, at no loss to our ego and no inconvenience to our usual way of life. . . .

Allowing the expression "Accept Christ" to stand as an honest effort to say in short what could not be so well said any other way, let us see what we mean or should mean when we use it.

To accept Christ is to form an attachment to the Person of our Lord Jesus altogether unique in human experience. The attachment is intellectual, volitional and emotional. The believer is intellectually convinced that Jesus is both Lord and Christ; he has set his will to follow Him at any cost and soon his heart is enjoying the exquisite sweetness of His fellowship. . . .

If this is what we mean when we advise the seeker to accept Christ we had better explain it to him. He may get into deep spiritual trouble unless we do.

Luke 18:9-14; John 1:11-13; Acts 16:30-31; Romans 10:8-10; Philippians 2:9-11
That Incredible Christian, 18, 19.

532. Gospel: accept Christ; Salvation: invitation to

But the Bible knows absolutely nothing about passive reception, for the word *receive* is not passive but active. We make the word receive into "accept." Everyone goes around asking, "Will you accept Jesus? Will you accept Him?" This makes a brush salesman out of Jesus Christ, as though He meekly stands waiting to know whether we will patronize Him or not. Although we desperately need what He proffers, we are sovereignly deciding whether we will receive Him or not. . . .

We have been taught that passive acceptance is the equivalent of faith when it is not. In the Greek, this word *receive* is active, not passive. You can go to any of the modern translations and you will find that they get across the idea of "take" and "took." "As many as took him," says one fine translation, "to them gave he the power to become the sons of God."

It is *taking* instead of *accepting*.... It is an act of the mind and of the will and of the affections. It is thus not only an act of the total personality, it is an *aggressive* act of the total personality.

When you bring that thought over into this text, the Holy Spirit is saying of the children of God: "As many as aggressively took Him with their total personality . . . ." There is no inference that they could sit and quietly accept. Every part of their being became a hand reaching forth for Jesus Christ. They took Jesus as Savior and Lord with all of their will and affections and feelings and intellect. That is why it says in the Greek: "As many as actively took Him. . . ."

John 1:11-13
Faith Beyond Reason, 10, 11, 12.

533. Gospel: accept Christ; Salvation: invitation to

Now the particular attitude revealed here about "accepting Christ" is wrong because it makes Christ stand hat-in-hand, somewhere outside the door, waiting on our human judgment.

We know about His divine Person, we know that He is the Lamb of God who suffered and died in our place. We know all about His credentials. Yet we let Him stand outside on the steps like some poor timid fellow who is hoping he can find a job.

We look Him over, then read a few more devotional verses, and ask: "What do you think, Mabel? Do you think we ought to accept Him? I really wonder if we should accept Him?"

And so, in this view, our poor Lord Christ stands hat-in-hand, shifting from one foot to another looking for a job, wondering whether He will be accepted.

Meanwhile, there sits the proud Adamic sinner, rotten as the devil and filled with all manner of spiritual leprosy and cancer. But he is hesitating; he is judging whether or not he will accept Christ.

My friends, look: doesn't that proud human know that the Christ he is putting off is the Christ of God, the eternal Son who holds the worlds in His hands?

Does he not know that Christ is the eternal Word, the Jesus who made the heavens and the earth and all things that are therein? . . .

The question ought not to be whether I will accept Him; the question ought to be whether He will accept me!

But He does not make that a question. He has already told us that we do not have to worry or disturb our minds about that. "Whoever comes to me I will never drive away" (John 6:37b).

Psalm 2:12; John 1:29; John 6:37, 44; Colossians 1:15-17
Christ the Eternal Son, 156, 157, 158.

534. Gospel: faith alone; Salvation: by faith alone; Faith: and works

There are so many who want to trust Christ plus something else. They want to trust Christ and add their own morals. They want to trust Christ and add their own good works. They want to trust Christ and then point to the merits of their baptism or church membership or stewardship.

Let me tell you straight out that Jesus Christ will never stand at the right side of a plus sign. If you will insist upon adding some "plus" to your faith in Jesus Christ, He will walk away in His holy dignity. He will ever refuse to be considered the other part of a "plus" sign. If your trust is in the plus—something added—then you do not possess Jesus Christ at all.

Matthew 19:21-22; Acts 13:38-39; Romans 3:28; Ephesians 2:8-10
Who Put Jesus on the Cross?, 64.

535. Gospel: moral implications

The fact is that the New Testament message embraces a great deal more than an offer of free pardon. It is a message of pardon, and for that may God be praised; but it is also a message of repentance. It is a message of atonement, but it is also a message of temperance and righteousness and godliness in this present world. It tells us that we must accept a Savior, but it tells us also that me must *deny* ungodliness and worldly lusts. The gospel message includes the idea of amendment, of separation from the world, of cross-carrying and loyalty to the kingdom of God even unto death.

To be strictly technical, these latter truths are corollaries of the gospel, and not the gospel itself; but they are part and parcel of the total message which we are commissioned to declare. . . .

To offer a sinner the gift of salvation based upon the work of Christ, while at the same time allowing him to retain the idea that the gift carries with it no moral implications, is to do him untold injury where it hurts him worst.

Luke 9:23-25; Titus 2:11-14; James 2:17
The Set of the Sail, 19, 20.

536. Gospel: need for understanding

A friend or neighbor may tell us, "Well, I have gone to this certain church all my life. I have been confirmed, baptized and all the rest. I am going to take the chance that it will get me through."

My friend, your odds are not that good—you do not even have a chance. If your relation to Jesus Christ is not a saving relation, then you are on your own, without a guide and without a compass. It is not a chance you have; it is suicide that you are committing. It is not a chance in ten times 10,000. It is either be right or be dead; in this case, be right or be eternally lost.

Matthew 1:21; John 14:6; Acts 4:12
Christ the Eternal Son, 159.

537. Gospel: need for understanding; Salvation: by faith alone

A few things, fortunately only a few, are matters of life and death, such as a compass for a sea voyage or a guide for a journey across the desert. To ignore these vital things is not to gamble or take a chance; it is to commit suicide. Here it is either be right or be dead.

Our relation to Jesus Christ is such a matter of life or death, and on a much higher plane. The Bible instructed man knows that Jesus Christ came into the world to save sinners and that men are saved by Christ alone altogether apart from any works of merit....

To the question "What must I do to be saved?" we must learn the correct answer. To fail here is not to gamble with our souls: it is to guarantee eternal banishment from the face of God. Here we must be right or be finally lost.

John 1:11-13; Acts 16:30-31; Ephesians 2:8-10; 1 Timothy 1:15-16
That Incredible Christian, 17.

538. Gospel: trust in Christ; Salvation: by faith alone

No man has any hope for eternal salvation apart from trusting completely in Jesus Christ and His atonement for men. Simply stated, our Lord Jesus is the lifeboat and we must fully and truly be committed to trusting the lifeboat.

Again, our Lord and Savior is the rope by which it is possible to escape from the burning building. There is no doubt about it—either we trust that rope or we perish.

He is the wonder drug or medication that heals all ills and sicknesses—and if we refuse it, we die.

He is the bridge from hell to heaven—and we take the bridge and cross over by His grace or we stay in hell.

These are simple illustrations, but they get to the point of the necessity of complete trust in Jesus Christ—absolute trust in Him!

John 1:11-13; Acts 4:12; Ephesians 2:8-10
Who Put Jesus on the Cross?, 63, 64.

539. Grace; Forgiveness

Now over against this set almost any Bible character who honestly tried to glorify God in his earthly walk. See how God winked at weakness and overlooked failures as He poured upon His servants grace and blessing untold. Let it be Abraham, Jacob, David, Daniel, Elijah or whom you will; honor followed honor as harvest the seed. The man of God set his heart to exalt God above all; God accepted his intention as fact and acted accordingly. Not perfection, but holy intention made the difference.

Nehemiah 9:17; Psalm 130:3-4; Acts 13:22
The Pursuit of God, 97.

540. Great preachers

I'm against the idea of putting the "big preachers" on tape and playing them back to the congregations that feel they are being starved by listening to "little preachers."

Fallacy, brethren—a thousand times, fallacy!

> *If we could have the Apostle Paul on tape recordings and let him stand here and preach, he could do no more for you than the Holy Ghost can do, with The Book and the human conscience....*

Oh, brethren, I would not detract from God's great men, but I can safely say that that's not what the church needs.

The church needs to listen to the inner voice and do something about it!

The Tozer Pulpit, Volume 1, Book 1, 108, 109.

H

541. Happiness

People are coming more and more to excuse every sort of wrongdoing on the grounds that they are "just trying to secure a little happiness." Before she will give her consent to marriage the modern young lady may ask outright whether or not the man "can make me happy." The lovelorn columns of the newspapers are wet with the self-pitying tears of persons who write to inquire how they can "preserve their happiness." The psychiatrists of the land are getting fat off the increasing numbers who seek professional aid in their all-absorbing search for happiness. It is not uncommon for crimes to be committed against persons who do nothing worse than "jeopardize" someone's happiness....

That we are born to be happy is scarcely questioned by anyone. No one bothers to prove that fallen men have any moral right to happiness, or that they are in the long run any better off happy. The only question before the house is how to get the most happiness out of life. The thesis of almost all popular books and plays is that personal happiness is the legitimate end of the dramatic human struggle.

Proverbs 14:12-13; Ecclesiastes 2:1-2; Romans 8:5-7
The Price of Neglect, 36, 37.

542. Happiness; Discouragement; Spiritual victory

I am quite sure that people in the average church are not the happy people that they ought to be.

The mood in most congregations is not a high, bright, happy key, but instead a low, growling, and gloomy key!

Many people who are professing Christians try to retain a cordiality socially, while inwardly they are heavyhearted, beaten and defeated. Inwardly they are bound and shackled, unhappy and a little bit frightened—yet they are Christians!...

> *It isn't the Lord that has us bound and discouraged—it is the devil. One simple act of the Holy Ghost will set a man free and give him victory.*

Lamentations 3:19-23; 2 Corinthians 2:14; Philippians 4:4
The Tozer Pulpit, Volume 1, Book 1, 141, 143.

543. Happiness; Eternity; Eternal perspective

We inhabit a world suspended halfway between heaven and hell, alienated from one and not yet abandoned to the other. By nature we are unholy and by practice unrighteous. That we are unhappy, I repeat, is of small consequence. Our first and imperative duty is to escape the corruption which is in the world as Lot escaped the moral ruin of Sodom. It is of overwhelming importance to us that we should seek the favor of God while it is possible to find it and that we should bring ourselves under the plenary authority of Jesus Christ in complete and voluntary obedience. To do this is to invite trouble from a hostile world and to incur such unhappiness as may naturally follow. Add to this the temptations of the devil and a lifelong struggle with the flesh and it will be obvious that we will need to defer most of our enjoyments to a more appropriate time. . . .

As I have said before, we can afford to suffer now; we'll have a long eternity to enjoy ourselves. And our enjoyment will be valid and pure, for it will come in the right way at the right time.

Genesis 19:15,29; Isaiah 55:6-8; John 15:18-21; Romans 7:24-25
The Warfare of the Spirit, 82, 83, 85.

544. Happiness; Holiness: first need

That we are born to be happy is scarcely questioned by anyone. No one bothers to prove that fallen men have any moral right to happiness, or that they are in the long run any better off happy. The only question before the house is how to get the most happiness out of life. Almost all popular books and plays assume that personal happiness is the legitimate end of the dramatic human struggle.

Now I submit that the whole hectic scramble after happiness is an evil as certainly as is the scramble after money or fame or success. . . .

How far wrong all this is will be discovered easily by the simple act of reading the New Testament through once with meditation. There the emphasis is not upon happiness but upon holiness. God is more concerned with the state of people's hearts than with the state of their feelings. Undoubtedly the will of God brings final happiness to those who obey, but the most important matter is not how happy we are but how holy. The soldier does not seek to be happy in the field; he seeks rather to get the fighting over with, to win the war and get back home to his loved ones. There he may enjoy himself to the full; but while the war is on, his most pressing job is to be a good soldier, to acquit himself like a man, regardless of how he feels.

2 Timothy 2:3-4; Hebrews 12:14; 2 Peter 1:4
Of God and Men, 48, 49.

545. Happiness; Holiness: first need

No man should desire to be happy who is not at the same time holy. He should spend his efforts in seeking to know and do the will of God, leaving to Christ the matter of how happy he shall be.

For those who take this whole thing seriously I have a suggestion: Go to God and have an understanding. Tell Him that it is your desire to be holy at any cost, and then ask Him never to give you more happiness than holiness. When your holiness becomes tarnished, let your joy become dim. And ask Him to make you holy whether you are happy or not. Be assured that in the end you will be as happy as you are holy; but for the time being let your whole ambition be to serve God and be Christlike.

1 Chronicles 16:25-29; Romans 6:11-19; 2 Corinthians 7:1
Of God and Men, 49, 50.

546. Happiness; Holiness: first need

Now, my brethren, I don't know whether I can make it clear or not. I know that things like this have to be felt rather than understood, but the wounded man is never a seeker after happiness. There is an ignoble pursuit of irresponsible happiness among us. Over the last years, as I have observed the human scene and have watched God's professed people live and die, I have seen that most of us would rather be happy than to feel the wounds of other people's sorrows. I do not believe that it is the will of God that we should seek to be happy, but rather that we should seek to be holy and useful. The holy man will be the useful man and he's likely to be a happy man too; but if he seeks happiness and forgets holiness and usefulness, he's a carnal man.

Matthew 25:44-46; Romans 12:9-13; Hebrews 13:1-3
Man: The Dwelling Place of God, 104.

547. Happiness; Trials: attitude toward

From the trials and triumphs of Paul, we gather, too, that happiness is really not indispensable to a Christian. There are many ills worse than heartaches. It is scarcely too much to say that prolonged happiness may actually weaken us, especially if we insist upon being happy as the Jews insisted upon flesh in the wilderness. In so doing, we may try to avoid those spiritual responsibilities which would in the nature of them bring a certain measure of heaviness and affliction to the soul.

The best thing is neither to seek nor seek to avoid troubles but to follow Christ and take the bitter with the sweet as it may come. Whether we are happy or unhappy at any given time is not important. That we be in the will of God is all that matters. We may safely leave with Him the incident of heartache or happiness. He will know how much we need of either or both.

2 Corinthians 12:8-9; Ephesians 5:15-18; James 1:2-4
We Travel an Appointed Way, 80.

548. Heart; Inner reality

Indeed it may be truthfully said that everything of lasting value in the Christian life is unseen and eternal. Things seen are of little real significance in the light of God's presence. He pays small attention to the beauty of a woman or the strength of a man. With Him the heart is all that matters. The rest of the life comes into notice only because it represents the dwelling place of the inner eternal being.

The solution to life's problems is spiritual because the essence of life is spiritual. It is astonishing how many difficulties clear up without any effort when the inner life gets straightened out.

1 Samuel 16:7; 1 Chronicles 28:9; 2 Corinthians 4:16-18
The Next Chapter After the Last, 82, 83.

549. Heaven: glory of

The true Christian may safely look forward to a future state that is as happy as perfect love wills it to be. Since love cannot desire for its object anything less than the fullest possible measure of enjoyment for the longest possible time, it is virtually beyond our power to conceive of a future as consistently delightful as that which Christ is preparing for us. And who is to say what is possible with God?

John 14:1-3; 2 Corinthians 5:1-8; Revelation 21-22
Born After Midnight, 138.

550. Heaven: glory of

Down here the orchestra merely rehearses; over there we will give the concert. Here, we ready our garments of righteousness; over there we will wear them at the wedding of the Lamb.

Matthew 25:10; Revelation 5:8-14; Revelation 19:7
Jesus, Author of Our Faith, 96.

551. Heaven: lack of interest in

The corrosive action of unbelief in our day has worn down the Christian hope of heaven until there seems to be very little joy and expectation concerning the eternal inheritance which God has promised.

I think we have a right to be startled by the thought that very few people really believe in heaven any more. Oh, we may hear a hillbilly with a guitar singing about heaven in a way that would make an intelligent man turn away from the thought of such a heaven. But, for the most part, we do not think about heaven very often and we talk about it even less!

Philippians 1:21-24; Philippians 3:18-21; 2 Timothy 4:6-8; 1 Peter 1:3-5
I Call It Heresy!, 90.

552. Heaven: lack of interest in; Affluence; Second coming: lack of interest in

In the United States and Canada the middle class today possesses more earthly goods and lives in greater luxury than emperors and maharajas did a short century ago. And since the bulk of Christians comes from this class it is not difficult to see why the apocalyptic hope has all but disappeared from among us. It is hard to focus attention upon a better world to come when a more comfortable one than this can hardly be imagined. The best we can do is to look for heaven after we have reveled for a lifetime in the luxuries of a fabulously generous earth. As long as science can make us so cozy in this present world it is hard to work up much pleasurable anticipation of a new world order.

Matthew 19:24; Mark 8:36-37; Luke 12:19-21
Man: The Dwelling Place of God, 154, 155.

553. Heaven: popular beliefs about

The man who knows himself least is likely to have a cheerful if groundless confidence in his own moral worth. Such a man has less trouble believing that he will inherit an eternity of bliss because his concepts are only quasi-Christian, being influenced strongly by chimney-corner scripture and old wives' tales. He thinks of heaven as being very much like California without the heat and the smog, and himself as inhabiting a splendiferous palace with all modern conveniences, and wearing a heavily bejeweled crown. Throw in a few angels and you have the vulgar picture of the future life held by the devotees of popular Christianity.

This is the heaven that appears in the saccharin ballads of the guitar-twanging rockabilly gospelers that clutter up the religious scene today. That the whole thing is completely unrealistic and contrary to the laws of the moral universe seems to make no difference to anyone.

Born After Midnight, 136.

554. Heaven: popular beliefs about; Death: preparation for; Unsaved; Funerals

I have been at funerals where the presiding minister preached the deceased right into heaven. Yet the earthly life of the departed plainly said that he or she would be bored to tears in a heavenly environment of continuous praise and adoration of God.

This is personal opinion, but I do not think death is going to transform our attitudes and disposition. If in this life we are not really comfortable talking or singing about heaven, I doubt that death will transform us into enthusiasts. If the worship and adoration of God are tedious now, they will be tedious after the hour of death. I do not know that God is going to force any of us into His heaven. I doubt that He will say to any of us, "You were never interested in worshiping Me while you were on earth, but in heaven I am going to make that your greatest interest and your ceaseless occupation!"

Jesus Is Victor!, 67, 68.

555. Heaven: rewards; Celebrities

Right now we live in a confused and mixed up world. Some people get the headlines who, if the truth were known, should be getting a striped suit in a prison somewhere.

There are other worthy persons who are completely ignored in this world and, if the truth were known, they would be on the front covers of the news magazines next week.

God is not mixed up, though. God is not confused! God continues to watch the human scene and He has His own process for sorting things out. Many a person receiving the praise and plaudits of the world today will be sorted out when God's time comes. He does not sort them out down here in our time. He did not even sort them out when His twelve disciples were with Him. Peter was a coward and Judas was a lover of money and a betrayer, but not until the last minute did He even mention it. But when Judas died he was sorted out. He died and went to his own place.

Death sorts us out and if we go to heaven it is because we have a nature that belongs there. It is not hard for the sovereign God to sort out all the natures that belong in heaven and take them there.

Matthew 13:29-30; Matthew 27:3-4; Acts 1:25
Echoes from Eden, 103.

556. Hell; Judgment of God: deserved

The idea of hell found in the Scriptures is so fearful that the first impulse of a loving heart is to wish it were not so. But human pity is both a beautiful and a dangerous emotion. Unless it is subjected to the sharp critique of moral judgment it may, and often does, put our sympathies on the side of the murderer instead of on the side of the dead man and the widow and children he has left behind him. Unholy sympathy moves starry-eyed ladies to send flowers to the criminal awaiting execution while the innocent child he may have raped and mutilated scarcely rates a fugitive impulse of pity.

In the same way uninformed and unreasoning sympathy tends to take sides with the fallen and rebellious race of men against the Most High God whose name is Holy. That He gave men life and intelligence, that He has been patient with them while they defied His laws, killed His only begotten Son and scorned His dying love, is overlooked completely. That men use their gift of free will to reject God, choose iniquity and with wide open eyes persistently work to prepare themselves for hell, seems not to matter to some people. In a welter of uncontrollable emotion they throw themselves on the side of God's enemies. This is unbelief masquerading as compassion.

Psalm 14:1-3; Isaiah 53:6; Romans 1:18; Revelation 16:7
The Warfare of the Spirit, 42.

557. Hero worship; Celebrities

I am sure that if we all saw God bigger, we would see people smaller. This is the day of the magnification of slick personalities, and as we magnify men, we minimize God. . . . We have whole meetings go by in which we never see God at all—we only see His servants. And the curlier the hair of the servant, the more we see the servant. And if he's been pardoned from murdering his grandmother's aunt, we magnify him still more. And if he's been half-converted from movie acting, we magnify him still more.

We always have some big wheel that we are down in front of, kissing the toe of. Then we wonder why the Holy Spirit doesn't bless us.... There is an awful lot of hero worship in the church of Christ.

Psalm 34:3; 2 Corinthians 4:5-7;
1 Thessalonians 2:4-6
Success and the Christian, 37, 38.

558. Hero worship; Imperfections of men

You will continue to have your longing after God, but you will no longer stumble over the imperfections of men and women around you. It was Thomas a Kempis who wrote in *The Imitation of Christ*: "If thou would'st have peace of heart, do not inquire too earnestly into other men's matters." If you spend time examining your Christian brother, you will find him lacking in some things. Don't forget that all idols have feet of clay.

We have plain teaching that the Lord does not want His children to become "saint-worshipers." He doesn't want you to become a preacher-worshiper or a teacher-worshiper. God wants to deliver you from the best man you know so that man can die and be removed and you won't backslide!

Jeremiah 9:23-24
I Talk Back to the Devil, 140, 141.

559. Hero worship; Imperfections of men

Do you suppose that young man, as he read my "prayer," thought of A.W. Tozer as some kind of a hero of the faith? That would have been a very inflated idea—far beyond the assessment held by Mrs. A.W. Tozer, for instance! Most of us are inclined to quote other people, particularly those we consider to be good examples. Probably it is a good thing that we do not know them as well as their families do! Otherwise we would have to be more cautious about our quoting them and holding them up for veneration.

Jesus, Author of Our Faith, 71.

560. Hindrances; Freedom

... yet I can understand how a religion that lay mostly in external observances could be forbidden. If true religion consisted in outward practices, then it could be destroyed by laws forbidding those practices. But if the true worshiper is one who worships God in spirit and in truth, how can laws or jails or abuses or deprivations prevent the spiritual man from worshiping?

Let a man set his heart only on doing the will of God and he is instantly free. No one can hinder him.

John 4:23-24; Acts 5:41-42; Romans 10:8-10
The Root of the Righteous, 129.

561. Holiness: commanded

You cannot study the Bible diligently and earnestly without being struck by an obvious fact—the whole matter of personal holiness is highly important to God!

Neither do you have to give long study to the attitudes of modern Christian believers to discern that by and large we consider the expression of true Christian holiness to be just a matter of personal option: "I have looked it over and considered it, but I don't buy it!". . .

Personally, I am of the opinion that we who claim to be apostolic Christians do not have the privilege of ignoring such apostolic injunctions. I do not mean that a pastor can forbid or that a church can compel. I only mean that morally we dare not ignore this commandment, "Be holy." . . .

But, brethren, we are still under the holy authority of the apostolic command. Men of God have reminded us in the Word that God does ask us and expect us to be holy men and women of God, because we are the children of God, who is holy. The doctrine of holiness may have been badly and often wounded—but the provision of God by His pure and gentle and loving Spirit is still the positive answer for those who hunger and thirst for the life and spirit well-pleasing to God.

Leviticus 19:2; 2 Corinthians 7:1;
1 Peter 1:14-16
I Call It Heresy!, 61, 62, 68.

562. Holiness: conditions for; God: His work; Trials: attitude toward

Yes, there is a dark night of the soul. There are few Christians willing to go into this dark night and that is why there are so few who enter into the light. It is impossible for them ever to know the morning because they will not endure the night. . . .

I think the more we learn of God and His ways and of man and his nature we are bound to reach the conclusion that we are all just about as holy as we want to be. We are all just about as full of the Spirit as we want to be. Thus when we tell ourselves that we want to be more holy but we are really as holy as we care to be, it is small wonder that the dark night of the soul takes so long!

The reason why many are still troubled, still seeking, still making little forward progress is because they have not yet come to the end of themselves. We are still giving some of the orders, and we are still interfering with God's working within us.

Psalm 30:5; James 4:7-10; 1 Peter 5:6-10
I Talk Back to the Devil, 81.

563. Holiness: unpopular subject

The true church understands that it must live a disciplined life. Although our High Priest loves us in spite of our weaknesses and failures, He encourages us to be a holy people because He is a holy God. Holiness may be an unpopular subject in some churches, but holiness in the Christian life is a precious treasure in God's sight.

What I say here may hurt, but I say it anyhow. We have lived with unholiness so long that we are almost incapable of recognizing true holiness. The people of God in the churches of Jesus Christ ought to be a holy people. But ministers have largely given up preaching Bible-centered sermons on holiness. Maybe they would not know what to do with hearers who fell under the convicting power of God's Word. Preachers today would rather give their congregations tranquilizers.

Leviticus 11:44-45; Deuteronomy 7:6;
Titus 2:11-14
Jesus Is Victor!, 61.

564. Holy Spirit: do not grieve

Because He is loving and kind and friendly, the Holy Spirit may be grieved. . . . He can be grieved because He is loving, and there must be love present before there can be grief.

Suppose you had a 17-year-old son who began to go bad. He rejected your counsel and wanted to take things into his own hands. Suppose that he joined up with a young stranger from another part of the city and they got into trouble.

You were called down to the police station. Your boy—and another boy who you had never seen—sat there in handcuffs.

You know how you would feel about it. You would be sorry for the other boy—but you don't love him because you don't know him. With your own son, your grief would penetrate to your heart like a sword. Only love can grieve. If those two boys were sent off to prison, you might pity the boy you didn't know, but you would grieve over the boy you knew and loved. A mother can grieve because she loves. If you don't love, you can't grieve.

When the Scripture says, "And do not grieve the Holy Spirit of God" (Ephesians 4:30a), it is telling us that He loves us so much that when we insult Him, He is grieved; when we ignore Him, He is grieved; when we resist Him, He is grieved; and when we doubt Him, He is grieved.

Psalm 78:40-41; Isaiah 63:9-10; Ephesians 4:30
The Counselor, 51, 52.

565. Holy Spirit: filling

Pentecost means that the Deity came to mankind to give Himself to man, that man might breathe Him in as he breathes in the air, that He might fill men. Dr. A.B. Simpson used an illustration which was about as good as any I ever heard. He said, "Being filled with the fullness of God is like a bottle in the ocean. You take the cork out of the bottle and sink it in the ocean, and you have the bottle completely full of ocean. The bottle is in the ocean, and the ocean is in the bottle. The ocean contains the bottle, but the bottle contains only a little bit of the ocean. So it is with the Christian."

We are filled unto the fullness of God, but, of course, we cannot contain all of God because God contains us; but we can have all of God that we can contain. If we only knew it, we could enlarge our vessel. The vessel gets bigger as we go on with God.

Ephesians 3:19; 2 Timothy 2:21-22
The Counselor, 68.

566. Holy Spirit: filling

It is the same with the fullness of the Holy Ghost. Evangelical Christianity believes it, but nobody experiences it. It lies under the snow, forgotten. I am praying that God may be able to melt away the ice from this blessed truth, and let it spring up again alive, that the Church and the people who hear may get some good out of it and not merely say "I believe" while it is buried under the snow of inactivity and nonattention.

How to Be Filled with the Holy Spirit, 19.

567. Holy Spirit: filling; Apathy

It may be said without qualification that every man is as holy and as full of the Spirit as he wants to be. He may not be as full as he wishes he were, but he is most certainly as full as he wants to be.

Our Lord placed this beyond dispute when He said, "Blessed are they which do hunger and thirst after righteousness: for they shall be filled." Hunger and thirst are physical sensations which, in their acute stages, may become real pain. It has been the experience of countless seekers after God that when their desires became a pain they were suddenly and wonderfully filled. The problem is not to persuade God to fill us, but to want God sufficiently to permit Him to do so. The average Christian is so cold and so contented with His wretched condition that there is no vacuum of desire into which the blessed Spirit can rush in satisfying fullness.

Psalm 42:1-2; Isaiah 55:1-2; Matthew 5:6; Ephesians 5:18-19
Born After Midnight, 8.

568. Holy Spirit: filling; Commitment

After a man is convinced that he can be filled with the Spirit he *must desire to be.* To the interested inquirer I ask these questions: Are you sure that you want to be possessed by a Spirit Who, while He is pure and gentle and wise and loving, will yet insist upon being Lord of your life? Are you sure you want your personality to be taken over by One Who will require obedience to the written Word? Who will not tolerate any of the self-sins in your life: self-love, self-indulgence? Who will not permit you to strut or boast or show off? Who will take the direction of your life away from you and will reserve the sovereign right to test you and discipline you? Who will strip away from you many loved objects which secretly harm your soul?

Unless you can answer an eager "Yes" to these questions you do not want to be filled. You may want the thrill or the victory or the power, but you do not really want to be filled with the Spirit. . . .

Before there can be fullness there must be emptiness. Before God can fill us with Himself we must first be emptied of ourselves.

Romans 14:7-9; 1 Corinthians 6:19-20; Ephesians 5:18
Keys to the Deeper Life, 51, 52, 54.

569. Holy Spirit: filling; Obedience: cost of; Lordship of Christ

Again, before you can be filled with the Spirit you must desire to be filled. Here I meet with a certain amount of puzzlement. Somebody will say, "How is it that you say to us that we must desire to be filled, because you know we desire to be. Haven't we talked to you in person? Haven't we called you on the phone? Aren't we out here tonight to hear the sermon on the Holy Spirit? Isn't this all a comforting indication to you that we are desirous of being filled with the Holy Spirit?"

Not necessarily, and I will explain why. For instance, are you sure that you want to be possessed by a spirit other than your own? even though that spirit be the pure Spirit of God? even though He be the very gentle essence of the gentle Jesus? even though He be sane and pure and free? even though He be wisdom personified, wisdom Himself, even though He have a healing, precious ointment to distill? even though He be loving as the heart of God? That Spirit, if He ever possesses you, will be the Lord of your Life!

I ask you, Do you want Him to be Lord of your life? That you want His benefits, I know. I take that for granted. But do you want to be possessed by Him? Do you want to hand the keys of your soul over to the Holy Spirit and say, "Lord, from now on I don't even have a key to my own house. I come and go as Thou tellest me"? Are you willing to give the office of your business establishment, your soul, over to the Lord and say to Jesus, "You sit in this chair and handle these telephones and boss the staff and be Lord of this outfit"? That is what I mean. Are you sure you want this? Are you sure that you desire it?

Romans 14:7-9; 1 Corinthians 6:19-20; Ephesians 5:18
How to Be Filled with the Holy Spirit, 42, 43.

570. Holy Spirit: filling; Obedience: need for

He will expect obedience to the written Word of God. But our human problem is that we would like to be full of the Spirit and yet go on and do as we please. The Holy Spirit who inspired the Scriptures will expect obedience to the Scriptures, and if we do not obey the Scriptures, we will quench Him. This Spirit will have obedience—but people do not want to obey the Lord. Everyone is as full as he wants to be. Everyone has as much of God as he desires to have. There is a fugitive impulse that comes to us, in spite of what we ask for when we pray in public, or even in private.

We want the thrill of being full, but we don't want to meet the conditions. We just don't want to be filled badly enough to be filled.

Ephesians 5:15-18; 1 Thessalonians 5:19-20; James 1:22-25
The Counselor, 76.

571. Holy Spirit: filling; Pastoral ministry: need for spiritual reality

Another thing that greatly hinders God's people is *a hardness of heart caused by hearing men without the Spirit constantly preaching about the Spirit*. There is no doctrine so chilling as the doctrine of the Spirit when held in cold passivity and personal unbelief. The hearers will turn away in dull apathy from an exhortation to be filled with the Spirit unless the Spirit Himself is giving the exhortation through the speaker. It is possible to learn this truth and preach it faithfully, and still be totally devoid of power. The hearers sense the lack and go away with numbed hearts. Theirs is not opposition to the truth, but an unconscious reaction from unreality.

Paths to Power, 55.

572. Holy Spirit: illumination

I would like to make an emphasis here and make it clearly: A revelation of the Holy Spirit in one glorious flash of inward illumination would teach you more of Jesus than five years in a theological seminary—and I believe in the seminary! You can learn about Jesus in the seminary. You can learn a great deal about Him, and we ought to learn everything we can about Him. We ought to read everything we can read about Him, for reading about Him is legitimate and good—a part of Christianity. But the final flash that introduces your heart to Jesus must be by the illumination of the Holy Spirit Himself, or it isn't done at all.

I am convinced that we only know Jesus Christ as well as the Holy Spirit is pleased to reveal Him unto us, for He cannot be revealed in any other way.... The Church cannot know Christ except as the Spirit reveals Him.

John 16:13-15; 1 Corinthians 2:12-16; 1 John 2:27
The Counselor, 28, 29.

573. Holy Spirit: illumination

That truth is in its essence spiritual must constantly be kept before our minds if we would know the truth indeed. Jesus Christ is Himself the Truth, and He cannot be confined to mere words even though, as we ardently believe, He has Himself inspired the words. That which is spiritual cannot be shut in by ink or fenced in by type and paper. The best a book can do is to give us the letter of truth. If we ever receive more than this, it must be by the Holy Spirit who gives it.

The great need of the hour among persons spiritually hungry is twofold: First, to know the Scriptures, apart from which no saving truth will be vouchsafed by our Lord; the second, to be enlightened by the Spirit, apart from whom the Scriptures will not be understood.

John 14:6,26; 2 Timothy 3:13-17
The Root of the Righteous, 37.

574. Holy Spirit: illumination; Textualism

The doctrine of the inability of the human mind and the need for divine illumination is so fully developed in the New Testament that it is nothing short of astonishing that we should have gone so far astray about the whole thing. Fundamentalism has stood aloof from the Liberal in self-conscious superiority and has on its own part fallen into error, the error of textualism, which is simply orthodoxy without the Holy Ghost. Everywhere among Conservatives we find persons who are Bible-taught but not Spirit-taught. They conceive truth to be something which they can grasp with the mind. If a man hold to the fundamentals of the Christian faith he is thought to possess divine truth. But it does not follow. There is no truth apart from the Spirit. The most brilliant intellect may be imbecilic when confronted with the mysteries of God. For a man to understand revealed truth requires an act of God equal to the original act which inspired the text. . . .

Conservative Christians in this day are stumbling over this truth. We need to re-examine the whole thing. We need to learn that truth consists not in correct doctrine, but in correct doctrine *plus the inward enlightenment of the Holy Spirit*. We must declare again the mystery of wisdom from above. A re-preachment of this vital truth could result in a fresh breath from God upon a stale and suffocating orthodoxy.

John 3:27; 1 Corinthians 2:12-16
The Pursuit of Man, 76, 77, 84.

575. Holy Spirit: indwelling

Deity indwelling men! That, I say, is Christianity, and no man has experienced rightly the power of Christian belief until he has known this for himself as a living reality. Everything else is preliminary to this. Incarnation, atonement, justification, regeneration; what are these but acts of God preparatory to the work of invading and the act of indwelling the redeemed human soul? Man who moved out of the heart of God by sin now moves back into the heart of God by redemption. God who moved out of the heart of man because of sin now enters again His ancient dwelling to drive out His enemies and once more make the place of His feet glorious.

John 14:15-17; 1 Corinthians 6:19-20
The Pursuit of Man, 100, 101.

576. Holy Spirit: inward witness; Apologetics; Claims of Christ

The Holy Spirit, whom Jesus also called the Spirit of Truth, has not come into this world to fool around. He will be found wherever the Lord's people meet, and in confirming the Word and the Person of Jesus Christ, He will demand moral action! ...

The Holy Spirit came to do a confirmatory work and He raised Him from the dead and since this mysterious witness is come, Jesus Christ is no longer on trial. It is no longer a question of "Was Jesus the Son of God?"

The Holy Spirit has taken that out of the realm of polemics and has put it in the realm of morals. The silent, immediate witness, this penetrating voice in the conscience of men tells us that this Person was indeed the very Son of God. . . .

Yes, the Holy Spirit's witness is a witness to the lordship and deity of the Son of God. Jesus Christ needs no more books written to prove that He is God. He needs no advocate pleading His cause before the unfriendly court of this world. He needs no witness to rise and say, "I know He is the Son of God."

The proof of the Sonship of Jesus has been removed from the realm of the intellect and placed where it has always belonged—in the realm of morals. And it is the Holy Spirit who has put it there.

John 15:26; John 16:8; Acts 17:30-31
Echoes from Eden, 25, 28-29.

577. Holy Spirit: inward witness; Apologetics; Testimonials

Our trouble is that we are trying to confirm the truth of Christianity by an appeal to external evidence. We are saying, "Well, look at this fellow. He can throw a baseball farther than anybody else and he is a Christian, therefore Christianity must be true." "Here is a great statesman who believes the Bible. Therefore, the Bible must be true." We quote Daniel Webster, or Roger Bacon. We write books to show that some scientist believed in Christianity: therefore, Christianity must be true. We are all the way out on the wrong track, brother! That is not New Testament Christianity at all. That is a pitiful, whimpering, drooling appeal to the flesh. That never was the testimony of the New Testament, never the way God did things—never! You might satisfy the intellects of men by external evidences, and Christ did, I say, point to external evidence when He was here on the earth. But He said, "I am sending you something better. I am taking Christian apologetics out of the realm of logic and putting it into the realm of life. I am proving My deity, and My proof will not be an appeal to a general or a prime minister. The proof lies in an invisible, unseen but powerful energy that visits the human soul when the gospel is preached—the Holy Ghost!"

Matthew 13:11,16-17; 1 Corinthians 2:12-16; 1 John 2:20
How to Be Filled with the Holy Spirit, 29, 30.

578. Holy Spirit: need for

In my sober judgment the relation of the Spirit to the believer is the most vital question the church faces today.

Keys to the Deeper Life, 57.

579. Holy Spirit: need for

David Brainerd once compared a man without the power of the Spirit trying to do spiritual work to a workman without fingers attempting to do manual labor. The figure is striking but it does not overstate the facts. The Holy Spirit is not a luxury meant to make deluxe Christians, as an illuminated frontispiece and a leather binding make a deluxe book. The Spirit is an imperative necessity. Only the Eternal Spirit can do eternal deeds.

John 15:1-7; Acts 1:8
Man: The Dwelling Place of God, 66.

580. Holy Spirit: need for; Dead churches; Church: Holy Spirit's work

I think we are going to have to restudy this whole teaching of the place of the Holy Spirit in the Church, so the Body can operate again. If the life goes out of a man's body, he is said to be a corpse. He is what they call "the remains." It is sad, but humorously sad, that a strong, fine man with shining eyes and vibrant voice, a living man, dies, and we say, "the remains" can be seen at a funeral home. All the remains of the man, and the least part about him, is what you can see there in the funeral home. The living man is gone. You have only the body. The body is "the remains."

So it is in the Church of Christ. It is literally true that some churches are dead. The Holy Spirit has gone out of them and all you have left are "the remains." You have the potential of the church but you do not have the church, just as you have in a dead man the potential of a living man but you do not have a living man. He can't talk, he can't taste, he can't touch, he can't feel, he can't smell, he can't see, he can't hear—because he is dead! The soul has gone out of the man, and when the Holy Spirit is not present in the Church, you have to get along after the methods of business or politics or psychology or human effort.

1 Thessalonians 5:19-20
The Counselor, 112, 113.

581. Holy Spirit: neglect of

Our insensibility to the presence of the Spirit is one of the greatest losses that our unbelief and preoccupation have cost us. We have made Him a tenet of our creed, we have enclosed Him in a religious word, but we have known Him little in personal experience. . . .

It will be a new day for us when we put away false notions and foolish fears and allow the Holy Spirit to fellowship with us as intimately as He wants to do, to talk to us as Christ talked to His disciples by the Sea of Galilee. After that there can be no more loneliness, only the glory of the never-failing Presence.

John 14:15-17
This World: Playground or Battleground?, 91, 92.

582. Holy Spirit: neglect of; Church: Holy Spirit's work

The continued neglect of the Holy Spirit by evangelical Christians is too evident to deny and impossible to justify. . . .

The only power God recognizes in His church is the power of His Spirit whereas the only power actually recognized today by the majority of evangelicals is the power of man. God does His work by the operation of the Spirit, while Christian leaders attempt to do theirs by the power of trained and devoted intellect. Bright personality has taken the place of the divine afflatus.

Acts 1:8; 1 Corinthians 1:26-29;
1 Thessalonians 2:4-6
God Tells the Man Who Cares, 108, 111.

583. Holy Spirit: neglect of; Church: Holy Spirit's work

A church without the Spirit is as helpless as Israel might have been in the wilderness if the fiery cloud had deserted them. The Holy Spirit is our cloud by day and our fire by night. Without Him we only wander aimlessly about the desert.

That is what we today are surely doing. We have divided ourselves into little ragged groups, each one running after a will-o'-the wisp or firefly in the mistaken notion that we are following the Shekinah. It is not only desirable that the cloudy pillar should begin to glow again. It is imperative.

Exodus 13:21; Nehemiah 9:19; Psalm 127:1-5
Keys to the Deeper Life, 50.

584. Holy Spirit: neglect of; Church: spiritual condition

This is the tragedy and the woe of the hour—we neglect the most important One who could possibly be in our midst—the Holy Spirit of God. Then, in order to make up for His absence, we have to do something to keep up our own spirits.

I remind you that there are churches so completely out of the hands of God that if the Holy Spirit withdrew from them, they wouldn't find it out for many months.

Ephesians 4:30
The Counselor, 52.

585. Holy Spirit: neglect of; Pastoral ministry: need for spiritual reality

"It is one thing," said Henry Suso, "to hear for oneself a sweet lute, sweetly played, and quite another thing merely to hear about it."

And it is one thing, we may add, to hear truth inwardly for

one's very self, and quite another thing merely to hear *about* it. . . .

We are turning out from the Bible schools of this country year after year young men and women who know the theory of the Spirit-filled life but do not enjoy the experience. These go out into the churches to create in turn a generation of Christians who have never felt the power of the Spirit and who know nothing personally about the inner fire. The next generation will drop even the theory. That is actually the course some groups have taken over the past years.

One word from the lips of the man who has actually heard the lute play will have more effect than a score of sermons by the man who has only heard that it was played. Acquaintance is always better than hearsay.

Luke 24:32; Ephesians 5:18-19; Colossians 3:16-18; 2 Timothy 3:13-17
The Root of the Righteous, 87, 88.

586. Holy Spirit: power of God

A definition of the word "power" means the ability to do. You know, because it is the Greek word from which our English word "dynamite" comes, some of the brethren try to make out that the Holy Spirit is dynamite, forgetting that they have the thing upside down. Dynamite was named after that Greek word, and the Holy Spirit and the power of God were not named after dynamite. Dynamite was discovered less than 200 years ago, but this Greek word from which we get our word "power" goes back to the time of Christ. It means "ability to do"—that is all, just "ability to do."

One man picks up a violin and he gets nothing out of it but squeaks and raucous sounds. That man doesn't have the ability to do. Another man picks up the violin and he is soon playing beautiful, rich melodies. One man steps into the prize ring and can't even lift his hands. The other fellow walks in and he has power to do, and soon the fellow who did not have the ability to do is sleeping peacefully on the floor.

It is the man with the ability to do who wins. It means the dynamic ability to be able to do what you are given to do. You will receive ability to do. It will come on you.

Luke 24:49; Acts 1:8
The Counselor, 61, 62.

587. Holy Spirit: spiritual gifts

For some time it has been evident that we evangelicals have

been failing to avail ourselves of the deeper riches of grace that lie in the purposes of God for us. As a consequence, we have been suffering greatly, even tragically. One blessed treasure we have missed is the right to possess the gifts of the Spirit as set forth in such fullness and clarity in the New Testament.

Romans 12:3-8; 1 Corinthians 12:1-11; Ephesians 4:11-16
Keys to the Deeper Life, 5.

588. Holy Spirit: spiritual gifts

In their attitude toward the gifts of the Spirit Christians over the last few years have tended to divide themselves into three groups.

First, there are those who magnify the gifts of the Spirit until they can see little else.

Second, there are those who deny that the gifts of the Spirit are intended for the Church in this period of her history.

Third, there are those who appear to be thoroughly bored with the whole thing and do not care to discuss it.

More recently we have become aware of another group, so few in number as scarcely to call for classification. It consists of those who want to know the truth about the Spirit's gifts and to experience whatever God has for them within the context of sound New Testament faith.

1 Corinthians 12:1-11
Keys to the Deeper Life, 40.

589. Holy Spirit: spiritual gifts

The time is more than ripe for a rethinking of the whole matter of spiritual gifts within the church of Christ. The subject has fallen into the hands of people for the most part extreme and irresponsible and has become associated with fanaticism in its various forms. This is a huge misfortune and is causing tremendous loss to the work of spiritual Christianity in our times.

Prejudices pro and con make the consideration of this subject extremely difficult, but its neglect is costing us more than we should be willing to pay. A revival of true New Testament Christianity must surely bring with it a manifestation of spiritual gifts. Anything short of it will create a just suspicion that the revival is something short of scriptural.

Romans 12:3-8; 1 Corinthians 12:1-11, 28-31
The Next Chapter After the Last, 80, 81.

590. Holy Spirit: spiritual gifts; Activity: religious; Pastoral ministry: need for spiritual reality

Let me shock you at this point. A naturally bright person can carry on religious activity without a special gift from God. Filling church pulpits every week are some who are using only natural abilities and special training. Some are known as Bible expositors, for it is possible to read and study commentaries and then repeat what has been learned about the Scriptures. Yes, it may shock you, but it is true that anyone able to talk fluently can learn to use religious phrases and can become recognized as a preacher.

But if any person is determined to preach so that his work and ministry will abide in the day of the judgment fire, then he must preach, teach and exhort with the kind of love and concern that comes only through a genuine gift of the Holy Spirit—something beyond his own capabilities. . . .

A Christian congregation can survive and often appear to prosper in the community by the exercise of human talent and without any touch from the Holy Spirit. But it is simply religious activity, and the dear people will not know anything better until the great and terrible day when our self-employed talents are burned with fire and only what was wrought by the Holy Spirit will stand.

1 Corinthians 2:1-5; 1 Corinthians 3:12-14; 1 Thessalonians 2:4-6
Tragedy in the Church: The Missing Gifts, 21, 22, 23.

591. Holy Spirit: spiritual gifts; Body of Christ; Church: Holy Spirit's work

The clear, emphatic teaching of the great apostle is that Christ is the Head of the Church which is His body. . . .

As a normal man consists of a body with various obedient members with a head to direct them, so the true Church is a body, individual Christians being the members and Christ the Head.

The mind works through the members of the body, using them to fulfill its intelligent purposes. Paul speaks of the foot, the hand, the ear, the eye as being members of the body, each with its proper but limited function; but it is the Spirit that worketh in them (I Cor. 12:1-31). . . .

The intelligent head can work only as it has at its command organs designed for various tasks. It is the mind that sees, but it must have an eye to see through. It is the mind that hears, but it cannot hear without an ear.

And so with all the varied members which are the instruments by means of which the mind moves into the external world to carry out its plans.

As all man's work is done by his mind, so the work of the church is done by the Spirit, and by Him alone. But to work He must set in the body certain members with abilities specifically created to act as media through which the Spirit can flow toward ordained ends. That, in brief, is the philosophy of the gifts of the Spirit.

1 Corinthians 12; Ephesians 4:14-16; Colossians 1:18
Keys to the Deeper Life, 43, 44.

592. Holy Spirit: spiritual gifts; Church: Holy Spirit's work; Church: spiritual condition

For a generation certain evangelical teachers have told us that the gifts of the Spirit ceased at the death of the apostles or at the completion of the New Testament....

The result of this erroneous teaching is that spiritually gifted persons are ominously few among us. When we so desperately need leaders with the gift of discernment, for instance, we do not have them and are compelled to fall back upon the techniques of the world.

This frightening hour calls aloud for men with the gift of prophetic insight. Instead we have men who conduct surveys, polls and panel discussions.

We need men with the gift of knowledge. In their place we have men with scholarship— nothing more.

Romans 12:3-8; 1 Corinthians 13:10; 1 Corinthians 14:1
Keys to the Deeper Life, 44, 45.

593. Holy Spirit: spiritual gifts; Fanatics; Extremes

This is a crude illustration, but let me tell you what we did after planting a field of corn when I was a young fellow in Pennsylvania. To save the field of corn from the crows, we would shoot an old crow and hang him by his heels in the middle of the field. This was supposed to scare off all of the crows for miles around. The crows would hold a conference and say, "Look, there is a field of corn but don't go near it. I saw a dead crow over there!"

That's the kind of conference that Satan calls, and that is exactly what he has done. He has taken some fanatical, weird, wild-eyed Christians who do things that they shouldn't, and he has stationed them in the middle of God's cornfield, and warns, "Now, don't you go near that doctrine about the Holy Spirit because if you do, you will act just like these wild-eyed fanatics."

1 Corinthians 14:27-33; 1 Thessalonians 5:19-20
The Counselor, 63.

594. Holy Spirit: spiritual gifts; Holy Spirit: need for

The important thing is that the Holy Spirit desires to take us and control us and use us as instruments and organs through whom He can express Himself in the body of Christ. Perhaps I can use my hands as a further illustration of this truth.

My hands are about average, I suppose—perhaps a little large for the size of my body, probably because I had to do a lot of farm work when I was a boy. But there is something I must tell you about these hands. They cannot play a violin. They cannot play the organ or the piano. They cannot paint a picture. They can barely hold a screwdriver to do a small repair job to keep things from falling apart at home. *I have ungifted hands.* . . .

You will agree that it would be foolish for me to try to bring forth any delightful organ music using such ungifted hands. Is it not appalling, then, to think that we allow this very thing to happen in the body of Christ? We enlist people and tell them to get busy doing God's work, failing to realize the necessity of the Spirit's control and functioning if there is to be a spiritual result.

1 Corinthians 12:1-11; Philippians 2:12-13
Tragedy in the Church: The Missing Gifts, 30, 31.

595. Holy Spirit: spiritual gifts; Holy Spirit: need for; Church: Holy Spirit's work

Much of the religious activity we see in our churches is not the eternal working of the Eternal Spirit but the mortal working of man's mortal mind.

That is raw tragedy!

From what I see and sense in evangelical circles, I would have to say that about 90 percent of the religious work carried on in churches is being done by ungifted members. I am speaking of men and women who know how to do many things but who fail to display the spiritual gifts promised through the Holy Spirit. . . .

The Spirit of God, His presence and His gifts are not simply desirable in our Christian congregations; they are absolutely imperative!

1 Corinthians 1:26-29; 1 Corinthians 12:1-11
Tragedy in the Church: The Missing Gifts, 25, 27.

596. Home; Entertainment; America: greatness

While it is scarcely within the scope of the present piece, I cannot refrain from remarking that the most ominous sign of the coming destruction of our country is the passing of the American home. Americans live no longer in homes, but in theaters. The members of many families hardly know each other, and the face of some popular TV star is to many wives as familiar as that of their husbands. Let no one smile. Rather should we weep at the portent. It will do no good to wrap ourselves in the Stars and Stripes for protection. No nation can long endure whose people have sold themselves for bread and circuses. Our fathers sleep soundly, and the harsh bedlam of commercialized noise that engulfs us like something from Dante's *Inferno* cannot disturb their slumber. They left us a goodly heritage. To preserve that heritage we must have a national character as strong as theirs. And this can be developed only in the Christian home.

Deuteronomy 6:4-9; Proverbs 24:3-4; Ephesians 6:4
Of God and Men, 127, 128.

597. Home; Family

It is vitally important that our homes be preserved. A nation is only as strong as its homes. No government can substitute for the ministrations of the family. Federal agencies cannot love and cuddle the baby, not kiss his bruised knee or hear his prayer at the close of the day. Fathers and mothers make homes; nothing else can. And whether our American homes produce delinquents or upright citizens will depend altogether upon what kind of fathers and mothers preside in those homes.

If the home is the oldest institution on earth the Church is the loftiest, and historically there has always been a close relationship between the two. The family that stays close to the church is the one most likely to hold together.

Psalm 127:1-5
The Price of Neglect, 116.

598. Honesty; Values; Character; Quakers

Do you know that one of the things that marked the lives of the original Quakers was their honest handling of the truth? They would not lie and they would not stretch the truth. They would not steal and they would not use flattering words. Someone in history wrote about the lives of the Quakers and commented that they "astonished the Christian world by insisting upon acting like Christians." In England they were often kicked around and some languished in jail because they insisted on honoring only God and refused to bow down to people who did not deserve it. In the midst of professing Christians who generally acted like the world, the honest, God-honoring Quakers were considered queer because they sought to live as Christians should.

Acts 5:29; Ephesians 4:25; Colossians 3:5-11
Who Put Jesus on the Cross?, 24, 25.

599. Hope

Hope is a nurse and comforter and enables us to go on after every reason for going on has disappeared. Hope has sustained the spirit of a shipwrecked sailor and given him strength to stay alive through the long days that seemed years till help and rescue came; hope has steeled the patriot to fight on and win at last against overwhelming odds; hope has saved from insanity or suicide the prisoner in his lonely cell as he checked off the years and months and days on his homemade calendar; hope has enabled the sick or injured man to wait out the pain and the nausea till health returned and the suffering ended; hope has made light the feet of the traveler hurrying home in near exhaustion to the bedside of someone he loved. . . .

So strong, so beautiful is hope that it is scarcely possible to overpraise it. It is the divine alchemy that transmutes the base metal of adversity into gold. In the midst of death Paul could be bold and buoyant because he had firm confidence in the final outcome. "For we who are alive are always being given over to death for Jesus' sake," he said, but his heart remained cheerful knowing that "our light and momentary troubles are achieving for us an eternal glory that far outweighs them all" (2 Corinthians 4:11, 17). . . .

The Christian's hope is sound because it is founded upon the character of God and the redeeming work of His Son Jesus Christ. For this reason Peter could call it "a living hope" (I Peter 1:3). It is living because it rests on reality and not on fancy. It is not wishful dreaming but vital expectation with the whole might of the Most High behind it.

Romans 15:13; 2 Corinthians 4:8-11, 16-18;
1 Peter 1:3-5
The Size of the Soul, 89, 90, 91.

600. Hope

Only a Christian has a right to hope, for only he has the power of God to give substance to his hope.

Hebrews 6:17-20
The Size of the Soul, 94.

601. Hope; Change

The Christian church cannot effectively be Christ's church if it fails to firmly believe and boldly proclaim to every person: "You can be changed! You do not have to remain as you are!" This is a hope held out not just to the desperate drug addict and the helpless drunkard; it is valid for every person the world over. . . .

Clay is not fixed. It is malleable; it can be shaped. After clay has been shaped by the potter, who gives it the form he wants it to have, he puts it aside to dry. Then he bakes it under intense heat, sometimes also adding a glaze, which is also baked on.

That piece of clay, once so malleable, is now permanently fixed. It is no longer subject to any changes. Once clay has been baked and glazed, the only way it can be changed is by destruction. The object can be shattered and ruined, but it can never be changed into something more beautiful or useful because it can never regain its malleable state.

For the apostle through the Holy Spirit to say, "Do not conform," is indication that the baking-glazing of our natures has not yet occurred. Thankfully, we are in a state of malleability regarding moral character.

There are two things that can be said to any person, whether an innocent youngster or a professional criminal on death row awaiting his fate for kidnapping and murder. The first is, "You can be changed!" The second, which is related, is this: "You are not finished yet!"

Romans 12:1-2; 2 Corinthians 5:17; 1 Peter 1:14-16
Tragedy in the Church: The Missing Gifts, 116, 117, 118.

602. Hope; Heaven: certainty of; Death: no fear of

Brethren, we have been born of God and our Christian hope is a valid hope! No emptiness, no vanity, no dreams that cannot come true. Your expectation should rise and you should challenge God and begin to dream high dreams of faith and spiritual attainment and expect God to meet them. You cannot out-hope God and you cannot out-expect God. Remember that all of your hopes are finite, but all of God's ability is infinite! . . .

I dare to say this to you, my friends—your Christian hope is just as good as Jesus Christ. Your anticipation for the future lives or dies with Jesus. If He is who He said He was, you can spread your wings and soar. If He is not, you will fall to the ground like a lump of lead.

Jesus Christ is our hope and God has raised Him from the dead and since Jesus overcame the grave, Christians dare to die.

Isaiah 25:8; Romans 8:35-39; 1 Corinthians 15:19-20, 51-57; 1 Peter 1:3-5
I Call It Heresy!, 41, 42.

603. Hospitality; Poverty

There is an evil which I have seen under the sun—one that grows and does not diminish. . . .

It is the evil of giving to them that have and withholding from them that have not. It is the evil of blessing with a loud voice them that are already blessed and letting the unblessed and the outcast lie forgotten.

Let a man appear in a local Christian fellowship and let him be one whose fame is bruited abroad, whose presence will add something to the one who entertains him, and immediately a score of homes will be thrown open and every eager hospitality will be extended to him. But the obscure and the unknown must be content to sit on the fringes of the Christian circle and not once be invited into any home. . . .

Our Lord warned us against the snare of showing kindness only to such as could return such kindness and so cancel out any positive good we may have thought we were doing. By this test, a world of religious activity is being wasted in our churches. To invite in well-fed and well-groomed friends to share our hospitality with the full knowledge that we will be invited to receive the same kindness again on the first convenient evening is in no sense an act of Christian hospitality. It is of the earth earthy; its motive is fleshly; no sacrifice is entailed; its moral content is nil and it will be accounted wood, hay, stubble before the judgment seat of Christ. . . .

Let us not become indignant at this blunt portrayal of facts. Let us rather humble ourselves to serve God's poor. Let us seek to be like Jesus in our devotion to the forgotten of the earth who have nothing to recommend them but their poverty and their heart-hunger and their tears.

Matthew 25:34-40; 1 Corinthians 3:12-14; James 2:1-5
We Travel an Appointed Way, 72, 73, 75.

604. Humanism; Opposition

Leaders and groups and nations often think they have something great and enduring and superior going for them in human society, and because we don't jump on the bandwagon and remark, instead, that "This, too, will pass away," we get a look of anger with the comment, "You are a cynical pessimist."

Let me say that it is very difficult to have any brains in this day in which we live and not get blamed for it. It is hard to have any insight and not be considered a cynic. It is hard to be realistic and not be classed with the pessimists.

But with most men and their methods and movements in society, a few months, at the most a few years, bring an entirely new perspective. People who disagreed with you and were engaged in flag-waving for someone's scheme or speech six months ago are probably looking back on that same thing and see it now just as you foresaw it.

It is a wonderfully exhilarating thing to be able to anticipate and foresee just a little bit—but it is also an ability that will bring you much criticism and hostility from those with lesser foresight and judgment.

Psalm 2; Psalm 73:15-20; Isaiah 40:12-15
Who Put Jesus on the Cross?, 78, 79.

605. Humanism; Redemption

The world is staggering on to no foreseeable future. We're having a mixed-up time of it because we are putting God down and putting men up. When humanism came along about a generation ago and made the human mind to be the criterion of all thought and put God down, theology ceased to be the queen of the sciences. The queen of the sciences became science itself, or humanism or sociology. Then, of course, we went down because we had not put God up. If you exalt God, God will exalt you. But if you put God down, you will go down. And the world is in the mess it's in because God has no place in the minds or hearts of the people.

The work of God in redemption is to restore this inverted order: to put God up and man down, in order that He might put man up. Now in order that He might do that, God came down—as far down as He could get.

Psalm 36:1-9; 2 Corinthians 10:5; Philippians 2:6-7
Success and the Christian, 136.

606. Humble service; Prayers

O God, let Thy glory be revealed once more to men: through me if it please Thee, or without me or apart from me, it matters not. Restore Thy church to the place of moral beauty that becomes her as the Bride of Christ: through me, or apart from me; only let this prayer be answered. O God, honor whom Thou wilt. Let me be used or overlooked or ignored or forgotten.

Keys to the Deeper Life, 66.

607. Humble service; Pride: human

We can never get too weak for the Lord to use us—but we can get too strong, if it is our own strength. We can never be too ignorant for the Lord to use us—but we can be too wise in our own conceit. We can never get too small for the Lord to use us, but we can surely get too big and get in His way.

Jeremiah 9:23-24; Romans 12:3-8; 2 Corinthians 12:9-10
Jesus Is Victor!, 63.

608. Humble service; Success; Servanthood

Had it happened in North America in our era, some publisher would have flown in to offer John a five- or six-figure check for book rights to his story. But I do not think John would have been concerned about turning a personal financial profit from his experience. The present-day financial value of a "born again testimony" was mercifully unknown in A.D. 95.

"Give your heart to the Lord, get born again, and your business will grow and grow and grow!" "If you want to become a top athlete and be well known, just accept the Lord and be born again!" "If you want your cows to give more milk. . . ." "If you want to be sure of getting better grades in college. . . ."

Possibly no one ever had a clearer, sweeter, stronger testimony of the grace and salvation that is in Jesus Christ than John. Humbly he related it: "I . . . [am] your brother and companion in . . . suffering. . . . [I] was on the island of Patmos because of the word of God and the testimony of Jesus."

In our day, the media would be asking, "What are you doing there on Patmos, John? You were the bishop at Ephesus. You should be at home among your people, presiding over your congregation. You were born again, were you not, John?"

"Yes," John would have replied meekly, "I was the Lord's disciple and companion, and I have been ministering and witnessing as He said. I am now His servant in exile."

John 13:23; Revelation 1:9
Jesus Is Victor!, 57.

609. Humility

We are to be a church of the living God, and not a gathering of the influential and the big shots. The big shots can come if they get on their knees—a big shot on his knees isn't any taller than anyone else, you know.

Luke 18:9-14; Philippians 2:3-4; James 2:1-5
The Counselor, 11.

610. Humility

True humility is a healthy thing. The humble man accepts the truth about himself. He believes that in his fallen nature dwells no good thing. He acknowledges that apart from God he is nothing, has nothing, knows nothing and can do nothing. But this knowledge does not discourage him, for he knows also that in Christ he is somebody. He knows that he is dearer to God than the apple of His eye and that he can do all things through Christ who strengthens him; that is, he can do all that lies within the will of God for him to do.

Romans 7:18; Romans 12:3-8; 1 Corinthians 4:7; Philippians 4:13
God Tells the Man Who Cares, 171, 172.

611. Humility

I once heard a brother preach on the fact that the church should be without spot or wrinkle. To get the wrinkles out of a sack, he said, you fill it. To get a wrinkle out of a rug, you lay it down and walk on it. God sometimes fills us, the preacher continued, but sometimes He just puts us flat down so that everyone can walk on us!

2 Corinthians 4:8-11; Ephesians 5:25-29
Men Who Met God, 117, 118.

612. Humility; Prayers

Lord, make me childlike. Deliver me from the urge to compete with another for place or prestige or position. I would be simple and artless as a little child. Deliver me from pose and pretense. Forgive me for thinking of myself. Help me to forget myself and find my true peace in beholding Thee. That Thou may answer this prayer I humble myself before Thee. Lay upon me Thy easy yoke of self-forgetfulness that through it I may find rest. Amen.

Matthew 11:28-30; Matthew 18:4; Philippians 2:3-4
The Pursuit of God, 107, 108.

613. Humility; Pride: human

Again, there is a close relation between humility and the perception of truth. "The meek will he guide in judgment: and the meek will he teach his way" (Psa. 25:9). In the Scriptures I find no shred of encouragement for the proud. Only the tame sheep can be led; only the humble child need expect the guidance of the Father's hand. When all the evidence is in it may well be found that none but the proud ever strayed from the truth and that self-trust was behind every heresy that ever afflicted the church.

Psalm 25:9; Proverbs 3:5,6; James 1:5-6
That Incredible Christian, 51, 52.

614. Humility; Pride: human; Spiritual warfare

The enemy never quite knows how to deal with a humble man; he is so used to dealing with proud, stubborn people that a meek man upsets his timetable. And furthermore, the man of true humility has God fighting on his side—who can win against God?

Strange as it may seem we often win over our enemies only after we have first been soundly defeated by the Lord Himself. God often conquers our enemies by conquering us.... When God foresees that we must meet a deadly opponent, he assures our victory by bringing us down in humbleness at His own feet. After that, everything is easy. We have put ourselves in a position where God can fight for us, and in a situation like that, the outcome is decided from eternity.

Numbers 12:3; 2 Chronicles 20:12; Philippians 2:3-4
We Travel an Appointed Way, 14.

615. Humility; Unworthiness

It has been the unanimous testimony of the greatest Christian souls that the nearer they drew to God the more acute became their consciousness of sin and their sense of personal unworthiness. The purest souls never knew how pure they were and the greatest saints never guessed that they were great. The very thought that they were good or great would have been rejected by them as a temptation of the devil.

They were so engrossed with gazing upon the face of God that they spent scarce a moment looking at themselves. They were suspended in that sweet paradox of spiritual awareness where they knew that they were clean through the blood of the Lamb and yet felt that they deserved only death and hell as their just reward.

Isaiah 6:5-8; Romans 7:15-25; 1 Timothy 1:15-16
Keys to the Deeper Life, 34, 35.

616. Humor: off-color

One of the most shocking things in the church is the dirty-mouthed Christian who always walks on the borderline. There is no place for borderline stories that embarrass some people, and there is nothing about sex or the human body that is funny if your mind is clean.

There was once a gathering of officers, and George Washington was present in the room. One of the young officers began to think about a dirty story that he wanted to tell, and he got a smirk on his face. He looked around and said, "I'm thinking of a story. I guess there are no ladies present." Washington straightened up and said, "No, young man, but there are gentlemen." The young officer shut his mouth and kept the dirty story inside his dirty head and heart.

Anything you could not tell with Jesus present, do not tell. Anything you could not laugh at were Jesus present, do not laugh at.

Matthew 12:34-37; Ephesians 4:29; Ephesians 5:3-4; James 3:5-6
Rut, Rot or Revival: The Condition of the Church, 67.

617. Humor: proper place of

We should all be aware by this time that one way the devil has of getting rid of something is to make jokes about it. Every one of us needs to be warned often about the corruption of our minds by the papers and magazines and entertainment.

There is a legitimate humor, and we all admit that. I think a sense of humor is in us by the gift of God.

But whenever that humor takes a holy thing as its object, that humor is devilish at once. . . .

There is plenty to laugh at in the world, including politics—which is usually funny anyway. But be sure that you do not laugh at something that God Himself takes very seriously.

Matthew 12:34-37; Romans 13:11-14; Ephesians 5:3-4
Echoes from Eden, 61, 62.

618. Hypocrisy

It would be a convenient arrangement were we so constituted that we could not talk better than we live.

For reasons known to God, however, there seems to be no necessary connection between our speaking and our doing; and here lies one of the deadliest snares in the religious life. I am afraid we modern Christians are long on talk and short on conduct. We use the language of power but our deeds are the deeds of weakness.

Matthew 23:2-3; James 3:17
Born After Midnight, 32.

619. Hypocrisy

I have long believed that a man who spurns the Christian faith outright is more respected before God and the heavenly powers than the man who pretends to religion but refuses to come under its total domination. The first is an overt enemy, the second a false friend.

Matthew 23:27-28; Revelation 3:15-17
Of God and Men, 39, 40.

620. Hypocrisy

Certainly the non-Christian is not too much to be blamed if he turns disgustedly away from the invitation of the Gospel after he has been exposed for a while to the inconsistencies of those of his acquaintance who profess to follow Christ. The deadening effect of religious make-believe on the human mind is beyond all describing.

The Root of the Righteous, 53.

I

621. Identity with Christ; Eternal perspective

We who are involved in the upward gaze of this long-range faith identify ourselves with Jesus Christ forever! We are satisfied that God is at work. We are satisfied to be misunderstood for Christ's sake. We are willing to be treated as the minority, for the people of God are always in the minority in this earthly context.

Our true identity is with Jesus Christ, our Savior and Lord. We have taken His cause as our cause. We have taken His way as our way. We have taken His place as our place. We have taken His future as our future. We have taken His life as our life. We have taken the long look of faith to the day of His triumph, and we know it will be our triumph as well....

Men and women committed to long-range faith can die with blessing and satisfaction even if they have not received the fulfillment of the promises. They have confessed themselves to be strangers and pilgrims on the earth. Their waiting is blessed because it is a waiting on God.

John 15:18-21; Colossians 3:1-4; 2 Timothy 1:11-12; Hebrews 11:13-16
Jesus, Author of Our Faith, 62, 63.

622. Idolatry

The fallen heart is by nature idolatrous. There appears to be no limit to which some of us will go to save our idol, while at the same time telling ourselves eagerly that we are trusting in Christ alone. It takes a violent act of renunciation to deliver us from the hidden idol, and since very few modern Christians understand that such an act is necessary, and only a small number of those who know are willing to do, it follows that relatively few professors of the Christian faith these days have ever experienced the painful act of renunciation that frees the heart from idolatry....

Grace will save a man but it will not save him and his idol. The blood of Christ will shield the penitent sinner alone, but never the sinner and his idol. Faith will justify the sinner, but it will never justify the sinner and his sins.

Joshua 24:14-15; 1 Kings 18:21; 1 Thessalonians 1:9
Man: The Dwelling Place of God, 89, 90.

623. Idolatry; Rivals of God

Now brethren, this is one of our greatest faults in our Christian lives. We are allowing too many rivals of God. We actually have too many gods. We have too many irons in the fire. We have too much theology that we don't understand. We have too much churchly institutionalism. We have too much religion. Actually, I guess we just have too much of too much!

God is not in our beings by Himself! He cannot do His will in us and through us because we refuse to put away the rivals. When Jesus Christ has cleansed everything from the temple and dwells there alone, He will work!

Matthew 21:12-13; Luke 16:10-13
I Talk Back to the Devil, 71, 72.

624. Illness

I'd run a mile to keep from having a needle put in my arm.

Once when I was ill, a heart specialist came to my house—somebody sent for him, I don't know who. He came upstairs to my room and sat down beside my bed. And when he came in, he had this huge rocket in his hand with a long sucker affair; and I saw it. And, brother, did I argue him down.

He said, "Now, I'll give you this and you'll sleep and you'll be all right. It's just a sedative."

I said, "You won't give me that."

And he said, "Well, if you are going to make so much of it, probably you'd be worse off if you took it." So he said goodbye and left. And I got better.

Success and the Christian, 82.

625. Imagination; Wonder

A purified and Spirit-controlled imagination is, however, quite another thing, and it is this I have in mind here. I long to see the imagination released from its prison and given to its proper place among the sons of the new creation. What I am trying to describe here is the sacred gift of seeing, the ability to peer beyond the veil and gaze with astonished wonder upon the beauties and mysteries of things holy and eternal.

The stodgy pedestrian mind does no credit to Christianity. Let it dominate the church long enough and it will force her to take one of two directions: either toward liberalism, where she will find relief in a false freedom, or toward the world, where she will find an enjoyable but fatal pleasure.

Born After Midnight, 94, 95.

626. Immortality; Eternity; Death: triumph in

It was then that Paul wrote a letter to a young friend, Timothy.

"For I am already being poured out like a drink offering, and the time has come for my departure" (2 Timothy 4:6), he wrote. He knew that death was near, so he wrote on:

"I have fought a good fight" (4:7)—past perfect tense!

"I have finished the race" (4:7)—past perfect tense!

"My testimony has been given. I am a martyr and a witness. I have done all that I could for Jesus. The war is over and I will take off my uniform. I have completed God's plan for me on earth."

According to the logic of death, the next words should have been "The End," for within a few days, Paul knelt on the flagstones of a Roman prison and the executioner severed his head from his body with a sword.

He had written his last testimony, but he did not say, "This is the end of Paul." Instead, he had purposely added one of those conjunctive words that speaks of a yesterday and connects it to a tomorrow.

"I have finished my course.... *Henceforth* (KJV)" (4:7-8).

Paul was testifying: "All of these things were a part of the human biography, but I am going on to another and better and eternal chapter!" For Paul, it was the blessed experience of coming to the next chapter after the last! ...

Thank God for the gracious chapter still being written, the chapter titled "Immortality." It is the chapter of God's tomorrows. It is the chapter of the henceforths known only to the children of God.

2 Timothy 4:6-8; 1 Peter 1:3-5
Who Put Jesus on the Cross?, 103, 104, 105, 107.

627. Immortality; Sin: consequences of; Man: spiritual searching

We take it for granted and we are not surprised at all about the eternal nature of God but the greater wonder is that God has seen fit to put His own everlastingness within the hearts of men and women. . . .

I believe that this is the truth about our troubles and our problems: We are disturbed because God has put everlastingness in our hearts. He has put a longing for immortality in our beings. He has put something within men and women that demands God and heaven—and yet we are too blind and sinful to find Him or even to look for Him! . . .

Men and women need to be told plainly, and again and again, why they are disturbed and why they are upset. They need to be told why they are lost and that if they will not repent they will certainly perish. Doctors and counselors will tell troubled men and women that their problems are psychological, but it is something deeper within the human being that troubles and upsets—it is the longing after eternity!

Ecclesiastes 3:11; Luke 13:3-5; Romans 3:10-18
Christ the Eternal Son, 52, 53, 54.

628. Imperfections of men

Our lofty idealism would argue that all Christians should be perfect, but a blunt realism forces us to admit that perfection is rare even among the saints. The part of wisdom is to accept our Christian brothers and sisters for what they are rather than for what they should be. . . .

There is much that is imperfect about us, and it is fitting that we recognize it and call upon God for charity to put up with one another. The perfect church is not on this earth. The most spiritual church is sure to have in it some who are still bothered by the flesh.

An old Italian proverb says, "He that will have none but a perfect brother must resign himself to remain brotherless." However earnestly we may desire that our Christian brother go on toward perfection, we must accept him as he is and learn to get along with him. To treat an imperfect brother impatiently is to advertise our own imperfections.

Romans 15:1; Galatians 6:2-3;
1 Thessalonians 5:13-15
We Travel an Appointed Way, 55.

629. Indifference; Apathy; Jesus Christ: His death

I once heard a very fine speaker, an effective preacher, describe what he had found in the emotional responses of an audience. He said he had told the story of a faithful old sheep dog. In the midst of a great storm, the herder knew that 11 young lambs were missing. Once, twice, three times he sent Old Shep, the dog, out for the missing lambs. And again and again, until the weary but faithful dog had returned with 10 of the lambs.

Once again the master took Old Shep to the door. "One more, Shep, one more," he said. "Bring him in!" The dog, utterly exhausted, went out into the storm again. Much later he returned, bearing the missing lamb. The old dog slowly placed the weak, wet lamb on the floor, then slumped to the floor himself.

As the shepherd finished caring for the stray lamb, he turned to Old Shep to express his gratitude. But it was too late. Shep was dead. The faithful dog had given his all to rescue the lambs.

The preacher who was describing his telling of the story said his audience was in tears as he finished. To that audience, then, he made the gospel application, deliberately and intentionally. He told of the faithfulness of the Son of Man as He was led to Calvary. He described the kind of love that motivated Jesus to die on Calvary's cross.

"I painted the picture of Jesus as vividly as I could," said the preacher in recounting the experience. "I let the Savior hang there for men and women to see."

And what was the result? "An obvious look of stony indifference came over those people," the preacher concluded. "They had been moved by the story of the faithful dog. They had been moved to tears. But the Savior's dying on the cross? They had heard that before—and they were no longer stirred by it!"

Matthew 27:27-31
Jesus, Author of Our Faith, 37, 38.

630. Indispensability: prideful thoughts of

I once preached a sermon in which I said that the Lord is self-sufficient and does not really need us. I bothered some people by that, for they thought the Lord really needed them. They thought that if they should resign or retire, the Lord would have to scramble to find someone who could take their place. What a low view of God! Could you get down on your knees and cry out to a God who needed you? I could not. A God who needed me would be a God in real trouble. God does not have to have me—or you, either. That may be bitter medicine for some to take, because we have come to believe that we are indispensable and that, when we go, a great tree will have fallen, leaving a vacant place against the sky. I am afraid that when some of us die, it will be like a stalk of grass eaten by a grasshopper, and nobody will notice the difference!

Faith Beyond Reason, 135, 136.

631. Influences; Music; Entertainment; Reading: dangers of

What can be said about the books and magazines you read? What you read will shape you by slowly conditioning your mind. Little by little, even though you think you are resisting, you will take on the shape of the mind of the author of that book you are reading. You will begin to put your emphasis where he puts his. You will begin to put your values where she places hers. You will find yourself liking what he likes, thinking as she thinks.

The same is certainly true of the power of modern films. If you give yourself over to their influences, they will shape your mind and your morals.

What about the music you enjoy? It seems almost too late in these times to try to warn against what many in our society seem to revel in—the vile, vicious, obscene gutter language of so much popular music. It is not overstating the case to insist that the kinds of music you enjoy will demonstrate rather accurately what you are like inside. If you give yourself to the contemporary fare of music that touches the baser emotions, it will shape your mind, your emotions, your desires, whether you admit it or not.

You can drink poison if you want to, but I am still friend enough to warn you that if you do, you will be carried out in a box. I cannot stop you, but I can warn you. I have not the authority to tell you what you should listen to, but I have a divine commission to tell you that if you love and listen to the wrong kinds of music, your inner life will wither and die.

Proverbs 4:23; 2 Corinthians 10:5; Philippians 4:8
Tragedy in the Church: The Missing Gifts, 125, 126.

632. Influences; Pleasures; Entertainment

You can drink poison if you want to, but I am still friend enough to warn you that if you do, you will be carried out in a box. I cannot stop you, but I can warn you. I have not the authority to tell you what you should listen to, but I have a divine commission to tell you that if you love and listen to the wrong kinds of music, your inner life will wither and die.

What about the pleasures you indulge in. If I should start to catalog some of your pastimes, you would probably break in and ask, "What's wrong with this?" "What's wrong with that?" There probably is no answer that will completely satisfy you if you are asking the question. But this is my best answer: Give a person ten years in the wrong kind of indulgence and questionable atmosphere, and see what happens to the inward spiritual life.

The pleasures in which we indulge selfishly will shape us and fashion us over the years. Whatever gives us pleasure has the subtle power to change us and enslave us.

Proverbs 4:23; 1 Corinthians 6:12; Ephesians 2:1-3; 1 John 2:15-17
Tragedy in the Church: The Missing Gifts, 126, 127.

633. Inheritance; Blessings: unlimited

It is openly taught from Genesis to Revelation that the true believer stands to benefit from an inheritance. God being who He is, His beneficence and His benefits are infinite and limitless.

I believe that God always touches with infinity everything that He does and this leads to the thought that the inheritance we receive must be equal to the God who gives it. Being God, He does not deal in things which are merely finite. Therefore, the inheritance that the child of God receives is limitless and infinite.

What a contrast to our small gifts and legacies and benefits on this earth! . . .

Even the world's richest man can only leave what he has—nothing more. Somewhere, the millions give out and every estate has a boundary. But, God being who He is, the inheritance we receive from Him is limitless—it is all of the universe! . . .

We humans should remember that when our high flights of imagination have taken wings upward we can be sure that we have never quite reached as high as His provision, because our imagination will always falter, run out of energy and fall weakly to the ground. In contrast, there is no limit to the infinite benefactions of God Almighty to His redeemed ones.

Matthew 7:7-11; Romans 8:16-17; 1 Peter 1:4
I Call It Heresy!, 77, 78, 79.

634. Insignificance: feelings of; Individual importance

No matter how insignificant he may have been before, a man becomes significant the moment he has had an encounter with the Son of God. When the Lord lays His hand upon a man, that man ceases at once to be ordinary. He immediately becomes extraordinary, and his life takes on cosmic significance. The angels in heaven take notice of him and go forth to become his ministers (Hebrews 1:14). Though the man had before been only one of the faceless multitude, a mere cipher in the universe, an invisible dust grain blown across endless wastes—now he gets a face and a name and a place in the scheme of meaningful things. Christ knows His own sheep "by name."

A young preacher introduced himself to the pastor of a great metropolitan church with the words, "I am just the pastor of a small church upcountry." "Son," replied the wise minister, "there are no small churches." And there are no unknown Christians, no insignificant sons of God. Each one signifies, each is a "sign" drawing the attention of the Triune God day and night upon him. The faceless man has a face, the nameless man a name, when Jesus picks him out of the multitude and calls him to Himself.

Psalm 8:3-5; John 10:3; Hebrews 1:13-14
We Travel an Appointed Way, 19.

635. Instant Christianity; Discipleship

It is hardly a matter of wonder that the country that gave the world instant tea and instant coffee should be the one to give it instant Christianity. If these two beverages were not actually invented in the United States it was certainly here that they received the advertising impetus that has made them known to most of the civilized world. And it cannot be denied that it was American Fundamentalism that brought instant Christianity to the gospel churches....

Instant Christianity came in with the machine age. Men invented machines for two purposes. They wanted to get important work done more quickly and easily than they could do it by hand, and they wanted to get the work over with so they could give their time to pursuits more to their liking, such as loafing or enjoying the pleasures of the world. Instant Christianity now serves the same purposes in religion. It disposes of the past, guarantees the future and sets the Christian free to follow the more refined lusts of the flesh in all good conscience and with a minimum of restraint.

By "instant Christianity" I mean the kind found almost everywhere in gospel circles and which is born of the notion that we may discharge our total obligation to our own souls by one act of faith, or at most by two, and be relieved thereafter of all anxiety about our spiritual condition. We are saints by calling, our teachers keep telling us, and we are permitted to infer from this that there is no reason to seek to be saints by character.

2 Timothy 2:14-16; 2 Peter 1:5-7; 2 Peter 3:18
That Incredible Christian, 23, 24.

636. Instant Christianity; Discipleship; Spiritual growth

Instant Christianity tends to make the faith act terminal and so smothers the desire for spiritual advance. It fails to understand the true nature of the Christian life, which is not static but dynamic and expanding. It overlooks the fact that a new Christian is a living organism as certainly as a new baby is, and must have nourishment and exercise to assure normal growth. It does not consider that the act of faith in Christ sets up a personal relationship between two intelligent moral beings, God and the reconciled man, and no single encounter between God and a creature made in His image could ever be sufficient to establish an intimate friendship between them.

By trying to pack all of salvation into one experience, or two, the advocates of instant Christianity flaunt the law of development which runs through all nature. They ignore the sanctifying effects of suffering, cross carrying and practical obedience. They pass by the need for spiritual training, the necessity of forming right religious habits and the need to wrestle against the world, the devil and the flesh. . . .

Instant Christianity is twentieth century orthodoxy. I wonder whether the man who wrote Philippians 3:7-16 would recognize it as the faith for which he finally died. I am afraid he would not.

Luke 9:23-25; 1 Corinthians 9:24-27; Philippians 3:7-16; 1 Peter 2:1-2
That Incredible Christian, 24, 25.

637. Intellect; Current conditions: shallowness; World: imitation of

A religious mentality characterized by timidity and lack of moral courage has given us today a flabby Christianity, intellectually impoverished, dull, repetitious and, to a great many persons, just plain boresome. This is peddled as the very faith of our fathers in direct lineal descent from Christ and the apostles. We spoon-feed this insipid pabulum to our inquiring youth and, to make it palatable, spice it up with carnal amusements filched from the unbelieving world. It is easier to entertain than to instruct, it is easier to follow degenerate public taste than to think for oneself, so too many of our evangelical leaders let their minds atrophy while they keep their fingers nimble operating religious gimmicks to bring in the curious crowds.

Well, I dare to risk a prophecy: The sheep are soon going to become weary both of the wilted clover we are giving them and the artificial color we are spraying over it to make it look fresh. . . .

Christianity must embrace the total personality and command every atom of the redeemed being. We cannot withhold our intellects from the blazing altar and still hope to preserve the true faith of Christ.

2 Corinthians 10:5; 2 Timothy 1:6-7
God Tells the Man Who Cares, 124.

638. Intellect; Thinking: need for

Then we must think. Human thought has its limitations, but where there is no thinking there is not likely to be any large deposit of truth in the mind. Evangelicals at the moment appear to be divided into two camps—those who trust the human intellect to the point of sheer rationalism, and those who are shy of everything intellectual and are convinced that thinking is a waste of the Christian's time.

Surely both are wrong. Self-conscious intellectualism is offensive to man and, I am convinced, to God also but it is significant that every major revelation in the Scriptures was made to a man of superior intellect. It would be easy to marshal an imposing list of Biblical quotations exhorting us to think, but a more convincing argument is the whole drift of the Bible itself. The Scriptures simply take for granted that the saints of the Most High will be serious-minded, thoughtful persons. They never leave the impression that it is sinful to think.

Jeremiah 9:23-24; Philippians 4:8; 1 Peter 1:6-9, 13
That Incredible Christian, 52.

639. Intellectualism; Mysticism; Holy Spirit: need for

The question being discussed by many these days—why religion is increasing and morality slipping, all at the same time—finds its answer in this very error, the error of religious intellectualism. Men have a form of godliness but deny the power thereof. The text alone will not elevate the moral life. To become morally effective, the truth must be accompanied by a mystic element, the very element supplied by the Spirit of truth. The Holy Spirit will not be banished to a footnote without taking terrible vengeance against His banishers. That vengeance may be seen today in the nervous, giggling, worldly minded and thoroughly carnal fundamentalism that is spreading over the land. Doctrinally, it wears the robes of scriptural belief, but beyond that it resembles the religion of Christ and His apostles not at all.

John 14:26; 2 Timothy 3:1-7; 1 John 2:27
We Travel an Appointed Way, 97, 98.

640. Intellectual snobbery

The snob whose claim to superiority is her material possessions is a comical figure, but because she is so pathetic she may with some effort be tolerated. The snob whose glory lies in her ancestors is less easy to endure, but she may be dismissed with the remark that since all she has to be proud of is her forebears the best part of her is under ground. But what shall we say of the intellectual snob? He is unbearable, a man difficult to love and impossible to like.

God Tells the Man Who Cares, 147.

641. Intolerance; Pharisaism

In fundamental circles a generation ago we had a hierarchy that was just as powerful and just as tough as the hierarchy that controls the Roman Catholic Church. Of course, they never had been elected; they just appointed themselves. And if you said anything that didn't jive with the notes of the Scofield Bible you were out on your ear, skidding across to the other curb.

Everybody had to believe exactly the same thing about everything, including the second coming and the antichrist and all the rest. Everybody had to believe exactly what everybody else believed. I grew up in that kind of an atmosphere and I was one of the first ones to rebel against it and fight it.

Matthew 23:23-24; Luke 18:9-14; Romans 14:5
Success and the Christian, 93.

J

642. Jacob: longing after God; Jacob: moral flaws; Longing for God; Complacency

If we had been neighbors to the household of Isaac and Rebekah and dependent only on our human judgment, we very probably would have selected Esau above Jacob as the brother more likely to succeed. We would have agreed that Esau was a good and promising young man.

To be sure, he had some rough edges, we would have said, but overall he had what it takes. He was a hunter and he was active and red-blooded. He smelled of the fields and the outdoors. He was kind to his parents. His character was unquestioned. His reputation was good.

On the other hand, everyone seemed to know about Jacob's moral shortcomings. If we were living in the same tent with Jacob, we would lock up our valuables at night. With scheming, cheating Jacob around, a person could not be too careful.

No, if we had to pick Jacob or Esau to live with, we would have picked Esau at that time in their lives.

But it turned out that Jacob had something Esau never possessed. Jacob had an inner longing for God. Yes, Jacob was deep in sin, but when it came to the time of soul crisis, he felt the tug and the lift of another, better world.

By comparison, Esau's controlling vice was his continuing and complete self-satisfaction. The thing that damned him was his spiritual complacency, his satisfaction and contentment in being just what he was. He had no desire to change, to be godly, to be God's man.

Genesis 25:25,27; Genesis 27:35-36; Genesis 35:14-15
Men Who Met God, 61, 62.

643. Jacob: longing after God; Longing for God; Complacency

Probably it would be difficult to find anywhere in history a more miserable or more lonely man than Jacob as he left mother and father and home.

Knowing the lives of Abraham and Isaac, we can surely believe there had been religious teaching in Isaac's household. Jacob must have known about the covenant-making God of his grandfather Abraham and the God of his father Isaac. We must conclude that Jacob, as he began his journey to Haran, not only hated himself for what he was and for what he had done, but he felt an inner longing for the knowledge and presence of God. Only God could answer his human need.

I think Jacob had come to a place of inner crisis in which he was self-stricken, hating himself for his sins and his flaws. He at last discovered that he had joined the great army of the discontented. Those conditions and that attitude added up to a deep, unsatisfied longing after God.

The person who is spiritually discontented has good reason to thank God with all his or her heart. Most people in our world have a feeling they are "good enough." They are complacent. They are quite well satisfied with themselves. Not bad enough to be much troubled by their consciences, they have no longing after God.

Genesis 28:5,10-22; Psalm 51; Luke 18:9-14
Men Who Met God, 52, 53.

644. Jacob: moral flaws

Looking beyond the household to Jacob's own person, we observe that he matured with many moral flaws. There were weaknesses in his character beyond the normal.

There was duplicity, there was dishonesty, there was greed. He cheated his own brother. He cheated his father. And he went on to cheat his father-in-law. Jacob seemed to be completely lacking in what we would call common honor. He showed a spirit of disloyalty and faithlessness in dealing with his brother and his father. . . .

I think we can safely say that the Jacob of those earlier years would have been voted the man least likely to get right with God. If we had been his judge and jury, we would have pronounced him hopeless.

But of all those looking at Jacob, there was One who disagreed. That One was God. God, with His eternal omniscience, saw in Jacob something worthwhile.

Genesis 27:35-36; Genesis 30:41-43; Genesis 35:9-12
Men Who Met God, 50, 51.

645. Jesus Christ: His authority

Now don't interrupt me by saying, "Jesus is our model." I know that He is our model—He ought to be our model. But the simple fact is that He is not. He ought to be the model for the churches, but Jesus Christ has about as much authority in the average Protestant church as I have in the average Catholic church.

Ephesians 1:22-23; Ephesians 5:23-24; Colossians 1:18
Rut, Rot or Revival: The Condition of the Church, 137.

646. Jesus Christ: His incarnation

We would suppose that God in stepping down would step down just as little as possible. We would think that He would stop with the angels or the seraphim—but instead He came down to the lowest order and took upon Himself the nature of Abraham, the seed of Abraham.

The Apostle Paul throws up his hands in wonder at this point. Paul, declared to be one of the six great intellects of all time, throws up his hands and declares that "the mystery of godliness is great" (I Tim. 3:16), the mystery of God manifest in the flesh. . . .

I think also that it is very becoming for us to enter into the presence of God reverently, bowing our heads and singing His praises, and acknowledging His loving acts on our behalf even with our words, "It is true, O God, even if we do not know or understand how You have brought it all to pass!"

John 1:18; Philippians 2:6-7; 1 Timothy 3:16
Christ the Eternal Son, 13, 14.

647. Jesus Christ: His incarnation

I confess that I am struck with the wonder and the significance of the limitless meaning of these two words, *He came.* Within them the whole scope of divine mercy and redeeming love is outlined. All of the mercy God is capable of showing, all of the redeeming grace that He could pour from His heart, all of the love and pity that God is capable of feeling—all of these are at least suggested here in the message that *He came*!

Beyond that, all of the hopes and longings and aspirations, all of the dreams of immortality that lie in the human breast, all had their fulfillment in the coming to earth of Jesus, the Christ and Redeemer. . . .

All of our hopes and dreams of immortality, our fond visions of a life to come, are summed up in these simple words in the Bible record: *He came!* . . .

There are times when the use of the superlative is absolutely necessary and you cannot escape it. The coming of Jesus Christ into this world represents a truth more profound than all of philosophy, for all of the great thinkers of the world together could never produce anything that could even remotely approach the wonder and the profundity disclosed in the message of these words, *He came!*

These words are wiser than all learning. Understood in their high spiritual context, they are more beautiful than all art, more eloquent than all oratory, more lyric and moving than all music—because they tell us that all of mankind, sitting in darkness, has been visited by the Light of the world!

John 1:11-14; John 8:12; Galatians 4:4-5
Christ the Eternal Son, 67, 68.

648. Jesus Christ: His incarnation

Nothing anywhere in this vast, complex world is as beautiful and as compelling as the record of the Incarnation, the act by which God was made flesh to dwell among us in our own human history. This Jesus, the Christ of God, who made the universe and who sustains all things by his powerful word, was a tiny babe among us. He was comforted to sleep when He whimpered in His mother's arms. Great, indeed, is the mystery of godliness.

John 1:14; Colossians 1:16; 1 Timothy 3:16; Hebrews 1:3
Jesus, Our Man in Glory, 35, 36.

649. Jesus Christ: His resurrection

The glory of the Christian faith is that the Christ who died for our sins rose again for our justification. We should joyfully remember His birth and gratefully muse on His dying, but the crown of all our hopes is with Him at the Father's right hand.

Paul gloried in the cross and refused to preach anything except Christ and Him crucified, but to him the cross stood for the whole redemptive work of Christ. In his epistles Paul writes of the incarnation and the crucifixion, yet he stops not at the manger or the cross but constantly sweeps our thoughts on to the resurrection and upward to the ascension and the throne. . . .

Should the Church shift her emphasis from the weakness of the manger and the death of the cross to the life and power of the enthroned Christ, perhaps she might recapture her lost glory. It is worth a try.

Acts 4:31-33; Romans 4:25; 1 Corinthians 2:1-5;
1 Corinthians 15:19-20; Ephesians 1:18-21
The Warfare of the Spirit, 118, 119.

650. Jesus Christ: His resurrection

Now, when we look at the Gospel we note an odd—and wonderful—thing. An extra chapter is added. Why?

Biography, by its own definition, must confine itself to the record of the life of an individual. That part of the book which deals with the family tree is not biography, but history, and that part which follows the record of the subject's death is not biography either. It may be appraisal, or eulogy, or criticism, but not biography, for the reason that the "bios" is gone: the subject is dead. The part that tells of his death is properly the last chapter.

The only place in world literature where this order is broken is in the four Gospels. They record the story of the man Jesus from birth to death, and end like every other book of biography has ended since the art of writing was invented. . . .

Then, for the only time in this history of human thought, a biographer adds to his book a new section which is authentic biography and begins to write a chapter to follow the last chapter. This time the story did not end with a funeral. . . .

That next chapter after the last is the source of all the Christian's hope, for it assures us that our Lord has put death in its place and has delivered us from the ancient curse. Death did not end the activities of our Lord. . . . And after three days, His spirit was reunited with His body and the new chapter began, the chapter which can have no ending.

Matthew 28:1-10; Acts 1:1-3; 1 Corinthians 15:3-4
The Next Chapter After the Last, 3, 4, 5.

651. Jesus Christ: His resurrection

True spiritual power does not reside in the ancient cross but in the victory of the mighty, resurrected Lord of Glory who could pronounce after spoiling death: "All authority in heaven and on earth has been given to me" (Matthew 28:18). Of this we need to be thoroughly convinced. Our power as Christians does not lie in the manger at Bethlehem or in the relics of Golgotha's cross. Our power lies in the eternal Christ who triumphed over death.

When Jesus died on the cross, He died in weakness. When Jesus arose from the grave, He arose in power. If we forget or deny the truth and glory of Jesus' resurrection and His present place at God's right hand, we lose all the significance of Christianity! . . .

Jesus died for us—true—but ever since the hour of resurrection, He has been the mighty Jesus, the mighty Christ, the Mighty Lord! Authority does not lie with a Babe in a manger. Authority does not lie with a Man nailed helplessly to a cross. Authority lies with the resurrected Man who was once in that manger, who hung on that cross but who, after He gave His life, arose on the third day, later ascending to the right hand of the Father. In Him lies all authority. . . .

Do we rightly understand the resurrection? It placed a glorious crown upon all of Christ's sufferings. Do we realize the full significance of Jesus Christ's being seated today at the Father's right hand—seated in absolute majesty and kingly power, sovereign over every power in heaven and on earth?

Matthew 28:18-20; Mark 16:19; Ephesians 1:18-21; Philippians 2:9-11
Tragedy in the Church: The Missing Gifts, 84, 85, 87, 88.

652. Jesus Christ: His resurrection

Many of the moral philosophers of the past dared to dream about a hope for tomorrow but they could never cope with the finality of death. They had always to take into account that fact that when a man is dead and buried he talks no more, he writes no more, he paints no more, he travels no more. No matter how beloved he has been, he speaks no more to his friends. The man is gone and that is the end. So, we write a respectful *finis* after the last of the biography and it is over.

The man is gone and with the passing of the man no other chapter is possible. The last chapter has been written.

It is against this factual background that we come to the biography of Jesus. . . .

Amazingly, we find another chapter and it is there because for the first time in human history, it became necessary to get out that pen again and add another chapter—authentic biography!

Matthew 28 is not annotation! It is not composed of footnotes or summary! It is not an editorial comment or human eulogy! It is an authentic chapter in the biography of a Man who had died one chapter before....

This is a new chapter because Jesus Christ, the Son of God, upset all of the old patterns of human life and existence. Jesus Christ took life into the grave and brought life out of the grave again and He who had been dead now lives again! For that reason, and for the first and only time in human history, it was necessary for the evangelist to add the chapter that has no ending.

Matthew 28; Acts 2:14-36; 1 Corinthians 15:19-20
Who Put Jesus on the Cross?, 98, 100, 101.

653. Jesus Christ: His resurrection; Death: triumph in

One thing the resurrection teaches us is that we must not trust appearances. The leafless tree says by its appearance that there will be no second spring. The body in Joseph's new tomb appears to signify the end of everything for Christ and His disciples. The limp form of a newly dead believer suggests everlasting defeat. Yet how wrong are all these appearances. The tree will bloom again. Christ arose the third day according to the Scriptures, and the Christian will rise at the shout of the Lord and the voice of the archangel.

1 Corinthians 15:3-4; 1 Corinthians 15:51-57; 1 Thessalonians 4:13-18
This World: Playground or Battleground?, 54.

654. Jesus Christ: His sufficiency

Christ is enough. To have Him and nothing else is to be rich beyond conceiving. To have all else and have not Christ is to be a cosmic pauper, cut off forever from all that will matter at last.

Psalm 73:25; Mark 8:36-37; John 6:68; 1 Corinthians 1:30-31
The Set of the Sail, 89.

655. Jesus Christ: intimacy with

One of the serious weaknesses of present-day evangelicalism is the mechanical quality of its thinking. A utilitarian Christ has taken the place of the radiant Savior of other and happier times. This Christ is able to save, it is true, but He is thought to do so in a practical across-the-counter manner, paying our debt and tearing off the receipt like a court clerk acknowledging a paid-up fine. A bank-teller psychology characterizes much of the religious thinking in our little gospel circle. The tragedy of it is that it is truth without being all the truth. If modern Christians are to approach the spiritual greatness of Bible saints or know the inward delights of the saints of post-biblical times, they must correct this imperfect view and cultivate the beauties of the Lord our God in sweet, personal experience.

John 17:3; Philippians 3:10; 1 John 1:1-3
We Travel an Appointed Way, 63, 64.

656. Jesus Christ: intimacy with; Spiritual warfare

Do you find your own heart sensitive to the Lord's presence, or are you among those who are "samplers" and "nibblers"? God help you if you are, for the child of the King isn't a sampler and a nibbler—he's a sheep who loves his Shepherd, and he stays close to his Shepherd. That's the only safe place for a sheep—at the Shepherd's side, because the devil doesn't fear sheep—he fears the Shepherd. Your spiritual safety and well-being lies in being near to the Shepherd. Stay close to Jesus and all the wolves in the world cannot get a tooth in you.

Psalm 23; John 10:11-15
The Counselor, 17.

657. Jesus Christ: judge

Which is He going to be for you—Saviour or Judge? He will be the one or the other.

I, for my part, can't afford to face Him as my Judge; I must have His protecting blood, and face Him as my Saviour.

He knows too much about me for me to dare to brazenly barge into His presence and let him judge me.

John 5:24-27; Acts 10:42-43; Acts 17:30-31
The Tozer Pulpit, Volume 1, Book 1, 100.

658. Jesus Christ: love for

Do you love the Lord Jesus Christ—*really?* Now I know we sing that we do. We sing things that aren't very true sometimes. Do you really love Christ?

A half-comical answer was given to Moody one time when he inquired of a man on the street, "Do you love Jesus?" He answered, "I have nothing against Him." I think that is about as far as a lot of people go. We have nothing against Jesus, but can we say we love Him? . . .

Do you love Jesus—*really?* It is possible to be a Christian, that is, to have faith in His power, in His work, in His atonement. It is even possible to have a vital relation to Him in the new birth and yet not have cultivated His fellowship to a point where we love Him very much. We're not finished until the love attachment to Christ has become so strong that it burns and glows and consumes.

Matthew 22:37-39; Luke 7:40-47; 1 Peter 1:6-7
Success and the Christian, 74, 75, 76.

659. Jesus Christ: love for; Music; Flippancy

Perhaps the most serious charge that can be brought against modern Christians is that we are not sufficiently in love with Christ. The Christ of fundamentalism is strong but hardly beautiful. It is rarely that we find anyone aglow with personal love for Christ. I trust it is not uncharitable to say that in my opinion a great deal of praise in conservative circles is perfunctory and forced, where it is not downright insincere.

Many of our popular songs and choruses in praise of Christ are hollow and unconvincing. Some are even shocking in their amorous endearments, and strike a reverent soul as being a kind of flattery offered to One with whom neither composer nor singer is acquainted. The whole thing is in the mood of the love ditty, the only difference being the substitution of the name of Christ for that of the earthly lover. . . .

Christ can never be known without a sense of awe and fear accompanying the knowledge. He is the fairest among ten thousand, but He is also the Lord high and mighty. He is the friend of sinners, but He is also the terror of devils. He is meek and lowly in heart, but He is also Lord and Christ who will surely come to be the judge of all men. No one who knows Him intimately can ever be flippant in His presence.

Song of Solomon 5:10; Matthew 11:19,28-30; Acts 17:30-31; Revelation 5:8-14
That Incredible Christian, 129.

660. Jesus Christ: modern view of

Scarcely anyone catches the imperious note in Christ's words. The Christian message has ceased to be a pronouncement and has become a proposition. Its invitational element has been pressed far out of proportion in the total scriptural scheme. Christ with His lantern, His apologetic stance and His weak pleading face has taken the place of the true Son of Man whom John saw clothed with a garment down to the foot, girt with a golden girdle, whose head and hair are white like wool, whose eyes are as a flame of fire, whose feet are like burnished brass and whose voice is as the sound of many waters. The Christ of the tentative smile and air of puzzlement is not the Christ of God. The artists have been guilty of inadvertent idolatry in presenting to the world a false image of Christ. Only the Holy Spirit can reveal our Lord as He really is, and He does not paint in oils. He manifests Christ to the human spirit, not to our physical eyes.

Ezekiel 1:26-28; Daniel 7:9-10; Revelation 1:13-16
The Set of the Sail, 55.

661. Jesus Christ: modern view of

Yet the teachings of Christ are wholly contrary to the beliefs of the modern world. The spiritual philosophy underlying the kingdom of God is radically opposed to that of civilized society. In short, the Christ of the New Testament and the world of mankind are so sharply opposed to each other as to amount to downright hostility. To achieve a compromise is impossible.

We can only conclude that Jesus is universally popular today because He is universally misunderstood.

Everyone admires Jesus, but almost no one takes Him seriously. He is considered a kindly idealist who loved babies and underprivileged persons. He is pictured as a gentle dreamer who was naive enough to believe in human goodness and brave enough to die for His belief. The world thinks of Him as meek, selfless and loving, and values Him because He was what we all are at heart, or would be if things were not so tough and we had more time to cultivate our virtues. Or He is a sweet, holy symbol of something too fine, too beautiful, to be real, but something which we would not lose nevertheless from our treasure house of precious things.

Because the human mind has two compartments, the practical and the ideal, people are able to live comfortably with their dreamy, romantic conception of Jesus while paying no attention whatsoever to His words. It is this neat division between the fanciful and the real that enables countless thousands of persons to say "Lord, Lord" in all sincerity while living every moment in flat defiance of His authority.

Matthew 7:21-23; John 15:18-21; Acts 8:3-4
The Warfare of the Spirit, 166, 167.

662. Jesus Christ: modern view of

We must be extremely careful that the Christ we profess to follow is indeed the very Christ of

God. There is always danger that we may be following a Christ who is not the true Christ but one conjured up by our imagination and made in our own image.

I confess to a feeling of uneasiness about this when I observe the questionable things Christ is said to do for people these days. He is often recommended as a wonderfully obliging but not too discriminating Big Brother who delights to help us to accomplish our ends, and who further favors us by forbearing to ask any embarrassing questions about the moral and spiritual qualities of those ends.

The Root of the Righteous, 23.

663. Jesus Christ: modern view of

Christians today appear to know Christ only after the flesh. They try to achieve communion with Him by divesting Him of His burning holiness and unapproachable majesty, the very attributes He veiled while on earth but assumed in fullness of glory upon His ascension to the Father's right hand. The Christ of popular Christianity has a weak smile and a halo. He has become Someone-up-There who likes people, at least some people, and these are grateful but not too impressed. If they need Him, He also needs them.

2 Corinthians 5:13-17; Ephesians 1:18-21; Philippians 2:5-11; Hebrews 2:9; Revelation 5:8-14
The Knowledge of the Holy, 57.

664. Jesus Christ: modern view of; Jesus Christ: judge

What is your concept of Jesus Christ, my brother?

If the "ten-cent-store Jesus" that is being preached by a lot of men, the plastic, painted Christ who has no spine and no justice and is pictured as the soft and pliable friend to everybody—if He is the only Christ there is, then we might as well close our books and bar our doors, and make a bakery or garage out of this church!

But that Christ that is being preached and pictured is not the Christ of God, nor the Christ of the Bible, nor the Christ we must deal with.

The Christ we must deal with has eyes as a flame of fire, and His feet are like burnished brass, and out of His mouth comes a sharp, two-edged sword. . . .

This is one of the neglected Bible doctrines of our day—that Jesus Christ is the judge of mankind. . . .

That makes me both love Him and fear Him! I love Him because He is my Saviour and I fear Him because He is my Judge.

Psalm 96:11-13; Acts 17:30-31; Revelation 1:13-16
The Tozer Pulpit, Volume 1, Book 1, 96, 97.

665. Jesus Christ: modern view of; Prayer: wrong use of; Pragmatism

Within the past few years, for instance, Christ has been popularized by some so-called evangelicals as one who, if a proper amount of prayer were made, would help the pious prize fighter to knock another fighter unconscious in the ring. Christ is also said to help the big league pitcher to get the proper hook on his curve. In another instance He assists an athletically-minded parson to win the high jump, and still another not only to come in first in a track meet but to set a new record in the bargain. He is said also to have helped a praying businessman to beat out a competitor in a deal, to underbid a rival and to secure a coveted contract to the discomfiture of someone else who was trying to get it. He is even thought to lend succor to a praying movie actress while she plays a role so lewd as to bring the blood to the face of a professional prostitute.

Thus our Lord becomes the Christ of utility, a kind of Aladdin's lamp to do minor miracles in behalf of anyone who summons Him to do his bidding.

Hebrews 13:20-21; James 4:3-4; 1 John 3:21-22
The Root of the Righteous, 24.

666. Jesus Christ: paintings of

All of the great artists of the past, all of them combining their talents on a gigantic canvas, could never have given us a true portrait of our Lord Jesus Christ or of His universal power....

Those celebrated European painters, whose works adorn the world's great art galleries, undoubtedly did their best to depict our Lord. They were limited, however, by their finite concepts of the Subject. To be frank, I do not want to hold in my mind an unworthy concept of my divine Savior....

It is a sad thought, but I suppose some Christians are going to be disappointed when they actually see Jesus. Their concept of Him has been shaped by the paintings and images they have seen of the human Jesus. The radiant, awesome Jesus of the Revelation is totally outside their perspective....

I cannot fully comprehend the power and the glory belonging to this One whose face will shine eternally with the brilliance of the sun! I do not have the words to explain that kind of brightness and light.

Daniel 7:9-10; Revelation 1:13-16; Revelation 19:11-16
Jesus Is Victor!, 53, 54, 55.

667. John 3:16

If we were to judge John 3:16 on the basis of its value to the human race, we would have to say that it is probably the most precious cluster of words ever assembled by the mind of an intelligent man; a 25-word compendium in which is contained the eternal Christian evangel, the message of genuine good news!

When we begin to grasp the radiance and significance of this text, we sense that it is as though God has compressed all of the deepest and richest meaning of the Scriptures into one brief, glorious segment of truth. . . .

If we will just let our imaginations soar a bit, we can properly say that the Holy Ghost has taken the redemptive evangel and has placed it under the emotional pressure of the triune God, so unbelievably strong and powerful that it has been crystallized into this shining diamond of truth.

Using our imaginations again, I believe that if we could place this John 3:16 text on one side of some vast eternal scale held in space by some holy one to measure its value to mankind, it would prove to be more precious than all of the books that have ever been written by men.

John 3:16
Christ the Eternal Son, 83, 84.

668. John 3:16; God: His love

I have heard that John 3:16 is a favorite preaching text for young preachers, but I confess that as far as I can recall, I have never had the courage to prepare and preach a sermon with John 3:16 as my text. I suppose I have quoted it as many as 15,000 or 20,000 times in prayer and in testimony, in writing and in preaching, but never as a sermon text. . . .

I think my own hesitation to preach from John 3:16 comes down to this: I appreciate it so profoundly that I am frightened by it—I am overwhelmed by John 3:16 to the point of inadequacy, almost of despair. Along with this is my knowledge that if a minister is to try to preach John 3:16 he must be endowed with great sympathy and a genuine love for God and man....

So, I approach it. I approach it as one who is filled with great fear and yet great fascination. I take off my shoes, my heart shoes, at least, as I come to this declaration that *God so loved the world.*

John 3:16
Christ the Eternal Son, 85, 86.

669. John the Baptist

I cannot refrain from asking you a question here: How do you suppose the Christian church as we know it today, would be inclined to deal with John the Baptist if he came into our scene?

Our generation would probably decide that such a man ought to be downright proud of the fact that God had sent him. We would urge him to write books and make a documentary film and the seminary leaders would line up to schedule him as guest lecturer.

But in that distant generation of mankind to whom the eternal Son of God presented Himself as suffering Savior and living Lord, John the Baptist gladly stepped down—allowing Jesus the Christ to displace him completely....

Actually, John the Baptist would never have fit into the contemporary religious scene in our day—never! He did not keep his suit pressed. He was not careful about choosing words that would not offend anyone. Something tells me that John the Baptist did not quote beautiful passages from the poets.

Some of the doctors of psychiatry in our day would have had quick advice for John the Baptist: "John, we have been observing you and the way you live and the way you talk and the way you dress. John, you really ought to get adjusted to the times and to society!"

Matthew 3:1-4; John 1:6-7; John 3:30
Christ the Eternal Son, 120.

670. John the Baptist; Pharisaism

The "Jews of Jerusalem," who supposedly knew all the prophetic Scriptures, could not find a card for John the Baptist. It was not that the Scriptures had not foretold his coming. The Jews did not recognize him because they had put his card in the wrong file....

John did not beat around the bush with these teachers. "I have been clearly foretold in your Scriptures," he said in effect. "Isaiah spoke of me, and you have overlooked his word. I do not fit into your plans because you want things your way. You want a dramatic prophet, a fiery Elijah. Of course you want the Christ, the King of Israel, to come. But on your terms. You have made no place in your expectations for someone who will disturb you morally. You want God to conform His intentions to your religious pattern, your religious tradition."

Isaiah 40:3; Malachi 3:1; Matthew 11:7-19; John 1:20-23
Faith Beyond Reason, 118.

671. Joy; Happiness

I am thinking about God's dear people always praying for joy, praying for light, praying for every benediction, and yet they don't receive. They work themselves up on Sunday, then go back down and stay on a lower level on Monday. Perhaps they work themselves up a little by Wednesday evening, but it never seems to stick. The bell loses its tongue, its clapper. It doesn't ring anymore.

Well, the joy and happiness of these disciples was now the joy and blessing and delight of the Holy Spirit. Their happiness was no longer the happiness of Adam—it was not the happiness of nature. Human beings are busy trying to work up a joy of some sort. . . .

No, the human race is not basically happy—we are anything else but! The joy of the Holy Spirit is not something worked up; it is a post-resurrection joy. Christ came out of the grave, and the Spirit of the risen Christ comes back to His people. The joy that we have is the joy that looks back on the grave.

Acts 2:46-47; Acts 5:41-42; 1 Corinthians 15:19-20
The Counselor, 146, 147.

672. Joy; Holiness: basis for joy; Holy Spirit: filling

I repeat: Most modern Christians live sub-Christian lives!

Most Christians are not joyful persons because they are not holy persons, and they are not holy persons because they are not filled with the Holy Spirit, and they are not filled with the Holy Spirit because they are not separated persons.

The Spirit cannot fill whom He cannot separate, and whom He cannot fill, He cannot make holy, and whom He cannot make holy, He cannot make happy!

2 Corinthians 6:17-18; Ephesians 5:18-19; 1 John 1:6-9
I Talk Back to the Devil, 31.

673. Joy; Moods; Faith: and feelings

The relation of faith to mood may be stated by means of a number of metaphors: if faith is the tree, mood is the blossom; if faith is the flower, mood is the fragrance; if faith is the instrument, mood is the melody. And who will deny the vital place of the blossom, the fragrance and the music in human life? . . .

Weather may be too hot, too cold, too dry, too wet to favor good crops, and the Christian's moods, in like manner, may be unfavorable to spiritual growth and fruitfulness. Christian service carried on during prolonged heaviness of heart may be as good as wasted. . . .

The Christian owes it to the world to be supernaturally joyful. In this day of universal apprehension when men's hearts are failing them for fear of those things that are coming upon the earth, we Christians are strategically placed to display a happiness that is not of this world and to exhibit a tranquillity that will be a little bit of heaven here below.

John 14:27; 2 Corinthians 4:8-11; Philippians 4:4,7
The Next Chapter After the Last, 51, 52.

674. Joy; Pleasure

The work of the Holy Spirit is, among other things, to rescue the redeemed man's emotions, to restring his harp and open again the wells of sacred joy which have been stopped up by sin. That He does this is the unanimous testimony of the saints. And it is not inconsistent with the whole way of God in His creation. Pure pleasure is a part of life, such an important part that it is difficult to see how human life could be justified if it were to consist of endless existence devoid of pleasurable feeling.

The Holy Spirit would set an aeolian harp in the window of our souls so that the winds of heaven may play sweet melody for a musical accompaniment to the humblest task we may be called to perform. The spiritual love of Christ will make constant music within our hearts and enable us to rejoice even in our sorrows.

Psalm 51:2; 2 Corinthians 6:10; James 1:2-4
The Pursuit of Man, 112, 113.

675. Joy; Spiritual victory

We are missing the mark about Christian victory and the life of joy in our Savior. We ought to be standing straight and praising our God!

I must agree with the psalmist that the joy of the Lord is the strength of His people. I do believe that the sad world is attracted to spiritual sunshine—the genuine thing, that is.

Some churches train their greeters and ushers to smile, showing as many teeth as possible. But I can sense that kind of display, and when I am greeted by a person who is smiling because he or she has been trained to smile, I know I am shaking the flipper of a trained seal. When the warmth and joy of the Holy Spirit are in a congregation, however, and the folks are spontaneously joyful, the result is a wonderful influence upon others. . . .

I have said it a hundred times: The reason we have to search for so many things to cheer us up is the fact that we are not really joyful and contentedly happy within. . . . But we are Christians, and Christians have every right to be the happiest people in the world.

Nehemiah 8:10; Philippians 4:4; 1 John 1:4
Tragedy in the Church: The Missing Gifts, 10, 11.

676. Judgment of God: future; Prophecy; Earthquakes

I am among those who believe that the judgments of God are certain. God is indeed going to shake the earth as it has never been shaken before. . . .

As these seals are opened, our earth experiences heavenly phenomena that rock and shake the planet. The earthquake that will take place will be devastating in its destruction.

I have never experienced an earthquake. Those who have say the greatest terror is the sudden and extreme loss of confidence in the earth itself. Psychologists confirm that such an experience can leave the human system in deep, long-term shock. Until the moment of the quake, the earth has been a stable, supportive friend. Suddenly it is that no longer! Floors, walls, ceilings are no longer fixed and certain. Everything—including the earth itself—seems to recede. The shaking, the rocking, the rumbling—all of these phenomena tell the finite human being that his or her life-long confidence in the *terra firma* has been a misplaced trust.

Haggai 2:6-7; Matthew 24:6-7; Revelation 6:12-17
Jesus Is Victor!, 106.

677. Judgment of God: future; Wrath of God

The justice of God and the wrath of God have been ignored and violated so long and so arrogantly that the day of reckoning must come. The divine lightning, the peals of thunder and the rumbling of judgment will go out from the throne.

Some who have misconstrued the meaning of God's grace will make light of such predictions. But the Bible is unequivocal: God's throne of grace will become a throne of judgment.

I confess that I am stirred within my being as I study these portions of the Revelation. If I were not a Christian, saved and forgiven, I would not wait. I would get down on my knees and plead for God's grace and mercy while there is time. I would not deceive my own soul with the excuse that "I do not have enough light" or "I do not understand all that Christ did" or "Why am I any worse in God's sight than my neighbor?"

Romans 1:18; Romans 3:10-18; Ephesians 5:6; Revelation 4:1-8
Jesus Is Victor!, 73, 74.

678. Judgment of God: present; Spiritual decline

Rarely does God send His judgment dramatically. I have wondered if we might learn our lessons of humility and obedience more quickly if God were to resist a man as one soldier to another, with the clash of sword and the letting of blood?

But it does not work that way. When God resists a man for the sins of his spirit and attitude, a slow, inward spiritual degeneration will take place as a signal of the judgment that has come. A slow hardening that comes from unwillingness to yield will result in cynicism. The Christian joy will disappear and there will be no more fruits of the Spirit. That man will sour as a jar of fruit sours—and it is not an exaggeration to say that the man who has earned the resistance of God will continue to sour bitterly in his own juice.

Psalm 32:3-5; Galatians 5:22-23; 1 Peter 5:5
I Call It Heresy!, 112.

K

679. Knowledge of God: church's need

.... *Acquaint thyself with God.* To regain her lost power the Church must see heaven opened and have a transforming vision of God.

But the God we must see is not the utilitarian God who is having such a run of popularity today, whose chief claim to men's attention is His ability to bring them success in their various undertakings and who for that reason is being cajoled and flattered by everyone who wants a favor. The God we must learn to know is the Majesty in the heavens, God the Father Almighty, Maker of heaven and earth, the only wise God our Saviour. . . .

Knowledge of such a Being cannot be gained by study alone. It comes by a wisdom the natural man knows nothing of, neither can know, because it is spiritually discerned. To know God is at once the easiest and the most difficult thing in the world. It is easy because the knowledge is not won by hard mental toil, but is something freely given. As sunlight falls free on the open field, so the knowledge of the holy God is a free gift to men who are open to receive it. But this knowledge is difficult because there are conditions to be met and the obstinate nature of fallen man does not take kindly to them.

Isaiah 6:1-8; 1 Corinthians 2:12-16; 1 Timothy 1:17; Jude 24-25
The Knowledge of the Holy, 180, 181.

680. Knowledge of God: church's need; Church: apathy

A great Christian of nearly 300 years ago, Nicholas Herman of Lorraine said that in his early Christian life he determined to cut through the tangle of religious means and "nourish his heart on high thoughts of God." I have always treasured that expression.

A cultivation of God through prayer, humble soul-searching and avid feasting upon the Scriptures would go far to awaken the church.

Psalm 1:1-3; Psalm 63:5-6; Psalm 139:23-24
Keys to the Deeper Life, 87.

681. Knowledge of God: continuous pursuit

There is a vast and important difference between a Pauline creed and a Pauline life. . . . Tens of thousands of believers who pride themselves on their understanding of Romans and Ephesians cannot conceal the sharp spiritual contradiction that exists between their hearts and the heart of Paul.

That difference may be stated this way: Paul was a seeker and a finder and a seeker still. They seek and find and seek no more. After "accepting" Christ they tend to substitute logic for life and doctrine for experience.

For them the truth becomes a veil to hide the face of God; for Paul it was a door into His very Presence. Paul's spirit was that of the loving explorer. He was a prospector among the hills of God searching for the gold of personal spiritual acquaintance. Many today stand by Paul's doctrine who will not follow him in his passionate yearning for divine reality. Can these be said to be Pauline in any but the most nominal sense?

1 Corinthians 9:24-27; Philippians 3:10-14; 2 Timothy 4:6-8
Keys to the Deeper Life, 29.

682. Knowledge of God: continuous pursuit

The modern scientist has lost God amid the wonders of His world; we Christians are in real danger of losing God amid the wonders of His Word. We have almost forgotten that God is a person and, as such, can be cultivated as any person can. It is inherent in personality to be able to know other personalities, but full knowledge of one personality by another cannot be achieved in one encounter. It is only after long and loving mental intercourse that the full possibilities of both can be explored.

John 17:3
The Pursuit of God, 13.

683. Knowledge of God: continuous pursuit

To have found God and still to pursue Him is the soul's paradox of love, scorned indeed by the too-easily-satisfied religionist, but justified in happy experience by the children of the burning heart.

The Pursuit of God, 14.

684. Knowledge of God: continuous pursuit

You and I are in little (our sins excepted) what God is in large. Being made in His image we have within us the capacity to know Him. In our sins we lack only the power. The moment the Spirit has quickened us to life in regeneration our whole being senses its kinship to God and leaps up in joyous recognition. That is the heavenly birth without which we cannot see the Kingdom of God. It is, however, not an end but an inception, for now begins the glorious pursuit, the heart's happy exploration of the infinite riches of the Godhead. That is where we begin, I say, but where we stop no man has yet discovered, for there is in the awful and mysterious depths of the Triune God neither limit nor end.

Genesis 1:26-27; Psalm 42:1-2; Psalm 63:1-2
The Pursuit of God, 14.

685. Knowledge of God: continuous pursuit

It is well that we accept the hard truth now: *the man who would know God must give time to Him.* He must count no time wasted which is spent in the cultivation of His acquaintance. He must give himself to meditation and prayer hours on end. So did the saints of old, the glorious company of the apostles, the goodly fellowship of the prophets and the believing members of the holy Church in all generations. And so must we if we would follow in their train.

Psalm 42:1-2; Psalm 63; Matthew 5:6; Acts 6:3-7
The Pursuit of Man, 5.

686. Knowledge of God: continuous pursuit

Pick at random a score of great saints whose lives and testimonies are widely known. Let them be Bible characters or well-known Christians of post-biblical times. . . .

I venture to suggest that the one vital quality which they had in common was spiritual receptivity. Something in them was open to heaven, something which urged them Godward. Without attempting anything like a profound analysis, I shall say simply that they had spiritual awareness and that they went on to cultivate it until it became the biggest thing in their lives. They differed from the average person in that when they felt the inward longing they did something about it. They acquired the lifelong habit of spiritual response. They were not disobedient to the heavenly vision. As David put it neatly, "When thou saidst, Seek ye my face; my heart said unto thee, Thy face, LORD, will I seek" (Ps. 27:8).

2 Chronicles 15:2; Psalm 27:8; Matthew 5:6; Acts 26:13-19
The Pursuit of God, 60, 61.

687. Knowledge of God: continuous pursuit; Communion with God

Oh, my friend, we are just beginning. God's personality is so infinitely rich and manifold that it will take 1,000 years of close search and intimate communion to know even the outer edges of the glorious nature of God. When we talk about communion with God and fellowship with the Holy Spirit, we are talking about that which begins now but will grow and increase and mature while life lasts.

Actually, I do find Christians these days who seem to have largely wasted their lives. They were converted to Christ but they have never sought to go on to an increasing knowledge of God. There is untold loss and failure because they have accepted the whole level of things around them as being normal and desirable.

The Holy Spirit is a living Person, and we can know Him and fellowship with Him! We can whisper to Him, and out of a favorite verse of the Bible or a loved hymn, we hear His voice whispering back. Walking with the Spirit can become a habit. It is a gracious thing to strive to know the things of God through the Spirit of God in a friendship that passes the place where it has to be kept up by chatter.

Galatians 5:16; 1 Peter 2:1-2; 2 Peter 3:18
The Counselor, 129, 130.

688. Knowledge of God: continuous pursuit; Longing for God

Come near to the holy men and women of the past and you will soon feel the heat of their desire after God. They mourned for Him, they prayed and wrestled and sought for Him day and night, in season and out, and when they had found Him the finding was all the sweeter for the long seeking. Moses used the fact that he knew God as an argument for knowing Him better. "Now, therefore, I pray thee, if I have found grace in thy sight, shew me now thy way, that I may know thee, that I may find grace in thy sight" (Exodus 33:13); and from there he rose to make the daring request, "I beseech thee, shew me thy glory" (33:18). God was frankly pleased by this display of ardor, and the next day called Moses into the mount, and there in solemn procession made all His glory pass before him.

Exodus 33:13,18; Psalm 42:1-2
The Pursuit of God, 15.

689. Knowledge of God: continuous pursuit; Meditation

Among Christians of all ages and of varying shades of doctrinal emphasis there has been fairly full agreement on one thing: They all believed that it was important that the Christian with serious spiritual aspirations should learn to meditate long and often on God.

Let a Christian insist upon rising above the poor average of current religious experience and he will soon come up against the need to know God Himself as the ultimate goal of all Christian doctrine. Let him seek to explore the sacred wonders of the Triune Godhead and he will discover that sustained and intelligently directed meditation on the Person of God is imperative. To know God well he must think on Him unceasingly. Nothing that man has discovered about himself or God has revealed any short cut to pure spirituality. It is still free, but tremendously costly.

Psalm 42:1-8; Psalm 77:11-15; Psalm 143:5-6
That Incredible Christian, 135.

690. Knowledge of God: divine encounter; Wonder

God always acts like Himself, wherever He may be and whatever He may be doing; in Him there is neither variableness nor shadow of turning. Yet His infinitude places Him so far above our knowing that a lifetime spent in cultivating the knowledge of Him leaves as much yet to learn as if we had never begun. . . .

So imperfectly do we know Him that it may be said that one invariable concomitant of a true encounter with God is delighted wonder. No matter how high our expectation may be, when God finally moves into the field of our spiritual awareness we are sure to be astonished by His power to overwhelm the mind and fascinate the soul. He is always more wonderful than we anticipate, and more blessed and marvelous than we had imagined He could be.

1 Chronicles 29:11-13; Psalm 33:6-9; Isaiah 55:8-9; James 1:17
That Incredible Christian, 38.

691. Knowledge of God: neglected; Busyness

I am convinced that the dearth of great saints in these times even among those who truly believe in Christ is due at least in part to our unwillingness to give sufficient time to the cultivation of the knowledge of God. We of the nervous West are victims of the philosophy of activism tragically misunderstood. Getting and spending, going and returning, organizing and promoting, buying and selling, working and playing—this alone constitutes living. If we are not making plans or working to carry out plans already made we feel that we are failures, that we are sterile, unfruitful eunuchs, parasites on the body of society. The gospel of work, as someone has called it, has crowded out the gospel of Christ in many Christian churches.

In an effort to get the work of the Lord done we often lose contact with the Lord of the work and quite literally wear our people out as well.

Psalm 4:4; Psalm 46:10; Luke 10:38-42
That Incredible Christian, 135, 136.

692. Knowledge of God: neglected; God: His presence; Communion with God

He has discovered Himself to some extent in nature, but more perfectly in the Incarnation. Now He waits to show Himself in ravishing fulness to the humble of soul and the pure in heart.

The world is perishing for lack of the knowledge of God and the church is famishing for want of His presence.

Psalm 19:1-6; Matthew 5:3-8; John 1:14
The Pursuit of God, 36.

693. Knowledge of God: neglected; Knowledge of God: continuous pursuit

Probably the most widespread and persistent problem to be found among Christians is the problem of retarded spiritual progress. Why, after years of Christian profession, do so many persons find themselves no farther along than when they first believed? . . .

The causes of retarded growth are many. It would not be accurate to ascribe the trouble to one single fault. One there is, however, which is so universal that it may easily be the main cause: *failure to give time to the cultivation of the knowledge of God*. . . .

The Christian is strong or weak depending upon how closely he has cultivated the knowledge of God. . . .

Progress in the Christian life is exactly equal to the growing knowledge we gain of the Triune God in personal experience. And such experience requires a whole life devoted to it and plenty of time spent at the holy task of cultivating God. God can be known satisfactorily only as we devote time to Him.

Psalm 1:1-3; Philippians 3:7-16; Hebrews 5:11-12; 2 Peter 3:18
The Root of the Righteous, 10, 11, 12.

694. Knowledge of God: neglected; Longing for God; Spiritual Growth; Complacency

I want deliberately to encourage this mighty longing after God. The lack of it has brought us to our present low estate. The stiff and wooden quality about our religious lives is a result of our lack of holy desire. Complacency is a deadly foe of all spiritual growth. Acute desire must be present or there will be no manifestation of Christ to His people. He waits to be wanted. Too bad that with many of us He waits so long, so very long, in vain.

Psalm 63:1-2; Matthew 5:6,8
The Pursuit of God, 17.

695. Knowledge of God: personal, intimate

It is possible to grow up in a church, learn the catechism and have everything done to us that they do to us, within reason. But after we have done all that, we may not know God at all, because God isn't known by those external things. We are blind and can't see, because the things of God no man knows but by the Spirit of God. . . .

We can hold the creed and not know God in His person at all. We can know the doctrine and not know spiritual things at all. The fearful consequence is that many people know about God but don't know God Himself. There is a vast difference between knowing about God and knowing God—a vast difference! I can know about your relative—and still not know him in person. If I have never met him, I do not know the touch of his hand or the look of his eye or the smile of his face or the sound of his voice. I only know about him. You can show me his picture and describe him to me, but I still don't know him. I just know about the man.

Jeremiah 9:23-24; Romans 10:1-3; 1 Corinthians 2:11-12
The Counselor, 20, 26, 27.

696. Knowledge of God: personal, intimate

God is a Person and can be known in increasing degrees of intimate acquaintance as we prepare our hearts for the wonder. It may be necessary for us to alter our former beliefs about God as the glory that gilds the Sacred Scriptures dawns over our interior lives. We may also need to break quietly and graciously with the lifeless textualism that prevails among the gospel churches, and to protest the frivolous character of much that passes for Christianity among us. By this we may for the time lose friends and gain a passing reputation for being holier-than-thou; but no man who permits the expectation of unpleasant consequences to influence him in a matter like this is fit for the kingdom of God.

John 15:18-21; John 17:14-16; James 4:3-4
The Knowledge of the Holy, 182, 183.

697. Knowledge of God: personal, intimate

To most people God is an inference, not a reality. He is a deduction from evidence which they consider adequate, but He remains personally unknown to the individual. "He *must* be," they say, "therefore we believe He is." Others do not go even so far as this; they know of Him only by hearsay. They have never bothered to think the matter out for themselves, but have heard about Him from others, and have put belief in Him into the back of their minds along with various odds and ends that make up their total creed....

Now personality and fatherhood carry with them the idea of the possibility of personal acquaintance. This is admitted, I say, in theory, but for millions of Christians, nevertheless, God is no more real than He is to the non-Christian. They go through life trying to love an ideal and be loyal to a mere principle.

John 10:27-29; John 17:3; 1 John 2:13
The Pursuit of God, 45, 46.

698. Knowledge of God: personal, intimate; Communion with God; Priorities

Without doubt the greatest need of the human personality is to experience God Himself....

All this is such a familiar part of evangelical theology that it may safely be assumed that the majority of my readers know it already. That is, they know it theoretically, but the experiential aspect of the truth is not so well known. Indeed large numbers of supposedly sound Christian believers know nothing at all about personal communion with God; and there lies one of the greatest weaknesses of present-day Christianity.

The experiential knowledge of God is eternal life (John 17:3), and increased knowledge results in a correspondingly larger and fuller life. So rich a treasure is this inward knowledge of God that every other treasure is as nothing compared with it. We may count all things of no value and sacrifice them freely if we may thereby gain a more perfect knowledge of God through Jesus Christ our Lord. This was Paul's testimony (Phil. 3:7-14) and it has been the testimony of all great Christian souls who have followed Christ from Paul's day to ours. . . .

To enjoy this growing knowledge of God will require that we go beyond the goals so casually set by modern evangelicals. We must fix our hearts on God and purposefully aim to rise above the dead level and average of current Christianity.

If we do this Satan will surely tempt us by accusing us of spiritual pride and our friends will warn us to beware of being "holier than thou." But as the land of promise had to be taken by storm against the determined opposition of the enemy, so we must capture new spiritual heights over the sour and violent protests of the devil.

John 17:3; Philippians 3:7-16; Hebrews 12;1-2
That Incredible Christian, 83, 84, 85.

699. Knowledge of God: personal, intimate; God: His immanence

What does the divine immanence mean in direct Christian experience? It means simply that God is here. Wherever we are, *God is here.* There is no place, there can be no place, where He is not. . . .

Men do not know that God is here. What a difference it would make if they knew. . . .

It will be a great moment for some of us when we begin to believe that God's promise of self-revelation is literally true, that He promised much, but no more than He intends to fulfill.

Our pursuit of God is successful just because He is forever seeking to manifest Himself to us.

Psalm 139:7-12; Jeremiah 23:23-24; John 1:18
The Pursuit of God, 56, 58, 59.

700. Knowledge of God: personal, intimate; Jesus Christ: intimacy with

To get acquainted with God is one thing; but to go on to experience God in intensity and richness of acquaintance is something more. Paul said, "I want to know Him in that depth and rich intensity of experience." As I have said many times, personality can't be fully known with one encounter. You may meet some people you don't particularly like at first. After you get to know them, you get to like them because you find the hidden potential in their personality that you didn't know were [sic] there. Christ is capable of increasing intimacy of acquaintance.

If I have anything to say to the Church of Christ in general it is this: that our great weakness is that not only are we not going on to know Christ in rich intimacy of acquaintance but we're not even talking about it. We don't even hear about it. It doesn't get into our magazines. It doesn't get into our books. It doesn't get onto our radios. It's not found in our churches—this yearning, this longing to know Him in increasing measure.

Philippians 3:10
Success and the Christian, 14, 15.

701. Knowledge of God: supreme value of

The man who has God for his treasure has all things in One. Many ordinary treasures may be denied him, or if he is allowed to have them, the enjoyment of them will be so tempered that they will never be necessary to his happiness. Or if he must see them go, one after one, he will scarcely feel a sense of loss, for having the Source of all things he has in One all satisfaction, all pleasure, all delight. Whatever he may lose he has actually lost nothing, for he now has it all in One, and he has it purely, legitimately and forever.

Philippians 3:7-16
The Pursuit of God, 19.

702. Knowledge of God: supreme value of

When God told Aaron, "You will have no inheritance in their land, nor will you have any share among them; I am your share and your inheritance among the Israelites," He in fact promised a portion infinitely above all the real estate in Palestine and all the earth thrown in (Numbers 18:20). To possess God—this is the inheritance ultimate and supreme. . . .

To know God, this is eternal life; this is the purpose for which we are and were created. . . .

Were we allowed but one request, we might gain at a stroke all things else by praying one all-embracing prayer:

> "Thyself, Lord! Give me Thyself and I can want no more."

Numbers 18:20; Joshua 13:33; John 17:3
We Travel an Appointed Way, 70, 71.

703. Knowledge of God: supreme value of

... God is so vastly wonderful, so utterly and completely delightful that He can, without anything other than Himself, meet and overflow the deepest demands of our total nature, mysterious and deep as that nature is.

The Pursuit of God, 39.

704. Knowledge of God: supreme value of; Earthly things; Prayers

Father, I want to know Thee, but my cowardly heart fears to give up its toys. I cannot part with them without inward bleeding, and I do not try to hide from Thee the terror of the parting. I come trembling, but I do come. Please root from my heart all those things which I have cherished so long and which have become a very part of my living self, so that Thou mayest enter and dwell there without a rival. Then shalt Thou make the place of Thy feet glorious. Then shall my heart have no need of the sun to shine in it, for Thyself wilt be the light of it, and there shall be no night there. In Jesus' name, Amen.

Matthew 5:3; Luke 16:10-13; 1 Timothy 6:17-19; Revelation 21:23
The Pursuit of God, 30.

705. Knowledge of God: supreme value of; Promises of God; God: His majesty

We must be concerned with the person and character of God, not the promises. Through promises we learn what God has willed to us, we learn what we may claim as our heritage, we learn how we should pray. But faith itself must rest on the character of God.

Is this difficult to see? Why are we not stressing this in our evangelical circles? Why are we afraid to declare that people in our churches must come to know God Himself? Why do we not tell them that they must get beyond the point of making God a lifeboat for their rescue or a ladder to get them out of a burning building? How can we help our people get over the idea that God exists just to help run their businesses or fly their airplanes?

God is not a railway porter who carries your suitcase and serves you. God is God. He made heaven and earth. He holds the world in His hand. He measures the dust of the earth in the balance. He spreads the sky out like a mantle. He is the great God Almighty. He is not your servant.

He is your Father, and you are His child. He sits in heaven, and you are on the earth.

Exodus 20:11; 1 Samuel 3:18; Psalm 2:1-4; Psalm 146:5-6; Isaiah 40:12-15; Revelation 4:1-8; Revelation 15:3
Faith Beyond Reason, 44.

706. Knowledge of God: through humble obedience

In every generation, the people who have found God have been those who have come to the end of themselves. Recognizing their hopelessness, they have been ready to throw themselves on the mercy and grace of a forgiving God.

Men Who Met God, 62.

707. Knowledge of God: through humble obedience

If God is the Supreme Good then our highest blessedness on earth must lie in knowing Him as perfectly as possible. . . .

In seeking to know God better we must keep firmly in mind that we need not try to persuade God. He is already persuaded in our favor, not by our prayers but by the generous goodness of His own heart. "It is God's nature to give Himself to every virtuous soul," says Meister Eckhart. "Know then that God is bound to act, to pour Himself out into thee as soon as ever He shall find thee ready." As nature abhors a vacuum, so the Holy Spirit rushes in to fill the nature that has become empty by separating itself from the world and sin. This is not an unnatural act and need not be an unusual one, for it is in perfect accord with the nature of God. He must act as He does because He is God. . . .

We all know how the presence of someone we deeply love lifts our spirits and suffuses us with a radiant sense of peace and well-being. So the one who loves God supremely is lifted into rapture by His conscious Presence. . . .

If only we would stop lamenting and look up. God is here. Christ is risen. The Spirit has been poured out from on high. All this we know as theological truth. It remains for us to turn it into joyous spiritual experience. And how is this accomplished? There is no new technique; if it is new it is false. The old, old method still works. Conscious fellowship with Christ is by faith, love and obedience. And the humblest believer need not be without these.

Luke 11:13; John 15:10; 1 John 2:3-6
That Incredible Christian, 65, 66, 67.

708. Knowledge: inadequacy of

Many... apparently overlook the fact that the Spirit of God never promised to fill a man's head. The promise is that God will fill the heart, or man's innermost being. The Word of God makes it very plain that the church of Jesus Christ will never operate and minister and prosper by the stock of knowledge in the heads of Christian believers but by the warmth and urgency of God's love and compassion flowing through their beings.

Now, don't throw your head away—you are going to need it! I am convinced that God has made it plain that man alone, of all the creatures on earth, is created so that he can have fullness of knowledge about the earth and all the wonders and glories that it holds. I believe that through grace man can have a fullness of knowledge even about the works of God—but this certainly does not mean that we find Him and know Him and love Him through thought processes and human wisdom.

It is utterly and completely futile to try to think our way through to knowing God, Who is beyond our power of thought or visualization. This does not mean that it is impossible for us to think about Him—but it does mean that we cannot think around Him or think equal to Him or think up to Him!...

If we are not in love with Christ Himself and if we are satisfied with a knowledge of the works of God and of systems of theology, our hunger for God will not be satisfied.

Romans 11:33-36; 1 Corinthians 8:1; Philippians 3:10
I Talk Back to the Devil, 101, 102.